ROLLARESQUE

or

THE RAKISH PROGRESS

OF

THE ROLLING STONES

A Tale of Loose Morals by
the Author of ZIGGYOLOGY etc.

IN FOUR VOLUMES
— with 8 Illustrations —
by **MR CHADWICK** Esq.

LONDON:

Published by Ebury Press at
Vauxhall Bridge Rd.
MMXV

1 3 5 7 9 10 8 6 4 2

Ebury Press, an imprint of Ebury Publishing
20 Vauxhall Bridge Road
London SW1V 2SA

Ebury Press is part of the Penguin Random House group of companies
whose addresses can be found at global.penguinrandomhouse.com

 Penguin
Random House
UK

Published by Ebury Press in 2015

www.eburypublishing.co.uk

A CIP catalogue record for this book is available
from the British Library

ISBN 9780091958350

Printed and bound in Great Britain by Clays Ltd, St Ives PLC

Penguin Random House is committed to a sustainable future
for our business, our readers and our planet. This book is
made from Forest Stewardship Council® certified paper.

CONTENTS

∽

BOOK THE FIRST

HEIRS

ec∽

BOOK THE SECOND

ORGY

❧

BOOK THE THIRD

GAMING

BOOK THE LAST

MADHOUSE

LIST OF ILLUSTRATIONS

All of the above plates by Mr Chadwick.

Front cover design by Mr Eldridge.

Endpapers 'Stroll-a-resque' map by Mr Goddard.

'But I have been a rolling stone, my good fellow.
Play – play has been my ruin! That and beauty.'

WILLIAM MAKEPEACE THACKERAY
The Luck Of Barry Lyndon, 1844

TO W.H.

Sir! – IT BEING the proper custom amongst works of this nature to commence with an honorary epistle, I nominate you as the person before whom I now humbly prostrate myself. And in doing so it is my hope that anyone else who may happen upon these pages will better understand their purpose, knowing that the Author has dedicated the work to your majestic self – the immortal William Hogarth.

To them, and to you, I must first address the obvious: that you did me the misfortune to croak your last all of two hundred and seven years, one month, three weeks and four days before I wailed my first. It, therefore, may easily be supposed by those cursed with only the weakest pulse of romance in their veins that this is not only a pointless exercise in séance by pen but, by proxy, damning documentary evidence of the shaky wits conducting the hand that wrote it. For such sour wretches, raised without nourishment of art or poetry, are all too plentiful in my trying times.

How my heart sinks when I compare *this* age with the elegance of *yours*. When sentences unfurled in rolls of silk, rippling over entire paragraphs embroidered with jewels of wit and pearls of punctuation, like those of your blessed friends, Messrs. Fielding, Smollett and Sterne. And how they, and you, would surely be aghast to see what has become of that language in the ungrateful paws of this epoch: one so frightened of expressive prose and its power to stir the soul from automated drudgery that some humans, even those of purportedly high intellect, ignore the infinite riches of our glorious vocabulary, preferring to communicate their emotions in infantile semaphore of punctuation marks. Indeed, you would scarce believe us to be the same species that gave the world The Bard!

But, I digress. Forgive me, Sir, and allow me to return to the intended theme of this prologue, a subject in which you yourself are a learned master: a treatise upon 'The English Rogue'.

I have often wondered why it is the people of these isles so love to read of rapscallions and their moral misdemeanours? Why it's ever been the case that the more our society condemns the temptations of vice, the more our tastes are whetted for bawdy tales of rakes, knaves and women of abandoned character? And why the Spanish were first to immortalise their *picaros* in print with the adversities of poor Lazarillo, but the march of culture has proven there is still nothing so English as a *picaresque*?

Why? Because the rogue, I tell you, is in their blood!* What is England if not beer, skittles and scallywags? Was ever a more fitting ambassador of that nation's spirit than the highwayman Dick Turpin, or the thief-taker Jonathan Wild? And were the English ever happier than in peacetime of Tyburn, the gibbet and a worn copy of the *Malefactors' Bloody Register* in every household?

I could long pursue this further into the rhetorical, but as you and I both know, the rogue is as dear to the English heart

---

* Being of Celtic extraction, Sir, I am thus unable to say 'our blood'.

as crumpets and tea to the English gut, since there was never more golden an age of roguery than your own: when Mr Sterne delighted us with his great cock and bull ode to squire *Tristram Shandy*; when Mr Smollett ravished our sensibilities with the exploits of that scoundrel, *Count Fathom*; and when your dear friend, Mr Fielding, spun his saucy history of the foundling *Tom Jones*, and in doing so discovered, as he articulated, 'a new province of writing' – THE NOVEL.

So the lovable rogue begat English literature, and it, in turn, has never lost its love for the rogue. Because was it not you – the divine Hogarth – who played midwife to that birth with easel, brush and engraving plate? You, the visual genius, creator of those episodic marvels so influential upon that frantic activity of ink in your peers: the perils of the syphilitic harlot Moll Hackabout, the cursed marriage of the cuckold Squanderfield and – rogue of rogues – Master Tom Rakewell, doomed by his own depravity to fritter away all fortune to fate of debtors' prison and madhouse.

It could have been that your beloved *Rake's Progress* would have minimal bearing on the society of centuries far beyond your time, were the rogue not a vessel so abundant in the English bloodstream, ubiquitous in fact of daily news as much as diverting thrill of fiction. The fashions change, revolutions in industry occur, wars are won and lost, parliaments sworn and laws are passed, but the rogue remains the same, whatever his chosen profession.

These shores have spawned so many spectacular examples of his kind in the two hundred and fifty years since you were lain under the sod in Chiswick (a fine tomb, might I add, which I've oft undertaken pilgrimage of visit), though one in particular stands out as bearing all the traits of your trade-marked artistry: as you called it, the 'Modern Moral Subject'. A story as true as Turpin and five times as thrilling – for it involves a whole quintet of Turpins, no less – which I simply *yearn* to share with your good self. But, then – perhaps I could?

To do so, in a manner that you would fully understand in your time – oh, for those merciful days when we all bathed in gin and were dead of dropsy at thirty-two! – I would have to convey their adventures in a style of narration and a rhythm of language that modestly bows in deference to the superior splendour of the same Fielding, Smollett, et cetera, so as you might find agreeably familiar. I would also have to adhere to the truth, of course, as annotated in the late-twentieth century, while moulding the narrative so as to concentrate on those aspects of vice, sin and scandal so revered by your own paying public of the eighteenth century. And should at any point the muse desert me I need only remind myself of my aim, to prepare a tale worthy of the humours at your favourite table in Old Slaughter's Coffee House on St Martin's Lane, and so speed its return.

Among your recorded quotations is a personal favourite of mine: that in which you describe your intentions as an artist, one so courageously radical, so inspiringly innovative, you 'endeavoured to treat my subjects as a dramatic writer'. So for you, the inimitable Hogarth, who painted many a great novel, I in turn would like to write as great a painting as my pen is worthy in the hope that you, and others, may not find it uninteresting.

Its subject: five of the boldest English rogues as have ever trodden their native soil.

Its form: that of the *picaresque*.

Or rather, this being the story of those infamous minstrels The Rolling Stones, as I have chosen to call it, a *Rollaresque*.

Your health, SIR!

The Author
MMXV

BOOK *the* FIRST

HEIRS

CHAPTER

I

≈

Shewing time and place through a pane of glass.

SATISFACTION! THEY BREATHED it in like oxygen. It fluttered the hairs inside their nostrils like a national perfume. In town and country, in street and field, every man, woman and child savoured its rich taste upon their tongues, swishing it around the corners of their mouths until its giddying effects had rendered them insensibly serene. A whole kingdom, gloriously drunk on the sacred juice which spurted from Old Blighty's breast into the grateful gullets of her fifty million sucklings. Sweet milk of satisfaction!

They were satisfied, for they were British, and as their right honourable Prime Minister had reminded them not five years earlier, they had 'never had it so good'. The blessed bearer of these tidings was one who, authoritative in nature as in moustache, was always right and always honourable; who had helped conquer that repellent Hun two wars running, first with bayonet, then with briefcase; whose earthly name, Harold Macmillan, all but disguised the fact he was less man, more superman, until such a time as one of his cheering subjects recognised his divinity in the glorious christening of 'Supermac'. And if Supermac told them they had never had it so good then they knew, absolutely, that they never had had it so good. For they were British, and therefore satisfied. And so the milk pumped, and on they suckled.

They suckled, and they smoked, just as Supermac smoked, for in his sixty-eight-year-old sagacity he had arrived at the singular wisdom of paying his respects to those twins of the treasury, tobacco and alcohol, by choosing one while abstaining from the other on a rotating year-on-year basis. It so happened that this year, Nineteen Sixty-Two, being one of his 'smoking years', Supermac made much public demonstration of the noble art of puffing, and so his faithful flock followed suit, blissfully blind to any notice in any paper demanding his government investigate spurious links between the joy of sucking the goodness out of a Bristol-tipped and the rare nuisance of lung cancer. For they were British, and superior in the knowledge, as the gospel according to Golden Virginia sayeth, that there was 'extra Satisfaction in natural tobacco'. And so the milk pumped as they suckled, smoking and coughing and doing their utmost not to die an inconvenient death, gleefully drowning in their own too, too satisfied phlegm.

And who amongst them would dare to kick anything so much resembling fate's shiny bucket, with all the ointments and creams and pills and tonics at their disposal: Zam-Buk for chilblains; Duramil for lumbago; Phosferine for grumpiness; Victory lozenges for pharyngitis; and Lifebuoy soap for the sorry hum of body odour. Even when that impatient reaper tried to import fresh pestilence with an outbreak of smallpox, Supermac's advisers were quick to deduce that this foreign lurgy had nothing whatsoever to do with the creamy-lipped Britons, but was the fault of scratching interlopers from the former Raj, all of whom, it was sensibly argued, should be barred from these satisfied isles forthwith. And so the milk pumped and on they suckled, happily immunised from pain, pus and Pakistanis.

And hadn't they ever had it so good thanks also to Mr Selwyn Lloyd, one of the many kind-hearted knights of the Tory order in Supermac's cabinet, whose privilege it was to satisfy their pockets as Chancellor of the Exchequer. Only last summer, Her Majesty's pound, as Mr Lloyd confessed, had been 'in danger' until he personally wrestled it from the dragon's jaw of recession, returning it to the safety of his red box and its incredible economic sorcery within. And how those simple womenfolk wishing to earn their crust nursing those whose lack of Zam-Buk, and other modern phenomena, had left their nervous systems temporarily dissatisfied, thanked Mr Lloyd for the daily reward of seven pretty pennies with which to happily feather their nest egg; hoping that one day it may be feathered enough to crack and give birth to the four shillings a week for a rented television set. And damn and blast that small coven of ungrateful stockinged hags who dared mutter that seven pennies' worth of *Z-Cars*, Arthur Haynes and *The Black And White Minstrel Show* wasn't reward enough for bed-bathing those moaning oafs in want of Zam-Buk. Because this was Supermac's Britain, land of the satisfied, and no place for shirkers, strikers, work-to-rulers and one-out-all-out-ers!

And so the milk pumped, and on they suckled: the gentlemen, with their Bass blue triangle, their Ford Anglias and their strip-joints and peepshows where nursemaids of a different sort offered soothing distraction with flesh, fire and fake snakes; and their wives, with their twin-tub washing machines, their Bri-Nylon lingerie and their Limmits 'meal-in-a-biscuit' to redeem any complacent heifers found guilty of sins against the slim. And if any husband and wife should cross words, be it over the difference between butter and Stork margarine or the corrupting pulchritude of Mademoiselle Brigitte Bardot, they could speedily find satisfaction in venting spleen and ballpoint pen to that clarion of wisdom and decency, the *News Of The World*; as was the case of one Middlesex gentleman describing a sorry domestic stalemate over table condiments, his spouse having recently vetoed the entry of vinegar into their household. 'She thinks it's common. I try to sneak it into the cabbage but she always sniffs it out and there's hell to pay!' A problem shared, a problem satisfied!

There were, nevertheless, more than a few hungry sucklers who, feeling they'd been denied their due turn at Supermac's teat, took it upon themselves to slake their thirst by blowing up safes, by robbing warehouses, by stealing mailbags, by poisoning elderly lodgers, or other such gruesome fancies according to their individual appetites for dynamite, lead or recreational psychopathy. The thrills of which were rarely worth the inevitable consequence of Her Majesty's noose, ready to shut the windpipe of those such as young master Hanratty, fingered as the notorious 'A6 killer' who, despite frantic bleatings of innocence, was hanged by his neck at Bedford gaol this first week in April, much to the satisfaction of all who agreed that one good corpse deserved another, that a wronged man hanged was better than the wrong of none hanged at all, with a 'hear, hear!', three cheers and 'God save the Queen!'

So 'Hurrah!' for the rope, and the cuffs, and the gavel and the birch! These, the tools of justice transforming the waters of disorder into the wine of discipline. For a disciplined Britain was a satisfied Britain, and so wine and milk pumped, and Supermac's litter obediently bowed to their decorated elders who'd fought and won two world wars so Old Blighty could continue these glorious lactations. And if an innocent man ended up dangling from the gallows once in a while, then that was simply an egg worth breaking so long as the resulting national omelette still contained tea and jam and *The Black And White Minstrel Show*.

But with such a prosperous litter – the acorns of conjugal satisfaction resulting in another seventeen-thousand Britons to suckle in the first three months of Nineteen Sixty-Two alone – it stood to reason that Supermac, Her Majesty and said monochrome minstrels with their 'Dry Bones', 'Dixie' and 'Polly Wolly Doodle' could expect to encounter their inevitable share of unruly young runts. As illustration of the character of this abominable breed, consider the adolescent mania of a schoolboy from Tunbridge Wells who, in a sudden desertion of all rules of polite society as had been meticulously beaten into him, decided to place a kipper in the bonnet of a car belonging to none other than his biology master. The effects of this incongruous alliance of smoked herring and sparkplug was that the master, naturally unaware that such a threat as fish sabotage existed in the minds of his pupils, turned his key in the ignition, thus short-circuiting his engine in a deafening bang, swiftly accompanied moments later by the nauseating odour of incinerated marine life. And yet, not being a capital offence, the culprit dunce was denied his deserved jig on the same stage as young Hanratty and merely suspended, having disgraced his family name and wasted what, to some noses present, smelt like an otherwise perfectly good kipper.

Mercy and leniency, so generously dished out, did little to improve the deportment of this runt generation who, having only recently been excused the improving powers of national service, manoeuvred themselves in sorry slouches while squawking about 'Banning The Bomb' and other such blasphemies against Queen, Country and Global Genocide.

Nor could their hot pulses be pacified by the national Hit Parade with its gay twang of 'Wonderful Land', the exotic hiccups of 'Wimoweh' or Mr Acker Bilk and the agreeable groan of 'Stranger On The Shore', but instead sought enslavement in a debauched mating dance called 'The Twist'. Fortunate for them that the much respected oracle of the country's loins, Marjorie Proops, was there to remind them in the pages of the *Daily Mirror* that 'pre-marital intercourse is impractical and idiotic', and thus a satisfactory state of untwisted chastity was reasonably assumed to have been restored thenceforth. And where words failed, and Proops was poo-pooed, and the sap of impudence still rose, the rod always succeeded; as in Peckham Manor School, where fifty boys who refused to wear caps were individually caned with a severity anyone insufficiently witted as to engage in such bald-headed anarchy would one day be thankful for.

Lest they forget, they were British, and whether suckled or strapped they would all learn satisfaction! And those that didn't learn the first time would be strapped and thrashed and leathered and if need be strangled for crimes they didn't commit until they recovered their love for Supermac, their taste for milk and their place at the back of their happy brethren queuing at the pump of plenty. The sensible benevolence of which was perfectly surmised in an address by a powdery wig to a court in Monmouthshire. 'We must not be sloppy or sentimental! We must be stern, strong and tough! There are too many young people who have too much money in their pockets! They have no regard for the Law!'

So there, in smoke and sickness, in bread and circuses, in pounds and shillings, in brassieres and vinegar, in Whitehall and blackface, in crime and punishment, in kippers and canings, we see the world through the window of April, Nineteen Sixty-Two. Satisfied Empire Of The Never Had It So Good.

And now, as our History properly commences, to find the stones to smash it.

II

*Of cracks and causes, ending cheerfully
in a convergence.*

THE CLIFF FROM whence these stones were quarried lay way out in the west of London, opposite the terminus of the District Line at Ealing Broadway where, latterly, runtish youth of a very specific rhythmic disposition had taken to gathering every Saturday evening to nourish their pleasures.

That first Saturday in April, as Her Majesty took rest in Windsor Castle, where that afternoon her royal patience had been tested by a display of French paratroopers marching around its quadrangle in Gallic monotony for a full fifteen minutes; as Supermac smoked in Chequers with Mr Lloyd discussing their following week's budget, together anticipating the satisfied gleam in the sweet teeth of their sucklings when told of its tax on gobstoppers; and as the sucklers themselves sat at home before their rented altars of two-channel distraction, spoilt for choice between Perry Mason's legal genius in solving *The Case Of The Startled Stallion* and Errol Flynn's Crimean folly in leading *The Charge Of The Light Brigade*, so into this valley of deafening vice rode the runt hundreds.

They arrived on train and bus, on foot, car and bicycle, pilgrims following a secret trail which, four weeks running, had been whispered for their ears only in the classified pages of those few periodicals primarily concerned with the sonic commotion commonly referred to as 'jazz'. The whisper ran thus:

'Alexis Korner's Blues Incorporated.

THE MOST EXCITING EVENT OF THIS YEAR!

Rhythm and Blues Club. The Ealing Club,
Ealing Broadway Station.

Turn left, cross at zebra and go down steps between ABC Teashop and Jewellers. Saturday at 7.30 pm.'

The whisper heeded, long before the stroke of seven the most eager pilgrims had already turned left and crossed the aforementioned zebra in anticipation: some congregating in the teashop of the Aerated Bread Company, where those in most urgent need of electric cacophony mourned the absence of any jukebox which might enliven their enjoyment of caffeine, cola and gaseous dough. Others took similar preparatory measures to build reserves for the imminent excitement with victuals from the adjacent chip shop, usually consumed in a snaffling queue along the chain-link fence overlooking the railway line at the foot of the sixteen steps to the threshold of the night's euphoria, thereby ensuring the stench of hot fat and vinegar lingered long enough to both torment the intestines of the famished and repel, should ever they stray there, that rarer breed of womankind who, as previously discussed, took apoplectic exception to said alkaline malt. At the appointed time the gate of this iniquitous Eden bolted open and in they spilled, wiping grease and sugar from their lips, breaths brown with coffee, green with mint or black with tobacco, the foolish relinquishing their coat to the cloakroom: an enigma of pegged oblivion from whence it would seldom return to its rightful owner.

The assembled tribe having yet to invent anything resembling their own uniform, those not lost in a non-descript scruffy purgatory clung, for better or worse, to the sartorial codes of that outnumbering peer group of 'trad jazz' apostles from which they had very recently splintered. Trad jazz being a serious business involving the precise sciences of banjo and clarinet, it merited the studious male armour of duffel coat with leather elbow-patches, a pair of corduroy trousers, a 'Ban The Bomb' badge, as weighty a bundle of books under their arm as could muster a comfortable illusion of braininess, and as thick a tuft of beard as the designs of mother puberty had seen appropriate. Their maidens similarly distinguished themselves with tight sweaters and long skirts, though not so long as to impair their ability to stir any base desires worth stirring beneath the intellectual chainmail of duffel and corduroy with the tight dance-floor spasm activity abruptly christened 'skip-jive'.

Months earlier, it was for such skip-jiving and confusing hollers of 'Dig!' despite neither earth nor shovel in sight that Supermac's lost sheep flocked to this same basement, where the rainwater dripped between the glass-blocks set in the pavement above directly onto the stage below; a constant leakage inspiring both a fashion for bowlers and other protective headwear amongst those whose task it was to lecture trad jazz in as preferably dry a humour as possible, and the club nickname 'The Moist Hoist'. Whereas now, as of mid-March, and as advertised, Mr Korner and his Incorporated friends had commandeered this humid cellar every Saturday to spread a new teenage virus: one yet to infiltrate the British airwaves, known only to the infected minority present, yet already contagious enough to threaten the unafflicted trad jazz majority for whom this 'Rhythm and Blues' was as disagreeable to their ears as the scent of vinegar to the nose of that domestic harpy now thrice referred to.

The vibrations of Mr Korner and his band were American in origin, not to mention 'negroid' as was the chief concern of their disapproving trad jazz forebears, comprising the loud amplification not only of guitar but also harmonica, saxophone, piano and bass over a syncopated beat while another of their number screamed metaphorical degeneracy about tigers in tanks, men who only choose to enter households from the back door, and the capabilities of an obscure piece of apparatus called 'a mojo'. The appeal of which was great enough to jam The Moist Hoist to a humid capacity worthy of its titular infamy.

Those who'd wisely dodged the cloakroom, having been admitted past the bar into the main club, were hit by such steamy torrents of perspiration as to provoke instant disrobing and the sudden eruption upon both floorboards and side benches of lumpy molehills of tossed fabric, primarily duffel. The heat was stoked by an epidemic outbreak of cigarettes, the smoke of which rose to form a thin stratosphere between the young heads of the assembled and the low ceiling, its aroma rivalled only by that of sweat, beer, cologne and a dizzying spike of 'reefer'; the latter ignited with flagrant nonchalance under the assumption, which proved correct, that none present were the slightest bit alarmed at being forced to inhale that prohibited Asian musk. And so, by degrees – the breathing space reduced to the point where any soul clumsy enough to drop a penny upon the floor would have to retrieve it by contortions so unacceptably intrusive to their neighbour as to fall under that unique category of molestation labelled 'frottage' – Mr Korner and his conspirators took their places upon the stage and commenced their musical depravity.

At length, as the overhead fog thickened, as the worshippers swayed in tightly packed unison as if in choreographed seasickness, skirts and corduroys flapping to the beat of the Blues and the sporadic thunder of a passing westbound express train,

Mr Korner paused their suggestive hubbub to make a public address. 'And now, we've got a guest on guitar. He's come all the way from Cheltenham, just to play for you. Give it up for – Elmo Lewis!'

With fateful synchronicity, it was then that two young rakes of no small significance to this chronicle, having crossed the zebra, turned left, descended the steps, inhaled the vinegar, joined the queue, paid the entrance, forgone the cloakroom and squeezed past the bar, savoured their first euphoric sip of The Moist Hoist just as Master Lewis took his place beneath the dripping ceiling and commenced some highly unusual electrified shenanigans. The impact of which upon our new arrivals was so profound as to transform their visages into frozen masks of wide-eyed, slack-jawed imbecility.

Perched upon a stool, half-facing the audience, this Lewis cradled a curvaceous Höfner, producing fluid wails by means of chaffing a steel bar against that part of the instrument ordinarily accustomed to more delicate minstrelship. The awestruck duo recognised the tune of these perverse tribulations as 'Dust My Broom' – originally performed by Elmore James, an American bluesman they themselves had studied at length, never anticipating to come across a fellow pupil their own age, nor one so skilled and courageous as to mimic the master in public. So much so, their uncontrollable impulse to share this admiration found eventual relief in the loud and fruity ejaculation: 'It's fucking Elmore James, man!'

His broom dusted, Lewis alighted from the stage to crackling applause and a ripple of 'Dig!'s, resuming his original position amongst those witnesses who had thus welcomed him so enthusiastically. After so popular a sweepage, as marked by the gauntlet of gratitude on his retreat to the bar, he was interrupted by a tap on his shoulder before he could order his liquid reward, bringing him face to face with that pair of exclamatory fanatics whose curiosity now demanded mutual introduction.

At which point in our story, we, like they, should pause the progress of further adventure in order to better make the association of these three stony specimens with due geological scrutiny.

CHAPTER

III

⁓

Portrait of a picaro.

WHILE IT WAS true that Master Elmo Lewis had indeed 'come all the way from Cheltenham' – that noted spa town in the county of Gloucestershire where people once flocked in order to cleanse their colons with its fresh waters which, in the age before Zam-Buk, were widely believed to perform similar miracles – the uncanny coincidence of his forename, Elmo, being so close to his hero, Elmore, made the revelation that this itself was a falsification at odds with the one scribbled by his parish registrar twenty years earlier all the less surprising.

His defence in administering this deception upon the public was his ambition to be received as an authentic bluesman, all of whom, as far as he had thus ascertained, had been blessed at the christening font with such worthy handles as 'Muddy', 'Sonny Boy', 'Howlin'' and, indeed, 'Elmore'. Whereas it had been his misfortune to be the apple of a parental tree which, lacking the foresight of Mr and Mrs Waters, Williamson, Wolf and James, had cursed him in accordance with their Welsh heritage, Lewis Jones. Had he designs on a life as the church organist in an obscure village in Gwynedd fussed over by spinsters, competing for his affections with the seductive density of their *bara brith*, then the history of procreation could never have received a so fittingly named Lewis Jones. But since, as is already apparent, young Jones' intentions were contrastingly heathen in outlook, such a handicap of appellation made that inoffensive charade, substituting fore-name for surname and abbreviating Elmore to Elmo, both excusable and necessary.

In a first hostile manoeuvre against this same birth mark, as a youth he'd already denied 'Lewis' the podium of his celebrity by instead choosing the former of his two middle names, Brian, with which to announce his personage amongst his fellow pupils at Cheltenham Grammar School; where he briefly excelled at clarinet and swimming until realising his talents would be better advanced by a curriculum of his own construction.

That their son would never amount to a holy melodist residing in Gwynedd notwithstanding, Mr and Mrs Jones, having already proven hasty in mislabelling their firstborn, were forced to pay for the consequences of that error when Brian's true temperament found its voice in pursuits which heaped more dishonourable manure upon the doorstep of their semi-detached oasis than their pruned hedges should ever require, were they to keep flourishing for another dozen millennia. Chiefly: an aptitude for classroom insolence, involving the institution of a trend amongst his susceptible fellow students to shirk the obligatory break-time repast of fresh milk in favour of brown ale; an addiction to jazz and other heinous phonographic vibrations, abetted by his endeavours with saxophone and all its shrill tortures; and a remarkable expertise in the art of fornication, in which he specialised in that particular discipline which shunned the protective saddle, choosing, as he would tell any friend enquiring as to his exploits, to ride 'bareback'. It was therefore fortunate for his appetites that there was no shortage of mares with which to canter, helped by their inexplicable attraction to a boy who, though possessed of angelic blond hair, a sweet, feathery voice and an effortless conversational charm, had a face prematurely preparing itself for the ravages of old age by the thin tracing of circles under his eyes, as guidelines for time's charcoal pencil to be applied, with indelible force, in adulthood.

Mr and Mrs Jones could ignore, as best they could, the brown ale and the saxophone wail, but their sixteen-year-old son's reputation as the town's most insatiable amateur biologist was less easily brushed under their napkins at meal times, especially when Brian confessed, to their understandable indigestion, that their proud family tree had, thanks to his bareback gardening, sprouted a new branch. That the fornicatrix who helped cultivate this twig of bastardy was all of fourteen summers further churned the moral diarrhoea which, once discharged, left so putrid a stain upon the straw boaters of Cheltenham Grammar that, with their firm consent, Brian would never have call to sport their crest ever again.

The disgraced moll being forced to surrender the crop of that twig for adoption, Brian was spared the shackles of matrimony and, thus liberated from school and altar, free to continue his ravishings of instruments reedy, stringed and skirted – habits his circumstances were now obliged to fund under pain of tolerable employment. The local guilds of coalman, shop assistant and bus conductor were each in turn blessed with his presence for as long as it took either he, or they, to deduce that none were a vocation fit for such a peppery squire, who happily relinquished all three; having learned only the furtive charity of the cash register, a hatred of soot and the rigmarole of fare collection as a dialogue which, with the skilful flourishes of his silvery tongue, occasionally concluded in a one-way ticket to paradise, bareback class. For the scandal that had so abruptly ended his education, thus bringing him to his present occupational limbo, failed to impress the obvious benefits of the saddle upon either mind or trousers. And so within a year of that first misadventure, he made another unintentional addition to the local census, this time with a married woman who decided to keep said mewling statistic, raising it with the compliant cuckold whose intimacy Brian had so boldly invaded.

Deciding to fledge from his ancestral house of disapproval into rented lodgings more sympathetic to his salacious customs, his hands – their rocking energies once again relieved of any responsibility to the cradle – instead availed themselves towards the practice of saxophone and also guitar, both of which he began to master with the same gleeful nimbleness previously demonstrated on zip and suspender belt. Further education was provided by a brief sojourn overseas, undertaking a busking expedition of the Nordic countries, returning with a more experienced ear and a bareback stamina greatly improved by extra tuition from those globally renowned daughters of Odin.

Upon his homecoming, Brian's prowess on brass was welcomed into the fold of The Ramrods, a Cheltenham 'rock'n'roll' ensemble who he happily tooted with for a few trifling engagements, exiting their ranks long before rare culinary tragedy befell their singer: his, the appalling misfortune to choke to death whilst eating a well-salted and heavily-vinegared bag of chips, not only a freak accident but a twofold catastrophe in its lending credence to the prejudice of that unreasonable harridan of the pantry immortalised, now, once too often in the pages of these adventures.

Brian's reputation, though dissolute, still wasn't so ill as to repel a local shop girl named Pat from rising to the challenge of becoming his steady sweetheart: one she bravely carried off to the predictable conclusion of his third seedling, her carriage of which left her indisposed to the more aerobic exertions of barebackery; as was proven when she discovered her love exercising those muscles with a wheezing surrogate only a few days before its delivery. However, it must not be supposed that our picaro's conscience was so slight as not to darken the maternity ward to furnish that exhausted haulier with a bouquet of flowers and their grizzling creation with a name: Julian.

The fresh threat of confetti looming over his head now added to the stagnation of heart and soul which he attributed to his isolated location, the very word 'Cheltenham' becoming a form of unutterable Hades. Imminent salvation from such Cotswolds fire and wedlock brimstone thus mercifully arrived one night at a trad jazz concert in the local Town Hall, where that future patron of The Moist Hoist, Mr Korner, provided small portion of entertainment; disturbing the assembled duffel coats with their first exposure to Rhythm and Blues, including Brian, whose ears, duly baptised by copper-wire and woe, heard the lock of his parochial gaol click open. Following Mr Korner to a nearby hostelry, this new disciple seized the opportunity to make his acquaintance, offering his eternal devotion of body and instrument to that Delta religion whose hymns, thus performed, had stoked such a sudden declaration of faith.

Bewitched by flattery, Mr Korner extended his generosity to the kitchen floor of his Bayswater flat, where Brian was invited to rest his head should ever he choose to visit the capital to assist in any preaching of the gospels of Muddy, Elmore and other saints of their exclusive canon. Unable to resist the hospitality of that tempting linoleum, Brian accepted his pilgrimage and headed east. This prosperous alliance of host and boarder, master and pupil, coinciding with the establishment of Mr Korner's proposals for The Moist Hoist, it was therefore a matter of course that, as 'Elmo Lewis', Brian should eventually join him beneath its trickling canopy and provoke that admiration which necessitated this biographical detour.

Of those two enthusiasts whose passions accosted him at the bar with tapping finger, the first to speak was a boy of noticeable facial orifice, his mouth large enough to swallow whole a suckling pig, yet his birdlike physique suggesting such advantages were rarely exploited. Receiving this pouting willow's opening compliments with good grace, Elmo introduced himself as Brian from Cheltenham. The mouth introduced itself as one 'Mick' from Dartford; which, once more, puts halt to our tale's forward thrust as we pause to unravel the thread which brought this remarkable fleshy aperture, and its owner, from thither to hither.

IV

And another.

DURING THAT BOISTEROUS era of shells and sirens when those Hunnish hawks took unusual liberties in reorganising London's urban character to their own smoky specifications, even Supermac, with the benefit of hindsight, may not have begrudged the Luftwaffe one extra crater knowing it had successfully annihilated a future ambassador of the abominable horseplay of youth that was set to become the scourge of his peacetime. The Kentish town of Dartford being directly under those Teutonic flight paths, it was only by mercy of Messerschmitt and luck of Lucifer that those fat and fated lips survived, much to the relief of Mr and Mrs Jagger.

The young Mick, still many years away from the mature harvest in which those spongy caressers would exert themselves with all the sensual benefits of their eloquent mutation, remained ignorant to their true purpose, and thus suffered the embarrassment typical of many adolescents who, upon consulting their reflection in the looking glass, conclude the size of their various bodily particulars to be the result of some monstrous evolutionary prank. The stigma of which wasn't in the least bit helped by his peers, a number of whom likened his arresting cakehole to that of the nation's favourite charlatan negroes, as seen hollering 'Coal Black Mammy' every Saturday night at the expense of the BBC licence payer.

He was, in spite of this, a child of confidence and reserve, neither top nor bottom of his class but hovering discreetly between, quietly drinking in the moods and motives of those around him, taking mental note and plotting human stratagem with a silent stealth not once betrayed by that innocuous blank mask with its gaping cavern suggestive of attachment to a mind of infinitely more gormless preoccupations.

Mick's father, being a school instructor in physical diversions, urged bodily development befitting that expertise, furnishing his son with dumb-bells and encouraging him in the practices of cricket, basketball and all things pertaining to the great outdoors. It was of particular pride to Mr Jagger that young Michael was 'a first-class camper', a boast far more prophetic than that gushing pater could have envisaged. For, much to his father's chagrin, 'camping' was the only skill accommodated by those slender muscles which, despite all other sporty toils, stubbornly resisted the masculine esteem of beefiness.

According to the selective curriculum of Dartford Grammar, Mick was considered academically average except in the study of French, a language which, having some notoriety in the advancement of feminine cajolery, greatly appealed to his formative subconscious. Otherwise, Kent's examining board setting no standards for mimicry, it was unfortunate that he should be denied the opportunity to attain top marks in this one field where his faculties of verbal imitation were in a league worthy of a scholarship to the dreaming spires of that great university, were its syllabus ever elastic enough to quarter honorary doctorates in copycatism.

This capacity for impressions, the delight of the playground where his lampooning of various masters aroused an early appreciation of his innate ability to enchant an audience, reached its zenith of excellence when applied to melody. So convincing were Mick's throaty deceits that Mrs Jagger would often cease the hanging out of her washing to sprint indoors, convinced that the serenade echoing through her kitchen window was being piped by Elvis Presley *in propia persona*, only to have that adulterous daydream shattered upon discovering the source of these scandalous temptations to be the quivering kissing jellies of her eldest son.

The shrieks and spasms of American rock 'n' roll so timed their arrival on British shores as to take priority in his doppelganger repertoire: simulations he soon put to use by testing his tonsils over the accompaniment of various friends, most of whose musical abilities were restricted by the peculiar codes of that rattling hullaballoo known as 'skiffle'. Sadly, such watery jangles fell far short of Mick's expectations as had been elevated by his latter exposure to the frisky confections of Little Richard and Chuck Berry; heights which, irrespective of his best efforts at howling caricature, were seldom scraped by means of washboard and broom-handle. It did at least prove fortuitous in cementing an alliance with a fellow pupil named Dick: a boy whose melodic passions flowed along identical currents, to the extent of accruing a slowly expanding collection of discs whose contents Mick was privy to share, thus unearthing those treacly tremors otherwise foreign to the majority of Dartford eardrums, so identified as 'the Blues', which heated his spirits with savage lightning.

Entering his eighteenth year, with his schooling now a finite matter of months, the likelihood of a career tailored to his epiglottal talents seemed too remote a whim to merit serious fantasy. Occupationally undecided, his modest employment history thus far stretched to the vending of iced desserts in the school holidays and a spell as porter in the local mental hospital. While neither stirred the boy's will to aspire to a permanent position in those posts, the latter was nevertheless memorable for the apprenticeship served in one of the asylum's store cupboards where a nurse, taking temporary leave of her responsibility to the many gibbering bedlamites under her charge, instructed Mick in the basics of that corporeal dialect which he was to grasp with a studious hunger exceeding that of French; helped in no small part by all that nature had generously bestowed upon him betwixt nostrils and chin.

Thus experienced in institutions of lunacy and clandestine trysts, his resolution to undertake preparatory measures for entry into the parliamentary life was most judicious. The London School of Economics and Political Science being willing to further him in that direction, he accepted a three year vow and accompanying striped scarf with which to distinguish himself as one of their envoys on his daily commute from Kentish town to Aldwych seminar room.

With his head surrendered to such calculus, his heart still ached for those vinylite excitements awakened by his friend Dick, whose library of records Mick now sought to rival with his own, channelling that determination into overseas correspondence and the postage of monies in exchange for those hallowed scriptures of Rhythm and Blues so far neglected by the British phonographic industry. The deliveries of which being the only threat to his economic textbooks' dominance of his wits during his voyages to and from the Dartford home where they were so euphorically received, it was sometimes the case that he undertook that journey bearing these same tokens of intellectual distraction which his covetous fervour forebade being parted from.

So it came to pass that one morning he boarded his train for the capital armed with yet another air-mailed marvel, the flagrant transport of which summoned the potent inquisition of another boy whose facial resemblance to the hairy associate of that celebrated Lord of the Jungle was not only striking, but somehow familiar. As Mick then recalled, a former neighbour: they'd attended the same primary school before both were cast their separate ways, now merged again on account of Chuck Berry's

Rockin' At The Hops, catalyst for the fevered excitations of this twin of Cheeta now sharing his carriage.

Henceforth the continuation of Mick's odyssey to The Moist Hoist being inextricably entwined with this hysterical other, in the interests of bringing these exploits back to speed with appropriate knowledge of all relevant parties, we must here delay that morning service towards Charing Cross, to be resumed after a short exploration of those symptoms specific to that fellow passenger.

CHAPTER

V

A trinity is coined and our History advanced.

THE RELENTLESS BLITZKRIEG upon the chimney stacks of Dartford which, as described in our previous episode, could have easily spared us of that great puckering organ might also have rid Supermac of this chimp-jawed accomplice had he too been smothered by Herr Hitler's explosive blanket; a historical hypothesis which would have surely gladdened the hearts of their future foes in its economical killing of two Stones with the droppings of one bird. The failure of which would greatly pique the interests of this second child of fortune who, in the throes of adulthood, took so a keen view of his potential assassin as to amass a modest archive of literature pertaining to the idiosyncrasies of said moustached dictator, for purposes of solitary amusement.

The undeveloped new-born mind usually lacking the permanence of memory, it might be supposed that these unpredictable shaves with the doodlebug left no lasting impression on this heaven-favoured tot. And yet, on the contrary, those budding shells yet to develop the simian contours so likening their carrier to a member of the primate order would never forget the wild halloo and brutal noise of warning siren and collapsing terrace; the cumulative effect of this destructive symphony being to heighten the child's instincts of human survival, resilience to harm, and self-preservation, beneficial traits he would hence grow to appreciate with a sentiment stopping just short of gratitude to the swastika squadrons who'd prepared him thus.

So the boy christened Keith first inhaled this world in that panicked air of dust and debris which had thankfully abated by the time his mother had cause to mark her only child's second birthday. To those harsh vibrations of aerial conflict first implanted in that pliable grey matter, Mrs Richards added the polished pulses of her favourite singers of jazz and big band, though the sound of brass in all its sundry executions coaxed no marked signs of wishful assimilation in her boy who, once of schooling age, was labelled by his class fellows with the affection, observant of his ears and their zoological incline, of 'Monkey'. Rather, it took his grandfather, a Huguenot minstrel, to uncork the dormant genie which neither trumpet nor trombone could disturb, allowing his tiny hands to first fondle a guitar, his maiden swipes with that weapon of wood and catgut sealing a betrothal between man and arms no less divine than the moment that eminent sovereign of Camelot withdrew Excalibur from its granite sheath.

His feet firmly in Dartford, his head was otherwise situated courtesy of the inflations of Saturday morning cinema which, pumping it to buoyancy necessary for transatlantic passage, had sailed it to the sun-scorched plains of the American Wild West. Commodore of his balloon of fancy was a Mr Roy Rogers, one of a succession of small-screen 'singing cowboys', whose screen life consisted of capering around cactuses on his horse, exhibitions with lasso and, as that epithet forewarned, yodelling a ceaseless catalogue of odes to frontiers, desert roses, 'injun' trails and ladies of the southern states – performed with sympathetic flourishes on that hollow instrument now uppermost in Keith's boyhood considerations.

His aspirations so shaped, he happily voiced his designs on becoming 'like Roy Rogers' to a casual playmate at Wentworth Primary School, being the same curiosity endowed of chops recently detailed herein; who, as the Reader should remember, was denied the continuation of that friendship into adolescence due, foremost, to a regrettable divergence of academic selection and, secondmost, a distinct lack of appreciation for the Stetsoned perpetrator of those gay warblings.

Cruelly cast into the untamed sierra of the local technical college, our lone cowboy, still the 'Monkey' of repute and more marmoset than baboon in stature, suffered the due buffets of the mob for as long as it took to muster like reprisal. Regardless, what bruises he bore were soothed in sound, be it that of his first phonograph – a revolving portal into the newly chartered dimensions of Elvis Presley, Little Richard and Chuck Berry – or his own attempts to recreate their unfathomable pluckings: a discipline which took such conspicuous precedence over his schoolbooks that – the troubadour's silhouette ever the truant's shadow, and his attendance being no better than if he were an inhabitant of neighbouring St Michael's churchyard – the observant governors of Dartford Tech, consulting their charity, so granted expulsion.

Seeking a campus more supportive of his salty humours, he favoured his chances in the nearest school of art, those blessed refugee camps of the scholastically shiftless: specifically, that four stops down the westbound branch line in Sidcup.

Exhibiting the good grace not to tax the lecturers of those delusive sciences with persistent enquiry, he removed himself to the gentlemen's lavatory, there spending the remainder of the academic calendar. Not on account of any infirmity in bowels or bladder which might impose that constant proximity to the porcelain throne, but as an echo chamber acoustically suited to serenade the digestive evacuations of his creative brethren with his impressively progressive guitar prangs, remarkably unimpaired by any distracting effluvia from the adjacent secretion of fresh human sewage.

So busking to a captive audience of cisterns, he was rewarded in comradeship with a pupil named Dick, being the same Richard who had latterly led our friend of over-ripened sip-pillows over the threshold of Rhythm and Blues paradise, where Keith now followed. Thus accompanied, life became a tempest of Chuck Berry, a fog of cigarettes and an avalanche of pharmaceutical bon-bons; those gelatine capsules whose manufacturers had promoted for the sole purpose of relieving menstrual cramps, thus failing to advertise their nobler benefits as a remedy for tedium in the adolescent male and, as Keith and Dick discovered, capable of similar jubilation in the animal kingdom following dietary experiments in a nearby park with a member of the feathery genus cockatoo, so named 'Cocky', who responded to these occasional treats with severe animation of wing and mandible.

The mutual acquaintance of Dick providing an obvious chaperone, fate nevertheless insisted Keith and Mick should encounter one another without intermediary obstruction, so propelling the former to platform two of Dartford railway station that same morning as the latter could be spied loitering with the holy grail of *Rockin' At The Hops* under his arm. And so, their train now lurching on to Charing Cross via Sidcup, and ours to Ealing, these journeys recover necessary motion.

There was nothing the scrolling vistas of Crayford and Bexley could offer these two crusaders to divert their cautious attentions away from reciprocal inspection of hair, face, mouth and trousers; nor their shared surprise in discovering an indigenous Dartfordian buck much like themselves so fluent in the recondite lexicon of Chuck Berry. With every second of speech, every yard of track, the recognition of a sibling quality rushed ever quicker to their shores of consciousness, breaking only when the announcement of Sidcup thwarted further colloquium on the subject.

The bond nevertheless sealed, arrangements were made to continue their dialogue at Mick's house, where Keith and his Excalibur were simultaneously initiated into a company of aspiring rock 'n' roll Templars who, for some months past, had been entertaining an impassive audience of settee and curtains. These knights branded themselves Little Boy Blue & The Blue Boys, with Mick adopting Arthurian charge over their order by means of that distinguishing prefix, proudly holding those attentions of valance and cushion with 'La Bamba': a popular tune of Latin extraction which, being untutored in Don Quixote's mother tongue, he interpreted with lolling vowels of his own nonsensical design, still managing to achieve phonetic ends capable of convincing those similarly unaccustomed with that swarthy nation of bull-skewering cranks of his ancestry in those quarters.

Their repertoire's one foreign body aside, the preponderance of their domestic disturbances followed the command of their latest secret dispatches from overseas, as now prescribed by Muddy Waters, The Lord Bo Diddley and the endlessly fulfilling Chuck Berry. These sounds set the tempos of their respective reveries during their hours of separation in lecture hall and washroom, neither anticipating that, in the vast duffeled dominion of the greater metropolis still skip-jiving to the placid puffs of trad jazz, they were not alone. Until chancing upon the announcement of a new club in Ealing: 'THE MOST EXCITING EVENT OF THIS YEAR.' Hence twenty-seven miles by car, hence sixteen steps, hence the faint trace of vinegar, hence five shillings entry, hence 'It's fucking Elmore James, man!'

And hence that gentle tap which first clattered our three stones together, here bringing these regressions to their timely conclusion.

'The Confidence Of Elmo Lewis'

VI

Of equations and chemistry, ending cheerfully
in a christening.

WHILE THAT PROVERB of the northern counties would have us believe 'give any fool a brick and they're more as likely to start a riot as build a house', in human practice the potential of such ammunition can only be achieved in the hands of those mentally endowed with a modest grasp of the mathematical laws of physics. So it was that only one of our trio was so skilled in those calculations of angle and velocity to guarantee destructive success. For though smitten with all that Apollo's plectrum had lately strummed upon their nineteen-year-old heartstrings, Mick and Keith were too malnourished of collective gumption.

Only Brian was so missile-minded as to initiate a contract with a destiny drafted to his own specifications; the aims of which formed the core of that first dialogue in The Moist Hoist, wherein he allowed these Kentish younglings – hitherto under the assumption he was permanently attached to Mr Korner's services – into the confidence of his plans to start a Rhythm and Blues band of his own; its members recruited according to his stringent criteria, and on the understanding that all successful applicants defer to his authority as their erstwhile First Fiddle, Chief Whip, Lord and Master.

Being the case that Mick and Keith were already committed to further entertainment of carpet and sideboard in the ongoing front parlour pupation of Little Boy Blue & The Blue Boys, they hesitated from submitting so rash a pledge, wishing Brian the best of luck and the promise of their vociferous applause upon the occasion of his new blues militia's first public foray. And yet, long after they'd bid him goodnight and trotted back to the tame heathlands of Dartford, the subject of Brian took permanent occupancy of their mental chambers, ensuring neither could speak, sleep nor lapse into idle trances of private fancy without reverential recall of his sandy hair, his Italian suit, his fretboard trickery, his plucky incantation of 'fucking Elmore James' and, least of all, his addictive perfume of human purpose.

Alas, this fixation of mind was by no means reciprocated, since matters domestic and financial demanding Brian's urgent attention, his economy of concerns could ill afford carefree thought of those two delightful sycophants when the want of a permanent London abode weighed so heavily upon his personage and all its spinal kinks after another eventful repose upon the floor of Mr Korner's scullery. The devil driving his needs, they galloped with haste to a Bayswater department store where he successfully applied for a vacant position as salesman of sporting accessories, a formidable achievement in view of his limited faculties in all fields of human exertion; save that one equestrian-inspired pursuit in which his competency had already been repeatedly proven with Olympian vigour.

This regular income assured, he found himself lodgings in the vicinity of West Hampstead, thereby putting an end to any further nocturnal agonies depending on the charity of Mr Korner and allowing himself the luxury of privacy – not lost upon a gentleman of his lusty convictions. Showing due appreciation of these favourable circumstances, he immediately extended his humble hospitality to a young lady he'd befriended shortly before leaving Cheltenham who, still being of that minor age accustomed to the chafe of hockey stick upon knee-socks, greatly appealed to Brian's athletic prerequisites.

Sadly, his happiness in this tutorial regime was agonisingly brief. No sooner had he established this bareback academy and debauched the sentiments of that first student when an unexpected visit from a former pupil effected cancellation of all further semester. For having been thus preoccupied with his new metropolitan existence, Brian had erred greatly in neglecting to sweeten the hometown vexations of the girl named Pat by way of regular correspondence assuring her of his commitments to their prenuptial fidelity and their child, Julian. The absence of such heartening epistles thereby giving rise to a distress typical of the under-taxed female mind, Pat invested all her worldly pittance in a one-way ticket to that distant capital, arriving unannounced with one suitcase – buckling; one Julian – bawling; and one heart – throbbing. All of which were greeted by one Brian – crumpling.

This deflation of spirit could only have been worse had the unforeseen rap of her knuckles upon his bolted entrance effected sudden interruption of another seminar with his teenage acolyte on the art of surrendering what little bulwarks of chastity hadn't already been decimated by her master's devoted one-on-one tuition. That he was caught in a solitary period of academic recess was the only favourable aspect of this situation which, taking cruel hostage of his obligations to wench and ward, he was forced to accept with a grimace as insincerely welcoming as it was libidinously defeated.

For the sorry consequences of this domestic invasion were manifold. His income, stretched as it was even with the bonus payments he frequently apportioned himself from the company cash drawer, was now prey to the pining bellies of two others who, quite possibly, were not so constitutionally hearty as to subsist on sharing his diet of half a tin of cold spaghetti hoops a day, served without ceremony of preparation in a teacup. More urgent still were the frets of his landlord, who while content for Brian's fellow lodgers to endure the corrective thuds and instructional moans of recent teachings, thought differently of the rasping chorus of the tot, Julian, whose incessant caterwauls, unsuppressed by all attempts to mute with cork of cold spaghetti hoops, necessitated an immediate change of surroundings.

Such were the impedimentary demons exhausting Brian's wits in the weeks that followed his unveiling of Elmo Lewis at The Moist Hoist, though none so obstructive of that same spirit of dust and broom that he failed in implementing that avowal so revered by our Dartford pilgrims. The gauntlet was thus swiped across page fifteen of *Jazz News* in the first week of May, in a boxed advertisement headed 'RHYTHM AND BLUES':

'Guitarist and Vocalist forming R. & B. Band, require
Harmonica and/or Tenor Sax, Piano, Bass and Drums.
Must be keen to rehearse.
Plenty of interesting work available.
Box No. 1277.'

The first game fellows to peek inside that box were mustered to the upper quarters of The White Bear, a hostelry just off Leicester Square, where Brian inspected his conscripts whilst liberally helping himself to the free stock of cigarettes housed in easy reach behind the bar. Only when the landlord alerted him to the fact that this was a generosity of his own invention did he have cause to seek alternative premises, burrowing further into the terraced flesh-pots of Soho and the function room above another alehouse named The Bricklayers Arms.

Thus bereft of complimentary nicotine, if comfortably relocated, Brian began sifting through the hopeful human dregs, securing only the allegiances of those genuinely sympathetic to his persuasions of rhythm. Which, after a couple of weeks, consisted of himself, a guitarist of earnest temperaments named Geoff and a pianist named Ian who, being surnamed Stewart, answered to the chirp of 'Stu', and whose Celtic heritage was embedded in a jawline so robust of contour as to prompt comparison to that famous hillock of Arthur's overlooking the Scottish capital.

This being a skeleton crew in dire need of muscle and blood, hope finally smiled upon Brian's persistence by driving two more emissaries of those hollering arts up the staircase of The Bricklayers Arms one early summer's eve. These he received with a smirk of recognition, being the very same fanatics who'd soaped him in foaming praise that halcyon Saturday night not so long ago in Ealing, unmistakably familiar in gob and auricle. Mick and Keith were just as pleasantly surprised that the key-holder of 'Box No. 1277' was none other than the esteemed Elmo Lewis, whose example had since inspired their own cameo appearance with Mr Korner's Blues Incorporated, after finally setting their sights on horizons beyond the net curtains of The Blue Boys' suburban incubator.

Their Dartford lances thus available for charter, they duly offered them to the advancement of Brian's campaign, pending agreeable chemistry of Mick's vocals and Keith's strings which, to the joy of all three, was immediately apparent. The marble chin of Stu wagged concurrence, though Geoff, whose blues orthodoxy was of a monastic order hostile to the impure shuck and boom of Chuck Berry and The Lord Bo Diddley, was coerced, by degrees, to remove himself from further practice of such sacrilege and seek a place of prominence in some History other than this.

The hearts of Brian, Mick and Keith beating as one, with Stu's maintaining a loyal boogie-woogie pace, they lacked only a bass player and drummer of similar stony calibre; persevering with assorted auxiliaries during interim weeks of open audition, hampered as they were by their leader's absences, more often on account of the familial chaos of swaddling robes and spaghetti hoops still playing havoc with his purse and patience. After another fruitless evening rehearsal with no sign of Brian, Mick volunteered to address this problem, promising to pay their missing comrade a visit the next day after college. Furnished with the directions to Brian's latest rented hovel in Notting Hill, he speedily found the property in question, ascended the steps, rang the doorbell and was greeted by the comely vision of Pat who, in bashful stops and starts, explained that Brian wasn't home, only she and their son, currently in a state of mercifully quiet sloth.

Mick, forming the opinion that the artful quadrille of his lips had raised in her breast certain fluttering emotions, appealed to her hospitality that he might be allowed inside to wait until his friend, her master, returned. Thus admitted, Mick accepted his host's offer of a hot cordial – nervously prepared under his assiduous watch – all the while putting his current course of fiscal study into practice; making quick assessment of Pat's vital statistics, the economic risks of personal profit and loss, the margins for error and the dividends if that gamble paid its potential reward. Satisfied with these calculations, casting an eye on the clock and an ear on the lock, having marked her as a bit o' jam worthy of his audit, Mick set the heavy machinery of that sentiment into motion with due speed of opportunity.

Herein lies a great lesson to the Reader, who having been supplied with so much data may have already made haste of their own arithmetic and, in so doing, added one plus one and confidently arrived at the sum of two. They would, of course, be wrong: for whatever addition or subtraction may or may not have occurred that day in Powis Square, the sum total, as tallied by Brian who eventually returned home after hours of mournful wanderings, was nothing. That is, a flat of nothing, Pat having taken all her belongings, little Julian included, transporting her reasons for this desertion into a scribbled note left upon the bed: its purpose to inform the father of that child that faced with a choice between spaghetti hoops and Cheltenham she'd chosen the latter, and so returned there accordingly.

Far from soliciting sobs of rejection, this annunciation was received with a soaring heart typical of a captive wretch unexpectedly liberated from their clammy dungeon, now savouring their first breath of the Creator's clean air. Felicity still conducting Brian's humours when he returned to The Bricklayers Arms, he vaulted up the stairs with a sportive gait, sharing the good news with his fellow minstrels, whose camaraderie was manifest in their compassionate smiles of surprisingly keen interest in his domestic affairs.

Recognising such brethren qualities, Brian thereby ventured two further points for group discussion. The first, a suggestion that he, Mick and Keith consolidate their aims by renting a suitable billet for three happy bachelor musicians to share as one. And second, that they distinguish their advancing Rhythm and Blues endeavours with a name, proposing that plucked from the sacred psalms of their beloved divinity, Muddy Waters. Both motions readily approved, the search thereby commenced to find a home worthy of these spunky young squires of infinite pep. To wit, and henceforth, 'The Rollin' Stones'.

VII

Descriptive of a habitat and its infestation.

Long has mankind wrestled with the mysteries of civic nomenclature and the sly logic with which its draughtsmen apply their perverse incongruity of lowly terrace and lofty title. So let us not dwell unnecessarily on the unfortunate disgrace of the family Grove, and their daughter Edith. For the name of Mademoiselle Edith Grove, conjuring as she does the tender apparition of a virtuous school mistress delicately arranging a vase of lupins, was never more brutally deflowered by brick and slate than the sordid vennel where our three heroes found themselves affordable domicile. Enough that poor Edith, bleak boulevard of paupers and tinks, lay her body down in that specific Chelsea ditch where daily thoughts of the four horsemen so burdened its natives – convinced as they were it could only be a matter of days before the disgusted Lord belched 'Good riddance!' and punted the whole squalid commune sliding into the Thames – that it identified itself as World's End.

If the Reader can bear to picture that stretch of pathetic Edith, stricken spread-eagled, her feet almost dipping in the river, her head finding cold tarmacked comfort at the western edge of the Kings Road, then it was somewhere an inch shy of her privy-counsel that Brian, Mick and Keith invaded her personage like thatch fleas, nesting in the first floor of Number Hundred-and-Two at a cost of sixteen pounds a week. In exchange for this beggar's ransom, they were granted privilege of: two chambers – one consisting of twin mattresses, each commandeered by Mick and Keith, the other a general living quarter illuminated by a single overhead bulb, where Brian bedded; a narrow kitchen, its surfaces destined for scenes of multiple botanical experiments in the cultivation of yeasts, mould and similar fungal cankers upon the crockery so quickly exhausted by these three foreigners to the common dishcloth; and a washing basin, its purpose all too rarely exploited, except by Brian, whose daily toilet so amused and exasperated his cotenants that he earned their ribald esteem of 'Mr Shampoo'. That one other necessary facility of human habitation was situated outside on the upstairs landing, which they shared with both the lodgers of the adjoining apartments and a few scampering descendants of those furred plague-carriers of ignominious legend. As bleak and filthy a space as could be found in woeful Edith's groin, but proud homestead to our three newly fledged Rollin' Stones.

The call of education still tightening its scarf around Mick's nape, he alone was blessed with fair excuse for daily escape while Brian, since discharged in shame from the department store after the genius of his regular supplements from counter till to private payroll was abruptly exposed, and Keith, having tired of Sidcup art school and all its commodes, held the fort of guitar practice and group plotting during their singer's daylight absence.

These enterprises were, alas, forever at the mercy of those elemental enemies of spirit, shiver and starvation. Their tenancy coinciding with the coldest English winter for two centuries past, it was common for both to remain all day in their candlewick cocoons rather than risk the pulmonary perils of exposing bare flesh beyond the bedclothes. The only available source of warmth being dependent on their regular feeding of shilling coins into a meter, the paucity of the former and the gluttony of the latter only maintained that frozen torpor.

Being that the average temperature of Hundred-and-Two Edith Grove was better suited to those tusked sea mammals of the Arctic north, our heroes were doubly disadvantaged in their shocking deficiency of blubber, of which there was little danger of accumulation on a diet dictated not by peptic desire and bodily needs but poverty, charity and opportunity. In the last of those aspects, Brian was superior of cunning, subjecting the shelves of the local corner shop to the same dextrous minuet between palm and pocket as he had many an employer's cashbox. The proprietor of that establishment being a Welshman, name of Morgan, such embezzled edibles were thus granted the prominence of shorthand in their lexicon: 'a Morgan Morgan'.

To this erratic supply were added the occasional parcel of tinned victuals from Keith's mother, and what booty they could plunder from their direct neighbours; whether by invitation to a communal soiree, the host enjoying their company for as brief a period it took to relieve their larder of all transportable contents, exiting in strange postures governed by restriction of conspicuously lumpy raiment; or by more fiendish initiatives, discovering hidden latchkeys with which to casually invade those same stores during their occupants' hours of vacation without having to resort to criminal delinquencies of chisel and jemmy.

While the divisions of a Morgan Morgan were more nourishing for all when split three ways rather than four, the state of their collected assets being so dire as to impose need of such strenuous self-sufficiency in the first instance, it was decided to share their burden of lease by increasing their household by an extra number. The chosen digit was an old Cheltenham acquaintance of Brian's named Dick – this History being full of Dicks, big and small, not to be confused with any mentioned fore or aft – who initially struggled with those metropolitan customs alien to a young man of his parochial traditions.

Fortunately, he had the kindly wing of Brian, who took cautions to instruct in the particulars of London etiquette: that Dick must surrender his warmest garments to the wardrobes of his new denizens; the obligations of Dick's singular purse to all their appetites at the local Wimpy bar; and Dick's duties as flat jester, beholden to daily capers as Brian would threaten him with pain of electrocution from loose guitar cables – which, incapable of that task, only improved their good cheer watching his pot-walloper hysteria of ignorance – or repel him from the premises in a state of undress during a snow blizzard, so as to enjoy those hilarious convulsions of frostbite and humiliation as witnessed through the grimy lens of their front window. As Brian's plump cherry on this sweet cake of japery, Dick's frequent glances pleading to be readmitted were, to the auxiliary of his icy dismay, rewarded by the sight of his friend perverting their visage with both hands so as to resemble as grotesque a demon as could be found upon the stony spires of Notre Dame cathedral. So effective was this mask, and so frequent its employment in Brian's daily repertoire of expression, that it, too, was accorded scientific definition in their vocabulary, so defined: pulling 'a Nanker'.

The unfortunate rupturing of Dick's appendix effecting immediate cessation of these frolics, and his tenancy, it became the honour of another young gentleman – surnamed Phelge – to enter this World's End fellowship of Morgan Morgan and Nanker. Master Phelge – being blessed with an onomatopoeic cognomen worthy of a hunchy villain terrorising the pages of the great Mr Dickens – showed due consideration in the expectations of his heritage by conducting himself in ways which, even those hitherto unfamiliar with that extraction, would still recognise as the essence of Phelgery. When Brian, Mick and Keith returned home from a night at The Moist Hoist to be welcomed by their new lodger, stark naked, wearing underpants upon his head, striped as they were with the umber echo of recent excreta, all agreed this behaviour was '*most* Phelge!' When he decided to decorate the living room walls with a series of frescoes executed in his own human tempera, artfully applied without brush but rather by colourful projections from the palette of his oesophagus, all concurred such novel adornments – christened 'Scarlet Jenkins', 'Yellow Humphrey' and the like depending on hue and translucency – were '*indubitably* Phelge!' And when visitors to this same gallery of secretions were introduced to the artist, who would thus shake their hand whilst deliberately extending a chandelier of mucus from his nostril, they would leave secure in the knowledge of having never had the privilege of meeting an individual so '*scrupulously* and *splendidly* Phelge!'

It might easily be assumed that, the mathematics of four rakes into two chambers, the parsimony of privacy in respect of those same sleeping arrangements, and the Phelgian décor – with its aesthetic limitations in the eye of the average female beholder – may have unfavourable consequence for their baser impulses. And yet, the Cyprian instruments of Brian, Mick and Keith demanding as much regular rehearsal as guitar and harmonica, their dedication in this field, combined with their individual virtuosities of blandishment and bareback seduction, sufficed in guaranteeing the extension of their hospitality to a succession of damsels, none so shy or discriminate in home furnishings as to forgo the disentitling of their honour in so public and pediculous a forum.

Had she means to scratch, our lamentable Edith would surely have tackled these most persistent itches in her nether crevice. Shame enough on her, and the family Grove, that they continued in similar irritation, without address, throughout that bitter winter, as the three musicians starved, and Morganed, and Nankered, and

Phelged, and swived, and practised; committed to amplifying their fame upon the club stages of London, yet still vexed by the instability in their ranks with regard to a permanent bass player, and drummer, worthy of that designation: 'a Rollin' Stone'. To which end, and with the emphasis very much on amplifying, the first of these problems was solved a few weeks before Christmastide, in circumstances related in the episode looming.

VIII

∽

*Chiefly relates to the importance of
William never being Ernest.*

THE READER THUS familiarised with the deplorable
Edith – supine with her toes towards the Thames and
her tresses strewn northwards – might easily imagine
that, at the moment of horizontal collapse, a bonnet slipped off
her head and found close station along the Kings Road. In doing
so, the Reader will now understand the position of that bonnet
and its close proximity to those *caput mortuum* tapestries of
Number Hundred-and-Two, being the same locus of The
Wetherby Arms, one of many World's End mughouses and that
selected by our Rollin' Stones for purposes of regular rehearsal.

It was there, in full embrace of Wetherby, one especially snowy
Friday in December, that Brian, Mick and Keith gathered
alongside Stu, the Scottish pianist of extraordinary jawbone whose
fidelity to the group remained solid, awaiting their latest trial
drummer, one Tony who – in his eager state of purgatory, pending
full certificate of approval – had promised to introduce them to
another musician friend he considered worthy of audition; hoping
to complement his efforts, and their rhythm section, with a bassist
of parallel talents.

When Tony arrived it was, indeed, with that candidate in tow:
one Bill Perks, whose neatness of dress, and hair set in the cropped

Edwardian fashion, stood in direct contrast to our three scruffy specimens. They greeted one another as three pots of oil might a pitcher of water, the trio as repulsed by his precision of collars and cuffs as he by their surly dishabille. Adding to such immediate misgivings was the suspicion that this soldier of hygiene was sufficiently etched of face to have already been subject to time's despoilments long before any of them had joined the gallop of life and, indeed, had been given such a head start in that race as to be of a mature age that reminisced of a childhood prior to the cursed advents of electricity, motor car and the female vote.

In this last assumption, though they were correct of instinct, they had somewhat miscalculated that gap, the immaculate Bill being roughly seven years older than Mick and Keith, five older than Brian, and fewer than two longer in molars than Stu. His history, like theirs, commencing in those territories south of Westminster, he was raised in Penge, a name lending further proof to The Almighty's genius for denomination, being a township every bit as evocatively Pengeish as our beloved Master Phelge was characteristically Phelgish.

So Pengeish was Bill's youth, his juvenile predicaments could not have been more impoverished had he been born in a coal scuttle and weaned upon the succouring drips of sooty rainwater trickling down from the chimney above. Bedevilled by poverty and all its odours, his mother and father educated him in the essential arts of thrift and graft necessary for Pengeian survival; learning to change his socks not more than once per week, and being corralled with his five siblings into family onion-peeling sessions at the behest of a local firm of picklers, engaging thereof until his tear ducts declared drought and his fingers assumed the ochre of jaundice.

Moulded by these and other Pengeish affectations, Bill learned to appreciate the value not only of common coinage, but also bookkeeping; developing into a young man whose meticulous notation of every shilling spent – upon what, in which place, on what date, at what time – though of a character in that undefinable no-man's land between habit and mania, meant that any hypothetical fears of ever being arrested in error for having pickaxed a Croydon pensioner Thursday last at a quarter-to-six were now obsolete; having documentary evidence of the fish and chip vendor in Beckenham whom he patronised at that same hour, with supplementary information relating to cost, size of portion, flakiness of cod, frangibility of batter and sufficient other easily verifiable data to suspend any unwelcome appointment with Her Majesty's executioner.

Furthermore, the added benefits of being so persistently Pepys a Perks from Penge were as exhaustive a record of his own actions as would be the envy of that exalted diarist of fire and plague, no detail too insignificant for the posterity of transcription; from the date of his entry into the Royal Air Force, being of that age when such service to the nation was compulsory, to his more pleasurable entry into a young woman from Humberside, the latter one of many romantic conquests annotated with the same rigorous attention to time, place and other vital statistics as his chronic thirst for minutiae decreed.

At the age of twenty-three, all conquests having reached their dramatic conclusion, Bill resigned to muzzling further investigations and coppiced his *arbor vitae* in the time-honoured tradition known as matrimony; a detail which, four years on from those sacred mutterings, gave cause for astonishment amongst Brian, Mick and Keith of a kind no more pleasant than that already provoked by his age and apparel. Taking full inventory of this applicant – being a Perks from Penge, being not only a husband but latterly a father, being shipshape of locks and polished of shoe – all three passed silent judgement that the formality of audition was probably unnecessary, seeing that he was so unacceptably habited as to be much worse than a Bill but, by point of fact, 'a real Ernie'. The qualities of which were defined in their elite dictionary of phrase as being descriptive of any regular gentleman who, lacking individual style, usually carried themselves in such a manner as to assume the eyes of the world regarded them with an admiration entirely the product of their own fantasy; thus compounding the buffoonery of one whose behaviour demanded that vulgar abbreviated form of Ernest, so applied.

Motion carried, Bill now charged with the felony of Ernie, all that remained was for Brian to dispatch him back to Penge with a parting Nanker, when his sudden generosity in purchasing them all a round of drinks and the production from his pocket of an entire carton of cigarettes, duly distributed, delayed sentencing for enough minutes to allow him to fetch the tools of his four-stringed trade from his car outside. That opportunity afforded, he returned lugging a speaker cabinet so monstrous as could be sublet for inhabitation by pygmies; being as large as a wardrobe, as bulky as an omnibus and as heavy as a frigate. The wooden colossus dragged into position, Brian, Mick and Keith stood gawping as might those druids of old in worship of an enormous stone monolith, each contemplating what force of decibels could be blasted from this frightful behemoth. To which their eager expectations were quickly rewarded by practical demonstration, its employment sending such throbbing ricochets through their skulls as hadn't been felt since their respective infancies when babes of the Blitz.

This miracle of amplification demanding a retrial, their assize was adjourned for a short rehearsal to test the compatibility of its firepower beside their own artillery, after which they reconvened. The final verdict, as delivered, being that no Ernie was capable of such ingenious assemblage of valve and carpentry, thereby nulling and voiding that former charge and declaring that, in interest of volume, they were willing to accept this Ernie at face value of Bill and offer him speedy ceremony of induction. That honour accepted, along with the request to join them for his maiden engagement in their service the following week, it was suggested that, for convenience of all, Bill should store his gargantuan device beside their own in their living quarters just around the corner. This Bill also accepted, transporting that treasure to Hundred-and-Two Edith Grove and so experiencing the delight common to all who entered that premises on catching their first glimpse of those rare exhibited works from the phlegmish school.

By degrees of tailoring, practice and performance, Bill methodically ridded himself of all tics of Ernie and all traces of Perks; borrowing the name of an old acquaintance from his days as a conscript, one Lee Wyman, and ingratiating himself ever further into the vital organs of Brian, Mick and Keith by regular procurement of cigarettes and fish suppers – all properly accounted for in his ledgers with his usual exhaustive diligence – and making efforts to alter his hairstyle with strategic metamorphosis from short, oily quiff to long, swarthy fringe.

In this improvement he first presented himself to his new colleagues in the café of the Aerated Bread Company hours prior to a turn at The Moist Hoist: whereupon all greeted sight of his adjustment of pompadour with laughter so incapacitating as to provoke grave fears from the patrons of neighbouring tables for their respiratory wellbeing.

With these convivial charades of affection, Bill thus passed his probation as a Rollin' Stone, a position of reverence he was sadly unable to share with his original nominee. For their drum-stool requiring sturdier buttocks supporting stronger elbows than those of Tony, the quest for such critical ligaments thereby became paramount as the year Nineteen Sixty-Two hurtled without pause into Nineteen Sixty-Three – just as this chapter bombards irreversibly into our next.

CHAPTER

IX

∽

Acquaints the Reader with an enigma.

IKE A TRIUMPHANT general dusting specks of rubble from his epaulettes while surveying the aftermath of battle, so Brian began the New Year reflecting on the state of that regiment he'd painstakingly assembled over the previous eight months. The spoils of his tenacity being a devoted pianist and van driver in Stu, a sublime singer in Mick, a capital guitarist in Keith and an impressively thunderous bassist in Bill. These were his men, and he their master, even if he'd had misfortune to relinquish the public recognition of such, at no small cost to his ego, after press notices for their past few concerts listed them as 'MICK JAGGER AND THE ROLLIN' STONES'. This liberty the named culprit blamed on a silly misunderstanding between himself and printer's devil, reassuring Brian he would never be so insolent a Brutus as to plunge this treacherous dagger into the heart of his beloved leader with any deliberate calculation of forethought, being that he already had enough calculations to occupy his mind, both in his studies at the school of economics, and the algebraic conversion of a downstairs neighbour into an upstairs nymphet.

This incident was, however, but minor irritation to Brian when compared with the continuing crisis of tempo remaining uppermost in his apprehensions; having previously meddled with another Mick, considered a Carlo and latterly toyed with Tony: none of whom were sufficiently personable of character or percussion as to earn themselves a permanent station in that platoon.

Confounding Brian's frustration was the knowledge that such a perfect specimen did exist, having first witnessed this messiah of rhythm many months ago at The Moist Hoist in the employ of Mr Korner's Blues Incorporated, and having, on numerous occasions since, failed to tempt this phenomenon into his service. The identity of this elusive prophet so haunted his thoughts that whenever he mentioned him by title it was with a whispered reverence, as if incanting the Holy Ghost itself. His evangelical belief in this syncopatic saviour was so contagious it quickly spread amongst his fellow Stones with the velocity of lice, until they too were only able of articulating those same two words in hushed religious mantra, the echo of his legend howling through the fixtures of Edith Grove like a spectral draft. Hallowed be thy name, of 'Charlie Watts'.

Charlie Watts wasn't merely a drummer but also an enigma, and since the engagement of the former meant contending with the latter, Brian had yet to learn the correct combination to unlock the inscrutable gateway to his humours. To what cerebral timpani the industry inside Charlie's mind kept pace was a mystery no living soul would ever deduce from the stillness of visage; the mouth so permanently tight that the lips seemed a careless crease in an otherwise vast drape of skin; the philtrum so long, its fleshy groove invited tempting rest to a fountain pen; and the eyes, two great hooded bulbs greeting every individual with their cool resignation that this world was chiefly populated by idiots, thus better to subject all strangers to that same preconception of their intellects.

These were the opaque blockades of human emotion Brian had to surmount if his dream of hiring Charlie Watts was ever going to be realised; which, as of the first dawn of January, Nineteen

Sixty-Three, seemed as likely a change in fortune as that of their good friend Phelge being suddenly summoned to the palace with instruction to utilise all those ejaculatory talents at his disposal to render, upon canvas, as close a likeness to Her Majesty as his exceptional facial sockets could marshal.

Brian's loyal troops, bonded by mutual fixation with this inscrutable pimpernel of snare and sticks, and sharing his dismay, volunteered to aid him in whatever efforts of persuasion they could administer. Much as the keenest huntsmen are those who hesitate in rash pursuit of the quarry in order to first accustom themselves with the second natures of that which they wish to consign to the casserole, they similarly prepared themselves with as full an intimacy of his person as could be scraped from the barrel of hearsay. That he was indeed a Charlie, son of Charlie, and by all accounts, a Watts; that he was born north of the river, but schooled in the south; that his first instrument was a banjo, which he didn't take to, until he removed the obstruction of neck and strings, banged the hollow body – and, Lo! – discovered the sensual bliss of his first tabor; that he'd been to art school and now worked in the city as a designer of commercial graphics; that he was a groom of fashion with, it was said, an impressive catalogue of handkerchiefs; that he'd parted with Mr Korner and had since located his frozen grimace behind the cymbals of a new group, Blues By Six; and that he was of the professional opinion that the carriage, erection and dismantling of a drum-kit being so laborious, it was only ever worth his undertaking that nuisance in exchange for a handsome sum not merely deserved of his remarkable metronomic agues of limb, but of subsidiary benefit to the extension of that already renowned collection of silken napkins.

It was this issue of imbursement which most worried Brian and his fellow trappers who, despite increasing sorties upon the club stages of the capital, had yet to find remuneration so great as to stem the mysterious shrinkage of comestibles from the shelves of that World's End storekeeper named Morgan. The grand sum of their enquiry being that they were paupers, and he a prince seemingly beyond their purses. Or so they feared, until optimism was restored with the realisation that, if this Charlie Watts was so thoroughbred an enigma, he would possess that one quality which all such sires of the indecipherable held dearest, and which, with delicate extractions of conversation, they could utilise to their long-term advantage. That is, a true enigma was an inherent enemy of the predictable, ally to the unexpected and rebel to conformity.

Reviewing their tactics in light of this intelligence, after careful rehearsal of a stratagem considerate of so skilled a contrarian, they made fresh approach that second week of January. The diplomatic dalliance commenced with Brian innocently asking Charlie about the state of play in Blues By Six. Charlie replied that, though he appreciated the work and all its linen dividends, he always considered his talents better suited to the swing of jazz than the wallop of Rhythm and Blues.

Mick interpreted their next move accordingly, echoing that sentiment and offering his sympathies to Charlie that he should be forced into such a humiliating position as to waste his precious gifts on common commotions he evidently despised. The bait tasted, Charlie begged correction: though his heart throbbed to be-bop, he was still governor of his ambitions, happy with his decisions and no drudge to duress. Keith, reading these signals, apologised on Mick's behalf, and expressed his joy that Charlie had chosen to play that faddish noise in so obvious a form as that sculpted by Blues By Six, rather than, dare he say it himself, the novel 'jazzy' abstraction of rock 'n' roll as cooked by their own humble concert party.

Charlie, now an inch from the hook, retorted that they were, again, in error if they seriously believed his capabilities fell short of their dreadful cacophony. Brian, feeling the line twitch and turning the reel, interjected with expression of regret that, despite that last disclaim, Charlie had declined their offer to join them, much as they fully respected his motives and wished him all happiness for future compromises. This final contrivance tugging the full force of his obstinacy, Charlie countered that, although his father surely wouldn't approve, damn his eyes! And damn the eyes of all others who dared try and stop him climbing behind their drum-kit for the rest of his natural life.

The matter settled in most agreeable disagreement, upon the twelfth day of January, Nineteen Sixty-Three, as London braced itself for another night dipping minus six degrees below zero; as the nation shivered for warmth from the cathode ray flames of *77 Sunset Strip* and *The Rag Trade*; and as the iced pavements of Ealing Broadway glistened like a jewellers' shop-front, only a few feet below, the enigma Charlie Watts took his place on The Moist Hoist stage; content that once again he had proved duke of his own destiny, impervious to all coercion, and thus thumped his first beat – till death do them part! – as drummer with The Rollin' Stones.

CHAPTER

X

A short one, introducing forces opposed to their progress.

PEERING THROUGH THE window of his bedchamber, his sloping eyes noticing yet another arrival to the fertile family of stalactites who'd taken firm residence in the Downing Street guttering since Christmas, even the illustrious Supermac was forced to admit that, though his satisfied peoples had still never had it so good, they surely had never had it so cold as in January, Nineteen Sixty-Three.

So cold that drizzle froze solid the moment it kissed the ground: renamed by weather-forecasters who now warned of the dangers of 'frizzle'. So cold the fountains in Trafalgar Square had frozen, the river Thames had frozen and even the sea along the Kentish coast, deferring to this latest meteorological fad, had adopted an appearance similarly frozen. So cold that millions of gallons of milk sucked from the blue udders of frozen cows went to ruin, since the roads connecting the dairies to the towns were impassable. So cold that London buses spluttered to a halt because their reserves of diesel congealed into an engine-buckling sorbet. So cold that the hypothermic sucklers drained the national grid, leaving cinemas, shops, banks and even the lights of Piccadilly Circus in shivering darkness. But amongst all that snow, sleet and frizzle, in all of the great capital – indeed, in all of Dante's ninth circle of hell – there was nothing so cold as the membranous tissue within the heads and ribcages of those masonic elite known as the Jazz Mafia.

The cause of this petrification of heart and mind was the gravity with which the owners of those organs accepted the responsibility of sentry duty to the stages of London's Clubland, each holding as they did the golden keys to the holy cellars of Soho, and each determined that no minstrel who didn't humbly submit to their etiquettes of entry should ever be granted the privilege of admittance. This etiquette involving various means and measurements to assess the aesthetic purity of their performance according to the mathematical laws of jazz, and calculated with the kindred vigilance of Sicilian business affairs, they so earned their notorious epithet – subjecting all who dreamed of glory upon their sacred boards to the full blizzard of their merciless scrutiny. None dared challenge the prudence of the Jazz Mafia, who for years had monitored their palaces of entertainment as a bored spinster of zealous horticultural habits might a privet hedge: taking their shears to any unsightly bud or twig that may threaten to pervert the uniformity of bush so obsessively groomed the instant it appeared.

It was the subject of such a grotesque botanical mutation that took precedent on the agenda of the Jazz Mafia's inaugural monthly council of Nineteen Sixty-Three, conducted in their usual secret chambers deep beneath the Soho slush of snow, grit and frizzle. All members swearing in, raising their right hands with praise to 'Dixieland', the chairman bid them seated and, with the secretary poised with quill and inkwell to commence the scribbling of minutes, declared the order of business now open. Item one: discussion of application to perform on the premises of the Jazz Mafia by 'The Rollin' Stones'.

The secretary already engaged in frantic transcription, the first right honourable member enquired as to which variant of jazz these 'Rollin' Stones' executed. To which the chairman made advance apologies, informing his Brothers that he was of firm authority they were victims of that new infection troubling the provincial clubs to the west of the city, known as Rhythm and Blues, so abbreviated as 'R&B', and already popularised by their traitorous Brother Korner.

This information greeted with hiss and murmur, a second right honourable member inquired as to whether these 'Rollin' Stones' – and, by the by, how in Jove's name that had anything to do with Dixieland was beyond all his phonographic knowledge – were of Brother Korner's standards, high as they were for such a low pursuit. The chairman paused to consult his notes, returning with the information that they were, to quote a witness, 'somewhat more flatulent'.

That information received with fierce gusts of tutting, a third right honourable member asked whether or not any of that party wore bowler hats. The chairman returned that none of their number was known to perform wearing a bowler hat and, since on matters of habit and cloth, were in fact entirely devoid of duffel, so rallying a violent chorus of 'Pshaw!'

Palpitations calming and order eventually resumed after much waving of hands, clearing of throats and slapping of temples, their right honourable treasurer was next invited to pass his opinion, based upon the accrued sacrilege so far discussed. That Brother rising to his feet, he unscrolled a length of paper upon which he had prepared a graph of musical excellence, the apex of which was marked in illuminated script 'Dixieland', the base of which the forefinger of his right hand now pointed with remark to the relative virtues of the candidates, being tradesmen of arts so flatulent and, let it be said, 'excessively negroid'.

A cheer of concurrence, roars of 'Hear, hear!', 'Huzzah!' and 'Hoo-hoo-lah!', the treasurer resumed his seat, the chairman thanked the right honourable members and, turning to the secretary with whispering advice to underline 'excessively negroid' three times, passed motion that the name of these heathens be added to the Jazz Mafia's blacklist, to be breeched under pain of immediate expulsion from that benevolent brotherhood, all hail Dixieland!

On the streets above their heads, the frizzle continued to fall, the buses continued to choke, the dormant Piccadilly bulbs of Guinness and Wrigley's continued to cast ghostly grey traces in dire want of flickering brilliance. And those icy daggers continued to dangle in defiance from the gutter in Downing Street, no closer to thawing than the vitrified souls of that miserable guild now conspiring to eliminate our Rollin' Stones.

CHAPTER
XI

⸫

*Their progress happily unobstructed, with encouragement
from four northern minstrels of absurd popularity.*

PRING ARRIVED, THE snow departed, and still our adven-
turers were no further in penetrating the fortifications of
those withering sentinels of latter acquaintance. Spurned
from Soho, they gathered force safe beyond such jurisdiction,
remaining in the west, having risen to become Ealing's resident
weekend attraction at The Moist Hoist, also straying cautiously
into the surrounding counties as far as the Royal Borough of
Windsor and an establishment named The Ricky Tick; housed in
the upper quarters of The Star & Garter Hotel, where Mick paid
his own respects to that military Order by choosing to acquaint
himself with the garters of a local girl of considerable charm and
breeding.

Miss Christine Shrimpton, or 'Chrissie' as she preferred, had
been schooled in style of nunnery, a misfortune which our
champion charitably sought to amend by enlightening this
seventeen-year-old innocent into communions superior to those
of the Eucharist, specifically the rites pertaining to the altar of
Venus in which he was fast becoming a learned specialist. Upon
his first attempt in this blessed task, he discovered he had grossly
underestimated the mental barricades those dreaded she-beasts of
Rome had set in place, inviting Chrissie to visit his parental home

in Dartford at a convenient hour when, with full likelihood of consequences he had foreseen, that abode would be deserted. These circumstances arousing much less ardour in his young lady than they did the nervous suspicions of her chastity, she fled without any success of consecration.

A second invitation, this time to his proper lodgings in Edith Grove, ended in equally dismal fashion, his unblemished belle-chose refusing to part with the spoils of her honour in sight of the viscid tableaux of its artist in residence, the most admirable Master Phelge.

Cumulative rejection only maddening Mick's appetite, he made urgent appeal to Chrissie's sensitivity of environment, suggesting she personally select the scene of her imminent disgrace. Interpreting this blazing curiosity of hips as a tender sickness of heart, the helpless damsel finally nominated an opportune date at her parents' home near Windsor, where the upholstery was infinitely more agreeable; so ensuring his conspiracy was at last concluded in blissful privacy, the dam of popery was demolished and the waters of nature's treasury flowed free.

While Mick was thus bucking in Buckinghamshire, Brian applied similar vigour in finding a new stage for their group to flourish closer to home. In this industry he was tremendously successful, making the favourable association of one of the few musical promoters to have slipped between the hoarfrosted fingers of the supercilious Jazz Mafia. His name was Giorgio, a gentleman of Soviet extraction and Italian emulsion: his chief interest making films; his chief subject matter live music, both passions colliding in the instigation of his own club night allowing him regular opportunity for fresh celluloid document.

Taking inspiration from The Moist Hoist, Giorgio chose a parallel location, similarly situated at a branch end of the District Line, similarly placed directly over the carriageway opposite that terminus, being the rear of The Station Hotel in the Surrey suburb of Richmond. The only disadvantages of this enterprise were his restriction to the use of that premises on the Sabbath alone, and his initial employment of a resident Rhythm and Blues band who, in respect of that obligation, exhibited a disheartening lack of punctuality. This new erudition prompting Brian's cunning into overture, he presented himself to Giorgio, offering deep condolence for upset caused by those tardy ingrates and volunteering his own reliable replacements: a provident solution very gratefully accepted.

So commenced The Rollin' Stones' weekly inhabitation of The Station Hotel, which was named every Sunday evening for their purpose 'The Crawdaddy Club', chosen from a favourite song in their repertoire by The Lord Bo Diddley about coursing for langoustine; the suitability of which would otherwise have caused immense confusion to those prompted to undertake vain investigation of the nearby Thames for any evidence of that boilable crustacean.

Were they not so encased in glacial bitterness, it would have surely shattered the hearts of the Jazz Mafia to witness the success of this venture, the audiences doubling, then trebling, week upon week, not a thread of duffel amongst them, their hair unkempt as troglodytes, their number so huge that both sexes splurged together as one in a depraved human chutney of lipstick, knitwear and Chelsea boot; jammed so tight that they danced with spastic constraint as if vertically engaged in bareback surrender with an invisible assailant of their own sordid fancy. Had the Jazz Mafia sufficient luxury of association with that old Dutch master Hieronymus Bosch so as to commission him to paint them a vision of Hell, even he would be unable to muster anything from his famous palette of horrors quite so turbulent in all its flatulence and negroid excess to their digestive tracts as the Crawdaddy Club.

By the first blossoms of April, this local commotion had attracted the attentions of the parish newspaper, the *Richmond And Twickenham Times*, whose full-page report, the first such appearance of The Rollin' Stones in any periodical, was so celebratory of their antics that – from the day of its publication – Brian kept a copy upon his person at all times, retrieving it from his wallet for personal perusal in quiet moments of reflection, as a trenchfooted infantryman in the bogs of Flanders might a crumpled photograph of their distant sweetheart.

Among the many observations its correspondent thought worthy of ink he regarded their barbering, being 'brushed forward from the crown' in a manner that the writer likened both to a sculpted bust of recent anthropological conjecture on the missing link between monkey and homo-erectus, and 'The Beatles Pop Group'.

These words – once appearing in newsprint – having the effect of supernatural summons, the day immediately following publication of this article the very same Beatles Pop Group were stood in attendance at the Crawdaddy Club to make their own follicular assessment. Their four members were identically dressed in long coats of suede, and identically combed in concealment of forehead, but otherwise individual of visage and temperament: John, with the smile of a schoolboy but the vicious eyes of a hungry sparrowhawk; Paul, his face one of perpetual vexation, as if still recovering from the news that the earth was round and he half expected to roll off at any moment; George, so quiet as to provoke immediate mystery as to whether he was a pensive genius or a mute simpleton; and Ringo, who left no such doubt in the latter respect, being a fellow of quite explicit idiocy. As a 'Pop Group', so described, they had been savouring the joy of national adulation for five months, having already scored two hit singles and that week primed to release their third, the promotion of which had brought them to London from their home in Liverpool; a detail betrayed by their drowsily bobbing speech patterns typical of that northern province; and a circumstance which, through special invitation from Giorgio, also afforded them free time to witness their budding competition from the south.

The music of The Rollin' Stones struck them as quite different from their own in many aspects: the Stones played frantic interpretations of American blues madrigals, delivered with savage emphasis on rumbustious rhythm and Dionysian abandon, helped in no small part by the debauched convulsions of Mick, whose eager hips and eely lips piped the woodwind of those fair sex assembled with a saucy tune all their own; The Beatles Pop Group mostly played songs of their own construction, being sweet, orderly and often distinguished by choruses in which John and Paul would pucker their mouths, jiggle their heads and release a quivering coo of painfully high pitch, the combined effect evocative of a parson with acute inflammation of the nancy who, having been ill-advised to calm that agony in an icy bath, had plunged his hind quarters into that receptacle with a speed as keen as it was audibly foolish.

It therefore struck these guests of growing celebrity that the Stones, by comparison, were agreeable imitators of no challenge to their position, being as alike as a eunuch and a Viking, and so congratulated them on their accomplishment of noise after that performance. Thus flattered, the Stones exhibited appropriate hospitality by inviting The Beatles Pop Group to continue their conversation back at their humble retreat in the lap of poor Edith. That motion accepted, those four gentlemen of the north proved unusual in their nonchalance at the marvellous, if frequently polarising, encrusted exhibits of Master Phelge; informing their hosts that this habitat was positively regal compared to their previous lodgings in the German port of Hamburg where they'd served apprenticeship; their beds, at that time, located in a dormitory squeezed behind a cinema screen reserved for the regular projection of adult nature subjects, their slumber thus serenaded by the calls of the wild in all their piercing ululations.

So bonded by monologues of squalor and kindred coiffuring, four nights later the Stones and The Beatles Pop Group reconvened at Kensington's Royal Albert Hall, where those Merseyside sensations were scheduled to perform as part of a variety bill organised by the British Broadcasting Corporation. Unable to afford the price of entry, the Stones gained admittance with skilful subterfuge, masquerading as porters in the employ of the main turn: the carriage of John's guitar case and Ringo's cymbals sufficient ruse to ferry them beyond security and assume a prime location to witness the evening's proceedings.

Despite the fiercest efforts of all other acts – including an antipodean responsible for rare feats of hyperventilating lunacy assisted by unusual oscillations of plywood – none could incite the eruption of brainsickly feminine derangement specific to The Beatles Pop Group. The more they grinned, the more they cooed, the more their fringes fluttered and their knees sprang, the more the shriek of the audience rose to that of a colony of herring gulls granted freedom of a pilchard factory, reaching such volume as to undo the dentistry and liquefy the inner ears of any unwise enough not to muffle those apertures with both hands. It was a sound that humbled the Stones – who until then had thought themselves masters of similar manipulation, now realising they had caused only a damp ripple of petticoats compared with this swamping tidal wave of several thousand underbodices – as much as it inspired them.

Maintaining the stagehand charade till the end, upon transporting the band's instruments out of the Hall, our heroes found themselves under siege by squealing skirts who, in their sodden delirium and blindness of mascara, could see no further than man, guitar case and shaggy mane, and so mistook them as the very members of The Beatles Pop Group. Only after close proximity of molestation, having fumbled Mick, groped Keith and yanked Brian's locks like a bell chain, did these wretched maidens appreciate their error, and so retreated, leaving their victims supremely gratified by this tactile worship.

For having tasted but a few drops of that sweet juice in tiny measure, their appetites were now irreversibly whetted with a view to scaling the tree and scrumping the fruit. Yet, to do so, they would first need to acquire new means of elevation, no stone being able to hit so high a target without the ballistic assistance of a catapult. One much like the youthful cove of supreme elasticity and intense leverage, here poised to alter the entire course of their History, and this.

CHAPTER

XII

Contains a dramatic discussion of farthings and flapdoodles, in
course of which a letter is added and a number subtracted.

THE YOUNG GENTLEMAN stood, or rather shook, outside
the entrance of Richmond terminus, alone with nothing
to occupy him except his own excited twitching. He
twitched his lips on a cigarette, twitched to check his watch, twitched
his neck as a buxom young brunette sashayed past him, twitched an
approving glance at the sparkle of his shoes and twitched a
scratching finger to his ear before repeating this same cycle with
ever increasing twitchiness. He was as perfectly tailored as he was
pitiably thin; all body fat having been exhaustively twitched away,
leaving only a well groomed vibration of skin, bone and the bare
minimum muscle to hustle. For he twitched not out of sorry
prayer to St Vitus, but out of happy struggle to contain the excess
of atomic energy coursing through his bloodstream, his a waxed
mind whizzing at forty-five rotations per minute, forced to live in
a world grinding at a leisurely thirty-three-and-a-third: thus
rendering him the jump scratch across the grooves of pedestrian
reality christened Andrew Loog Oldham.

It was to the utmost disgrace of one of the finest boarding schools
in the land that they had failed to reduce the speed of this sprite,
despite their proudest traditions of dormitory cruelty, classroom
lobotomy and sports field pugnacity. These having quite the adverse

effect of increasing his twitchy momentum, he blasted free of their tender suppression, grazing through the fringes of the fashion trade until concentrating all force of his havoc on popular music: a sphere he entered through ingenious means of persuasion, feigning previous acquaintance with key persons of influence who, too proud to admit to any shabbiness of memory in not knowing this garrulous twitcher from Adam, obliged themselves to acquiesce in his confusing charade to full advantage of his future prospects.

At the age of nineteen, this young man born a bastard of wartime had successfully catapulted himself to positions of responsibility for the publicity of a variety of recording artistes, including The Beatles Pop Group. His twitching intensified by exposure to those nodding northerners' tempestuous effect upon the female pulse, he'd not long taken to fantasies of discovering such a troupe capable of inciting similar delirium to nurture for his own when fate, in form of a journalist friend, pointed him towards the novel disturbance taking place every Sunday in the rear of Richmond's Station Hotel.

Undertaking due investigation, he ventured alone, passing through the doors as a parish pauper whose bony lips knew only the weak taste of gruel might on waking up to find themselves suddenly transported to a world made entirely of treacle tart. In all his nineteen summers, no sensation had ever skewered Andrew's heart, dry-cured his tongue, grilled his ears, pummelled his teeth, goose-stepped the length of his spine, made marimba of his ribs, twanged his tendons, boxed his loins and French-kissed his soul like sight and sound of the hairy shamans upon the stage of the Crawdaddy Club. Though his faculties of speech had been blown much too askew to consider immediate introduction, with the grime of all opposing ambition flushed from his head, he left with his new monomaniacal purpose decided: to secure, post haste, management of The Rollin' Stones.

The success of this scheme dependent on the assistance of an established business partner whose years of experience in that field was necessary redress for his own shortcomings in aspect of youth, he turned to the nearest available candidate, one who had already proven sympathetic to Andrew's progress in allowing him shared rent of their Piccadilly office space at an especially attractive rate.

Mr Eric Easton was considerably older, considerably greyer and considerably less southern than Andrew; being a former organist at Blackpool Tower where he serenaded the clogged and capped and, it was rumoured, an employer of those same peasants as owner of a cotton mill. As a music agent, his most recent success was a management contract with a middle-aged saloon pianist from London's East End named Gladys Mills, whose joy in being able to thump out 'The Sheik Of Araby' and popular selections from *No, No, Nanette* with all the delicacy of a cooper's mallet, while miraculously never quite crushing the bones of recognisable melody, betrayed itself in a fixed facial expression permanently that of one second to midnight on New Year's Eve.

Grinning Gladys and her ivory clangs being typical of the entertaining breezes spinning Mr Easton's mental windmills, Andrew was understandably cautious in approaching him with so stormy a proposition as The Rollin' Stones, stressing all emphasis on the financial harvest should they prove anything as popular as that much admired Beatles Pop Group, who that very week were chuckling their way to the top of the charts with their latest castrato yodel. His northern fancy easily seized by thoughts of shiny farthings, the next obstacle was coaxing a commitment to witness them in person that coming Sabbath in Richmond: a request which tested Andrew's skills as verbal hypnotist to its limits, involving as it did damnable sacrifice of Mr Easton's favourite television programme, *Sunday Night At The London Palladium*.

And so, as he stood waiting outside Richmond station at the appointed time, Andrew's twitchings disguised no undue jig of panic that Mr Easton may yet forfeit their rendezvous, this worry only evaporating at first sight of the familiar grey scalp ascending the steps from platform to concourse. That scalp swiftly chaperoned across the road and into the rear of the Station Hotel, Andrew prayed its owner could tolerate the orgiastic crush of youth long enough to acknowledge his sagacious instincts with regard to the profitability of its conducting delinquents. Though Mr Easton was, indeed, deafened, dampened and jostled to the very thresholds of trauma, he concurred that Andrew may have found, if not quite a golden goose, then at the very least a silver hen whose lewd menstruations, if of a quality he could never appreciate with the same enthusiasm as his beloved Gladys and her wrecking-ball ragtime, could most likely be packaged and sold for enough shillings and pence to be worth his while.

Thus instructed to strike on their joint behalf, after waiting until the end of their rackety fermentations, Andrew waded through the swamp of pubescent exhaustion, approached the stage and introduced himself to Mick, assuming him to be their spokesperson according to his centrifugal presence on stage and his superior artillery of face for that capacity. The folly of this deduction, however innocent, was very swiftly highlighted in the singer's blank expression and jerking thumb towards Brian, who Andrew thereby understood, not without some twitch of surprise, to be their appointed superintendent.

Corrected in the course of his objective, Andrew put pause to his volley of enchantments, their rapid fire only resuming once he had full attention of Brian, whose ego he caressed with such floods of flattery as might, in different circumstances, set in motion the purchase of gold bands, silk gowns and perfumed confetti. The quarry swooning, Mr Easton next manoeuvred

'The Unlikely Leader Revealed'

himself into position, so relieving his partner of further mediation while he and Brian plotted their possible association in terms of tight contracts and loose change, agreeing to continue this same discourse later that week in the older gentleman's Piccadilly office.

Having reassured his five colleagues that he would never be so rash as to sign a single docket which might jeopardise group interests, Brian strode with confidence of purpose to the appointed place at the appointed hour where, sinking into Mr Easton's soft furnishings and bathed by Andrew's increasingly sweet torrents, his powers of attorney became so fogged by scrumptious dreams of fame, fortune and boons of fornication as to render him insensible: the consequences of which were that, before Brian was requested to autograph the bottom of the contract prepared, he was obliged to indulge Andrew in two trifling caveats. The first: a delicate issue of grammar, that their name, as spelt Rollin' with a dangling apostrophe in lieu of consonant, expressed sloppiness of intent and would benefit greatly from reinstatement of the crudely amputated seventh letter. And the second: that being six Stones they were, alas, simply one too many for public consumption.

The muscles of Brian's forehead agitated by this latter stipulation, after narrowing his eyes, rubbing a forefinger under his lips and emitting a knowing sigh, he replied that he too harboured his misgivings about Mick's vocal energies and, though it pained him to deny their audience a vision of male comeliness almost as magnetic as his own, he fully approved of their shrewd request to eject him forthwith.

Andrew smiled politely, clearing his throat before offering gentle apology for any misconstruction. To clarify, he detailed his quintet concern as purely aesthetic, the group currently looking like five Romany princes with the unfortunate appendage of a piano player reminiscent of that jigsaw of cadavers electrocuted to life on the pages of Miss Shelley. Brian now edified as to the identity of the sacrificial lamb being moreover a sacrificial mammoth, Andrew reiterated his regret that – although their chunky *compadre* could still assist them off stage in the recording studio and continue, should he wish, his duties as governor of group transportation – there was no place for Stu's unsightly millstone mandible in any operation so dependent as theirs on winning the gurgling approval of the nation's flapdoodles.

This new perspective being enough to alarm Brian's baser instincts, he consented that business being business, flapdoodles being flapdoodles, for the good of his group, their future and his whistle and bells, he hereby signed over all management at the agreed cost of one punctuation mark and a stocky pianist. In exchange, Mr Easton vowed to prove that Gladys Mills hadn't exhausted his Midas touch by securing them a phonographic recording deal, while in the meantime waging him a weekly retainer to be shared five ways. Brian expressed his gratitude, yet begged permission to wonder aloud whether that administrative responsibility ought to be acknowledged in kind, and so secured himself an extra five pounds a week, to be paid in strictest confidence.

All ink dried and hands shaken Brian departed, congratulating himself on his cunning of negotiation having greatly improved his purse. Mr Easton, too, congratulated himself on *his* cunning of negotiation having used Andrew's charm to win him effortless proprietorship of a potentially lucrative teenage vogue along the lines of The Beatles Pop Group. But neither congratulated themselves quite so heartily as that twitching youngster whose cunning of negotiation was of a genius so great as to allow both the aforementioned separate illusions of victory in a game he alone had won. For so long as Brian and Mr Easton busied themselves in fiscal pettifoggery, having exposed themselves as, respectively, a transparent Machiavelli who'd garrotte his best friend for a shake in the sheets, and a starched pinchpenny who'd

73

sign a bronchial ass if he heard a sovereign in its feathery honks, Andrew could be left alone to improve the recipe of his treacle tart until every flapdoodle in Christendom drooled at the faintest whisper of, the now named, now five, 'Rolling Stones'.

CHAPTER

XIII

◦⸎◦

The catapult employed and the pane broken.

RETURNING TO EDITH'S filthy bosom and informing his accomplices of all that had transpired, Brian was disappointed that his courageous duties as custodian of their trusts should be rewarded, not with huzzahs, hugs and jubilation, but with suspicion and alarm over the sudden execution in their ranks.

The one exception in this ugly remonstrance was the condemned pianist himself who voiced no protest, being sufficiently aware both of his shortcomings of pulchritude with regard to female excitations, and of the inherent skulduggery in their appointed leader. Thus Stu graciously complied to remain, as suggested, their transport chief and session stalwart: a minor consolation to Keith, who expressed no shortage of emotion on the subject, while Mick's distrust took interrogative shape of a lengthy cross-examination, with special focus on the breakdown of their invigorated finances. In particular, the contractual implications to their residency at the Crawdaddy Club and their patron, Giorgio, thus far under the impression he would retain his share in the Stones' commercial evolution. To which Brian was forced to admit that having already buried one poniard in the back of their Scottish amigo, he saw no reason not to repeat assassination upon their Richmond Caesar who, it saddened him to say, had indeed become another unfortunate casualty of their progress, the conduction of which now rested instead with their new benefactor Mr Easton, and his twitching confederate.

The murmurs of discontent ceased and cautious harmony was restored by a visit from that very same stirrer of the sands of monotony, who at his first sight of the hallowed hangings of Phelge and first smell of their festering kitchen recrement became prone to thoughts of disgorging his breakfast. Resisting this impulse for as long as it took to herd them away from Edith's sour aromas of juice and decay, and steering them to the refreshingly fragrant emporiums of Carnaby Street, Andrew informed them they were to be habited – at his and Mr Easton's expense – with new vestments.

In answer to Keith's enquiry as to why they need dispense with their old vestments, Andrew gently reminded them of the etiquette of the entertainment world, with its institutionalised abhorrence of the scruff: making reference to the uniform stitchings of the much admired Beatles Pop Group and, ipso facto, their obligation to follow suit with suits if they were to have any hope of chasing those footsteps to the heights of similar celebrity. This answer being enough to quell debate, including the bubbling umbrage of Charlie, whose exquisite tailoring rarely passed without compliment, Andrew proceeded to dictate their wardrobe: matching houndstooth jackets, rollneck jumpers, leather waistcoats and black denim inexpressibles, to be worn in varying combinations, as instructed, whenever they next prepared themselves for the posterity of camera lens.

Thus festooned with fresh cloth, Andrew further rejoiced their spirits with the news that he and Mr Easton had that week hired them an afternoon in a studio in which to record their first seven-inch waxing, the choice of which was naturally theirs, though he begged they consider its primary aim to infiltrate the Hit Parade, so suggesting they forgo the tribal excesses of their stage act –

prone as they were to repeating The Lord Bo Diddley's cannibalistic clip-clops for fifteen minutes uninterrupted – and instead constrain their sympathies to melody and brevity.

The challenge accepted with supreme enthusiasm, the five Stones retreated to their lair for emergency conference. After whittling the candidates from their current setlist down to almost nil, they leafed through their slim library of gramophone recordings in hope of inspiration, and so came upon a lesser composition by Mick and Keith's bonding Cupid, the estimable Chuck Berry; its libretto concerning a young man's scalding of heart and its ensuing hoodoo upon his affairs of automobile and telecommunications, the article being less than two minutes from start to finish and titled with apposite urgency for their current circumstance: 'Come On'.

Taking pains to customise its flavour as required – replacing jerky pulse with frantic throb and adding a fanfare of harmonica to lend it a nod and a wink vaguely reminiscent of The Beatles Pop Group – after rehearsing its arrangement to a state of competence, they reconvened that Friday afternoon at the chosen chamber of commitment, a converted synagogue in the vicinity of Piccadilly Circus named Olympic Studios.

They were greeted by Andrew, who presented himself as now not merely their managerial overseer but also their producer, volunteering for that task with a violent alacrity wholly disproportionate to his experience in that office; being, in truth, ignorant of the workings of the most basic recording appliances and utterly reliant on the charitable advice of a young engineer named Roger, whose first duty was to inform the twitching novice of the necessity of amplifiers in answer to his query as to why the band couldn't simply, as he'd presumed, 'plug into the wall'. Mick's exiguity of optimism in these clueless proceedings was complemented by the bundle of textbooks he brought with him, having yet to surrender his economic studies: ill convinced as he still was of spiting academia to risk his entire wellbeing on such shabby exploits, including his own Kentish approximation of Mr Berry's command of idiom which – with a week's hindsight – he himself felt obligated to dismiss with that crude syllable expressive of faecal ejecta.

Their enterprise was nevertheless comfortably achieved in the three hours allotted, or so Andrew thought until Roger politely raised the issue of 'mixing': a process still alien to the virgin choragus, who suggested his eager engineer be much better suited to that mysterious task; arranging to retrieve the finished article the following Monday when he planned to commence the next phase of his stratagem.

Andrew had already decided that there was only one Goliath worthy of felling with his twitchy sling, being another of those numerous Dicks which the Reader, as forewarned in a previous chapter, will hopefully have accepted as a regular eventuality of these adventures. Mr Rowe was, at that time, among the biggest Dicks in the industry, a consensus of opinion based on his reputation as the man who a decade earlier rammed '(How Much Is) That Doggie In The Window?' to number one on the pop charts, thus establishing himself as arch potentate of artist and repertoire at the Decca recording company, under the auspices of its celebrated founder and knighted sexagenarian, Sir Edward Lewis.

His professional esteem in that position had, however, recently been tarnished after forfeiting a first opportunity to acquire The Beatles Pop Group; declining due to his belief that guitar-based bands such as they were 'on the way out', thus repelling those Scouse-bred scamps into the clutches of his rivals at Parlophone, whose subsequent fortunes made such harsh mockery of his error in judgement as to disturb his sleep like Irish toothache. Mr Rowe thus being not merely a big Dick, but a sore one, Andrew deduced an opportunity to soothe his throbbing with the balm of his five treacle tarts, whose glory would surely afford him ample compensation by restoring his status as a man with a golden ear, and recouping dividends of envy not experienced since he unleashed that glorious hymn inquisitive of canine purchase upon the British public ten years past.

In this endeavour Andrew was aided by Mr Rowe's previous profitable dealings with Mr Easton, who accompanied him to Decca's main fortress upon the Albert Embankment: the twitcher armed with the freshly mixed ointment of 'Come On', and determined to apply maximum pressure to Dick's tender spot by comparing their charges to The Beatles Pop Group – who that week were still number one in the nation's singles charts – with such regularity as to agitate the tidal current of his ordinarily smooth sentences like a linguistic hiccough.

Once admitted into that gentleman's office, the intended effect of this premeditated torture upon Mr Rowe was manifest in his squirms of compliant agony, so evidently crippled by excruciating pulsations that he all but begged to be allowed lease of these irresistible Beatles-Pop-Group-Doppels: his delirium for relief being so insatiable that he pledged to haste 'Come On' upon the market as soon as feasible as salve to his distress, pencilling in the first week of June as that due occasion.

With the surrender of Mr Rowe, the rest, as Andrew saw to gerrymander, was simply a matter of mischief and effortless manipulation. In victorious steps, he walked out of Decca's citadel, hailed a hansom cab and informed its driver to ferry him in direction of Chelsea. To tell his five chosen picaros, Mick, Keith, Brian, Bill and Charlie, to fill their sacks, that the adventure had begun, the Stones now thrown, and all pray hark!

For was e'er a sound so sweet as the crisp shatter of solid glass.

BOOK *the* SECOND

ORGY

CHAPTER

XIV

⌒℘⌒

Our picaros finally plunge headlong into public life;
encountering no shortage of hostilities in societies high and low;
with incidental account of their talents of construction when
their humours are crossed.

T HE DRONES AND drudges, men and women, who slid
through the gates of the Decca pressing plant in New
Malden – who stamped their clock cards, who hung up
their coats, who switched on their lathes and who squashed
bucketfuls of polyvinyl chloride into boxfuls of 'Come On' by
The Rolling Stones – were oblivious to any complicity in so
lobbing those grenades amongst society; being much too
preoccupied with thoughts of shock and confusion regarding their
beloved Supermac, whose authority over their hearts had that
week been called into question in the most ignominious
circumstances. The sordid particulars, as regrettably conveyed by
the dutiful members of the popular press, concerned the conduct
of his cabinet minister for war; or rather the conduct of that
minister's pikestaff, which in an unfortunate excess of combatant
spunk had cause to skirmish with a young lady of society who,
unbeknownst to him, was also routing with an emissary from
Russia. These hot-blooded diplomacies now exposed and made
newsprint of a kind which the combined chip fryers of England
were unable to exhaust – and with each day increasing that supply

with fresh forensic horrors of the who, where, how and 'he would do' – Supermac's evidently inadequate grip upon his cabinet, and its abuse of arms, had thrown his once-happy sucklers into a state of moral consternation.

By early July, these serialisations of vice continuing to absorb the country's appetite for grease, salt and vinegar – and congratulate me, dear Reader, on abstaining from reviving mention of that condiment's domestic nemesis, whom I vowed to dispatch to literary Coventry in the previous volume, so observed! – the exhausted populace sought succouring reprieve in their television screens. Whereupon, the second Saturday of that month, the elasticity of their disgust was further strained by the popular music variety show *Thank Your Lucky Stars*; containing as it did a vision so heinous as to incite multitudes to spew their repulsion on parchment and post to the culprit producers at the Associated British Corporation in Birmingham.

The specifics of offence contained in this spectacle, broadcast between the dining hours of six and seven p.m. – and so unfortunately optimum in causation of mass discomposure of the public's entrails – related to five young gentlemen, all of whose collar-tickling locks exhibited so unacceptable an aversion to the barber's chair as to confuse the established parameters of the male gender; a panic of androgyny which found rudest manifestation in their singer, main muse to the fury of pen and ink which, executed in such haste as to abjure poetic deliberation, declared that woolly hermaphrodite 'a lout', 'a yob' and, at worst, 'a beast'. For such was the manner in which the first missile was thrown through the nation's television screens, so introducing the world to the five fiends of decency, our subjects, The Rolling Stones.

It was thanks to the machinations of their elder sponsor Mr Easton, who also represented *Lucky Stars* host Pete Murray, that they managed to invade that primetime pop cavalcade; so guaranteeing an exposure ordinarily denied a band of their comparatively fresh status. The programme's intentions were to offer pleasant perspective on the temperaments of youth, assembling a vaudeville of their favourite melodians, with weekly space also devoted to the novelty of 'Spin-a-disc'. Purporting to be a musical critique of the latest releases as judged by members of the public, the latter feature was, in actuality, an excuse for a local maiden named Miss Nicholls to amuse the nation with her abnormality of dialect: being inherently indiscriminate as to award every song a maximum score of five, so mutated by her spasms of accent into the altogether more mysterious syllable 'foyv'.

This oblivious jester to the Queen's English was, by fixture of demand, there to witness The Rolling Stones at this juncture in their history, where she, and they, were joined on set by the following bill of fare: the popular nightingale Helen Shapiro, a remarkable specimen of sixteen years with a voice of a woeful gin-hag thrice that age; the American sensation Johnny Cymbal, who had made rare artistry of stuttering in his paean to a certain 'Mr. Bass Man'; and a brigade of brightly uniformed cadets from the Emerald Isle.

The Stones had driven the hundred-and-twenty-five miles from London to the television studios in north Birmingham with Andrew, who regaled them on the journey with the tale of his previous visitation to *Lucky Stars* during his brief tenure with The Beatles Pop Group, and his confidence that they would be received in similarly warm humour. As a provision, Andrew had instructed they wear matching houndstooth jackets, so as to present an image every stitch as agreeable to the viewer as their celebrated Liverpudlian predecessors, unaware that such efforts of costume were scarce distraction to their impropriety of scalp.

This oversight of decorum was first brought to their attention by Mr Murray, whose keenness to distance himself from their association in sight of the cameras took the form of an introductory quip, informing the audience that, following tonight's programme, the Stones would suffer ordeal by an angry deputation from the guild of hairdressers. The stain of enmity and ridicule was so shaped for the performance itself, whereupon a member of the production team ushered Andrew aside, gently advising him that his hairy charges' only hope of progressing in the affections of the public were dependent on losing the singer, whose lips they described as 'tyre-tread', with similar criticism of his accompanying visage; the collected evaluation being no less than 'vile-looking'.

Despite these bitter choruses of disapproval and a minor scuffle behind the cameras between Keith and the Irish cadets – who turned on his person after he made some disparaging remarks about their military attire, punctuated with that common truncation of 'cunnigate', which rarely fails to arouse the passions of Celtic fists – Andrew considered their television debut a tremendous success. In its aftermath, as he waited for 'Come On' to climb towards the top forty, ably assisted by his furtive high street myrmidons, he busied himself with a scheme to improve the Stones' native geography, dispatching them to play in provinces far beyond the safety of the capital. Andrew himself remained at home during these reconnaissance missions, preferring the comforts of London and the second-hand titillation of reports from their receptions in the wildernesses of Middlesbrough and Wisbech; usually involving robust inspection of the local petticoats, so provoking troubled sentiments in their unsophisticated male suitors; these typically expressed in jeering promise of physical dismemberment and accompanying projectiles of coin and bottle.

By way of antidote to these baptisms of bumpkin intolerance, upon their homecoming Andrew planned to placate them with a booking where they were assured full hospitality at expense of the peerage. That is, employed to provide musical accompaniment to the occasion of the entry into polite society of the youngest daughter of the venerated Baron Killearn. After having first been furnished in life with a godparent no less noble than Sir Winston Churchill and a name no less elegant than Roxana, at the saucy age of seventeen this privileged child of Empire instead chose to distinguish herself by answering to the call of 'Bunty'. Being thus susceptible to the illogical impulses of fashionable youth, Bunty had decided that her debut in society should be appropriately 'groovy'; so requesting the presence of The Rolling Stones, whom she had been led to believe through a handful of press notices and personal recommendations to embody that very quality.

The prospect of molesting the sensibilities of the aristocracy amused and excited the group's fancies with swish thoughts of admittance into some fine palace or castle, filling their bellies with sweetmeats and fortified wines, and pocketing appropriate souvenirs, whether pawnable silver candlestick or satiated Viscountess's affections. To which trances Andrew was forced to make modification, informing them that Miss Bunty, being of blue blood but beatnik veins, desired these proceedings take place in a system of caves etched into the cliffs of Hastings: already the scene of previous youthful gatherings, which had become so antagonistic to the equilibrium of the nearby town that its council had taken the impatient measure of spraying these rocky grottoes with foul-smelling toxins to dissuade further juvenile capers. A disclosure which Brian surmised aloud as the difference between being invited to play a stately home and, indeed, 'a shitty cave'.

While his fellow Stones presumed that the sole author of Brian's deflation of spirit was an environmental concern for the whereabouts of Miss Bunty's 'hop', he made pains to mask its true scribe: his grievances over their recent promotional encounters with the press, all of whose representatives had not only exhibited the same surprise upon discovering him to be their leader, but had impudence to ignore that distinction by presenting the majority of their questions to Mick. His credit of enthusiasm for the band being thus in arrears that week, upon the drive from London to the Sussex coast, Brian entered a symphony of coughs and shivers, building to a green-faced crescendo which, by group consensus, excused him from performing, making temporary sickbed of the backseat where he remained for the duration; so sparing himself all intimacy of Miss Bunty's cave which, as he was subsequently told, exuded a far more pleasant aroma than his crude predictions might have supposed.

The accumulated *bon vivants* being either young friends of around Miss Bunty's pedigree or venerated fruits and nuts of her family tree in all its endowments of Lords, Ladies, Countesses and Barons, Andrew and the Stones' arrival was cue for much jingling of pearls, flapping of jaw and choking of cigar amongst the older branches; a sensation of appearance eclipsed only by Miss Bunty herself, who affected an even greater bobbery of disbelief: waiving all sartorial expectations of a debutante hostess by entering in a pair of white Bermuda shorts.

Alas, what hopes the Stones harboured of serenading that garment into pleasing gyration evaporated on first sight of the limited electrical supply, the conversions of seaside cave into society ballroom being only a moderate success. In lieu of amplification, such were Miss Bunty's ecstasies over their mere presence, declaring them sufficiently 'groovy' company for her purposes, she insisted they remain as her guests, so granting them full liberty of the banquet buffet: a feast they gratefully assaulted with such violence of hunger as their fellow hobnobbers normally only witnessed when releasing their hounds upon the trespassing peasants who dared ramble over the hedgerows of their country estates.

Stuffed to belching satisfaction, they next turned that same vigour of appetite upon the endless liquid refreshment until they spoke as much in fumes as in phrases, bellowing both in the ear of whichever bejewelled young damsel caught their eye; forced into dialogues of a decidedly 'wizard' and 'tip-top' humour, which they endured in hope of gaining trust enough to be admitted more private audience to inspect the treasures of their trinket boxes. In doing so, the Stones would thus learn that the southern man of rank and his northern yeoman counterpart were not so very different in matters of chivalry: being equally protective of their women and their trinket boxes, whom they were prepared to defend in accordance with the Marquis of Queensberry, as conveyed in shaking voice of 'steady old man!', 'what the jiggins!' and 'I say, chappie!' with much flushing of cheek and trembling of lip.

After a few hours of such trinket-picking endeavours – having exhausted the generosity of Miss Bunty's larder and angered enough of her invited dandiprats to incite demands of satisfaction in various woodland clearings with the seconds of their choice – a young photographer friend named Philip suggested to Andrew that he and the Stones could best avoid continued threat of duelling pistol by prolonging their insobriety elsewhere, knowing of a castle not thirty miles away, home to a dear friend of his. Most castles having cellars and those cellars casks of the finest creature, Andrew, Mick and Keith agreed this was a capital idea, and since Philip's vehicle was room enough to carry only these three, they alone accompanied him on his crusade, leaving their comrades to seek alternative retreat.

The castle and its casks of sudden legend lay eastward over the border in Kent, set in two hundred acres near the village of Lympne. Once the seat of medieval priests, who still clung to its cloisters in moaning echoes and ectoplasm, it was now throne to the family Margary, whose eldest son, Aubyn, was the 'dear friend' of their parched objectives. To account for the character of this young man, the Reader need know only two morsels of his personal history: that at the age of only twenty-one he was already guilty of attempted fratricide, having accidentally shot his brother in the eye with a rifle; and that he was committed to promoting 'decorative dress in the English male' by taking to silk breeches, lace handkerchiefs, a silvery wig and the consumption of snuff in his self-designated post as Chairman of the elite association christened 'Twentieth Century Fops'.

These unpredictable qualities, both lethal and elegant, boded for a thoroughly entertaining nightcap; or so Philip hoped as their vehicle screeched to a halt of smoking rubber at the top of the carriageway in front of the castle's impressive oak doors which, very soon, were booming to the rhythm of their thirsty enthusiasm as their combined limbs beat passionate request of entry. These ricochets, embellished with some choice hollers imploring they be welcomed in with open decanters, were duly answered by a silhouetted head poking from one of the upper windows, which, presumably being that of Aubyn in a condition far from sympathetic to the interruption of his slumbers, reminded them of the late hour of their unexpected visit in the indelicate fashion of 'Fuck off! It's four in the morning!'

Their prayers to Bacchus so rudely silenced, all focused their hazy intellects on an immediate scheme of revenge. The Devil thus made sterling work of their idle indignation in bringing to attention the restoration of a cottage close by in the castle grounds; its partial completion evident by the large heap of building materials sat outside. These serendipitous tools appealing to Andrew's genius with speed of lightning, they soon threw themselves into heavy labour, shifting masonry by moonlight, calling upon all instincts of siege amongst their Anglo-Saxon forefathers by creating a formidable stone blockade across the castle driveway to seal the enemy within and prevent escape. The full majesty of which was demonstrated at the first light of dawn, whereupon Aubyn's father emerged, yielding all hopes of his morning commute to the Admiralty, along with the best of his wits, to great halloos of vindication from the architects of his woe, together observing his confusion from a discreet vantage point the other side of their proud effort.

Retreating with haste back to the capital, Mick and Keith made sleepy repair to Edith Grove, where they were greeted with the vision of Brian, since carted home and left lying in grumpy recuperation in the living room, where they proceeded to subject him to hot ravings of all he had missed in way of Morgan Morgans, fizz and bubbles, Miss Bunty's shorts, trinket boxes, 'by Jingo!'s, caves, castles and cordons. All of which served to corrupt Brian's features in a jealous grimace no more repulsive than had his face been struck with a palsy so severe as he himself might catch glimpse in a mirror and diagnose as an incurable case of 'the Nankers'.

CHAPTER

XV

*Their fortunes prosper when deficiency of inspiration is
lent a helping hand by two familiar acquaintances of
near intolerable celebrity.*

THE STRUCTURAL ALTERATIONS to Lympne Castle
were as much a mystery to poor Mr Margary as they
were to the local constabulary, who failed to collar the
nocturnal tradesmen responsible, lacking as they did the
confidence of his eldest son's candour: Aubyn being privately
possessed of advanced suspicions, based upon his rude awakening
at the strike of four and the catalytic motives his salty conduct in
that briefest of discourses may have planted in the culprits. And
so the guilty Stones were spared any pain of interrogation, their
progress as blissfully unhindered as that of their first disc, which
by early August had finally bumped its way inside the hallowed
top forty Hit Parade.

By dint of a popularity unfathomable to the producers of *Lucky
Stars*, they were summoned back for a second televised appearance: this time dispensing with the cosmetic appeasement of
houndstooth jackets, choosing instead black leather waistcoats,
conducive to the small screen tableau of five collectors of refuse,
all still exhibiting that same scandalous determination to place
increasing strain on the steady finances of those who made their
livelihood servicing the nation's follicles.

With no Irish cadets to spar with, they found alternative sport in the show's star guest: a former milkman named Terry Perkins who had since become Cinderella of the dairy trade; reinventing himself as a warbling pretty boy and assuming the glamorous appellation of 'Craig Douglas'. It was unfortunate for Master Douglas that his many talents stopped short of clairvoyance; else he surely would have refrained from passing negative comment upon 'Come On' in the recent pages of the *Melody Maker* – expressing a fierce dislike of Mick's diction while despairing of its whole arrangement as being 'very, very ordinary'. Unfortunate, for it was now his awkward fate to cross paths with the victims of his scorn while those typeset pellets were still very freshly imbedded in their minds.

Presented with chance opportunity to return their respects, the not so ordinary five considered it fair riposte to remind the former Perkins of his humbler origins, which had thus earned him the epithet 'The Singing Milkman': making quick and stealthy inventory of the studio premises with purpose of collecting every available empty receptacle associated with the delivery of that bovine ambrosia. These they positioned with exquisite care outside their opinionated target's dressing room door, in such number as would guarantee clinking cacophony should he step out with any suddenness of gait, their bottlenecks containing scribbled chits of 'Two pints please!' and similar ilk intended to stir nostalgic flashbacks to his halcyon days rattling crates to dawn's chorus in white cap and coat. And yet in reception to such gaiety, Master Douglas revealed himself strangely lactose intolerant, voicing urgent petition to the producers to eject the Stones from the building forthwith and veto their broadcast: a demand which, he was very regretfully informed, they were no more able to fulfil than their beloved Miss Nicholls could correctly pronounce that vowel-perverting digit betwixt four and six.

Our champions were not, however, long amused by these vain chimeras of horseplay, which soon vanished a few days hence before other reflections of more importance. Their old foes, the Jazz Mafia, had that summer perished under the relentless infestation of negroid rhythms and flatulent blues, which swamped Soho like a bubonic plague feasting on the carrion of their Dixieland dead. As a spoil of this victory, the Stones had shifted their rehearsals to the heart of town, hijacking the jazz club named Studio Fifty-One behind Leicester Square underground station, where one Tuesday lunchtime in early September Andrew confronted them on the sore subject of industry. Their first disc now peaking on the cusp of the top twenty, he reminded them of their pressing obligation to provide a sequel with which to nurture their already modest infamy, and so demanded they excavate their repertoire for a song ripe for that very purpose before the day was out.

An hour later, Andrew could feel a profound increase in his affinities for that starving pooch of the widow Hubbard, having been subject to various borrowed American strummings and realising, to his dismay, that their cupboard was no better stocked than that same notorious tormentor of the canine appetite. The aggregate sum of their twangs asphyxiating his tempers, he excused himself for a breath of air and so escaped into the grey light of mid-afternoon; his feet in automatic motion to speed away from their hopeless echoes, but otherwise vacant of destination.

With his mood lowering to a state utterly indifferent to his fate, he trod as if under spell of Haitian witchcraft, off the kerb, into the road and directly into the path of oncoming vehicles, daring to be relieved of the day's managerial agony under the wheels of a Hackney carriage. At which moment, Dame Fortuna answered his prayers and threw such a stagecoach his way: not to crush his slender bones upon Charing Cross Road, but to haul Andrew from his mental sewers with the two passengers who stopped its driver and disembarked directly in front of him.

They and Andrew recognised one another in an instant: he, as that amiable speedy-tongued chap who'd once been employed in their promotions department; they, as the core of that collective of unwipable northern grins which that week had, yet again, cooed and 'ooh!'-ed their way to number one in the charts with their newest knock-kneed plucking, 'She Loves You' – being none other than John and Paul of The Beatles Pop Group.

Their cheeks a little ruddier than Andrew remembered, in greeting him they explained they were fresh from attending a liquid luncheon courtesy of the Savoy Hotel, during which they'd been called upon to accept a trophy as the year's 'Top Vocal Group' by the Variety Club of Great Britain. His respondent congratulations being so feeble, they begged enlightenment on the cause of these anxious tumults of mind so transparent in his disposition, and listened as he sketched the contours of his misery regarding the Stones and their creative poverty.

Their characters having just been polished by fine wine and silverware, John and Paul were at that moment easily predisposed to benevolence, stocktaking the particulars of Andrew's predicament as a rich man might the sorrows of a beggar: between them moved to such pangs of sympathy that they made offer to nurse the worm of grief that preyed upon his vitals. It being part of the phenomena of The Beatles Pop Group that John and Paul were possessed of a dark magic hitherto unknown in their sphere, having presumption to compose both words and music of each one of their hits so far, their pity was moved to spare these needy waifs some crumbs from their loaf of endless invention.

The surprise entrance of the two saviours in their manager's tow immediately silenced the Stones' noisy scrambles in the foot-hills of Rhythm and Blues, as they laid down tools to welcome their celebrated peers in loud and delighted raptures. The commotion settled, John relayed that Andrew had allowed he and Paul confidence of their delicate situation, to which end they'd come armed with the restorative tonic of an original song – so fresh its ink still smeared to the touch – which they selflessly volunteered as a port of stimulus in their storm of banality.

This salvation gratefully received, behind the twinkles of John and Paul's exterior civilities, their Mersey minds were, nevertheless, not so foolish as to risk furnishing these potential usurpers with any prize crowns from amongst their treasure chest. But they considered them at least worthy of a small, unpolished opal they'd already relegated as ballast upon their next long player; to be donated with equal cunning of foresight, knowing any success these southern greenhorns may furnish upon it at speed of forty-five revolutions-per-minute would still bring cheer to their accountants in the oblong shape of a publishing royalty cheque.

Borrowing Keith and Brian's utensils of melody, John and Paul took position opposite one another and commenced their vibrations of string; lips piping, both heads oscillating like buoys in rough waters as they shined, best they could, this coarse jewel which, minutes later, took finished form of repeated appeals for romantic intimacy to a tight if colourless air – and noticeably devoid of their signature 'ooh!'s of that stricken parson – so titled 'I Wanna Be Your Man'. Mick and Keith stood transfixed by this process, considering it no less miraculous than had they just witnessed John and Paul nourish five thousand bellies with seven loaves of Mother's Pride and a Bird's Eye finger of fish.

Come their turn to follow suit with full band its simplicity, to their relief, required minimum trial and error: even if, to John and Paul's ears, their sweet entreaty for a maiden's kiss had been distorted by Mick's savage leer and the sleazy frolics of Brian's slide guitar into the more savoury sentiments of Don Cypriano.

The afternoon's missionary work done, John and Paul extracted themselves from that munificent position with a cheer of good luck, two waves, a wink and a foxy eyebrow, returning to whichever abode of the blessed had evidently sent them. The Stones now had their song, and Andrew's faith in destiny was restored, if temporarily. For, by nightfall, his dejected twitches spoke of the harsher lesson learned – that they couldn't rely on chance encounters with The Beatles Pop Group every time their skins needed saving – and his funk of wits resumed more savage than before. So, as is often the case in life, good fortune in such a short, sharp dose removes one cast of melancholy only to replace it with contortions far ghastlier in its wake.

CHAPTER

XVI

Descriptive of dramatic changes in habit and habitat.

A FULL CALENDAR had elapsed since our three picaros took paupers' chambers in those dirty drawers of Edith; shivering through frizzle, existing on theft of Morgan Morgans, diverted only by their musical furtherance and constant wonder at the abstract embellishments of their fellow occupant and maestro of bronchus, the august legend Phelge.

But now their pockets sagged with the comfort of Mr Easton's weekly retainer, Brian's all the heavier for his added confidential annuity; now their domestic attachments had suffered strain of clashing vanities, which invade friendships with Mongol fury once placed under even the palest glow of limelight; and now that their appreciation of Master Phelge had long since peaked with his pièce de respiratory résistance, 'Green Gilbert Gottfried'; this conspiracy of circumstances propelled them to evacuate that trollop of Chelsea for separate, and more salubrious, lodgings befitting their improved tastes and financial standings.

Brian removed himself from the city altogether, seeking sanctuary in Windsor, long the scene of one of the group's regular bookings, where he'd since focused his southern appetites on a teenage admirer named Linda. Her affections towards him were an evidently hereditary condition, her parents also transported to rare exultations in his company, sentiments which he happily reciprocated, if in a manner naturally less demonstrative than that vigorously applied to their daughter. Light-headed at the honour of playing host to a recording celebrity, Linda's parents beseeched Brian to make their house his home, and her bed his, and in doing so pray allow them to rechristen their dwelling, 'Rolling Stone'.

This appealing to his most basic needs of a roof over his head, a pedestal for his pride and a cotton plain to ride bareback in sumptuous privacy, he graciously accepted, failing to mention that, amongst his few personal effects, he'd since acquired an item of livestock which, by necessity, would have to be granted paradise of the family garden. The particulars of which were only manifest the day he arrived on their doorstep with suitcase, box of records, guitar and pet goat. His attachment to this charm of Capricorn, affectionately baptised 'Billy G', was such that he'd even taken pains to suit it with collar and leash, so as to parade, master and beast, on the local byways to the vexation of Linda, her parents and all privy to this uncommon spectacle on the streets of that Royal Borough.

While Brian was thus engaged in exploits carnal and caprine in Berkshire, Mick and Keith chose to remain as one in London; neither the least fraction sorry to see the last of his morning Nankers, and furthermore elated to replace him in the formation of another terrible trident. It was Andrew's suggestion that he should be its third prong, seizing their change in tenancy as divine occasion to install himself in their new home with a view to exerting absolute influence upon their every temper: his mind having already arrived at a scheme to fix their ongoing crisis of composition, and so smother his mental flames of anguish, which fitted these circumstances to perfection.

The trio thus formed, an agreeable domicile was found in Kilburn, to the north west of the city; of advantageously close distance to Andrew's mother's home in Hampstead, and of advantageously sanitary furnishings – in aggressive contrast to

Mick and Keith's previous titivations of filth, fungus and phlegm. So too its location, within a detached Victorian house set in a residential avenue cautiously sprinkled with species of *platanus hispanica*, was advantageous of privacy; with few of their curtain-twitching Mapesbury Road neighbours familiar enough with the current whims of youth to recognise a party of Rolling Stones had just taken occupancy of Number Thirty-Three.

The stage set, Andrew spared no time in commencing his puppetry of their cognisance, with sights firmly affixed on the trophy of his wiles: the conversion of Mick and Keith into a respective John and Paul as authors of their own Rhythm, Blues and possibly wobbly-headed 'ooh!'s. Accelerating his concern was the group's first effort, assembled for the reverse of the new single; an impudent goosing of the popular instrumental 'Green Onions', upon which Mick spoke at intervals in a very curious state of distraction about being 'Stoned': that title assumed by the rubber stamps at Decca to be in reference to that sport of the ancient world, similar to the modern coconut shy but with those hairy exoticisms substituted by the shivers of the village strumpet. None of the band being so proud as to demand public recognition for this falderal of theft and nonsense, they accredited it to a creation of their own fancy, choosing the two words most precious to their sentiments; thereby inflicting upon society the fictitious partnership of Nanker & Phelge. Of whom Andrew formed the sagacious opinion they could no more place their hopes for continued success in the dubious hands of Mr Nanker and his accomplice than they could in finding a brass lamp which, when gently rubbed, produced a mystic vapour in shape of their Scouse Samaritans each time the muse abandoned them.

The course of his enterprise revealed, Mick and Keith expressed no small amount of reluctance to assume this mantle, both being of the opinion that the art of songwriting was the craft of a magus elite; and though their proficiency of throat and fingers might indicate a favourable predisposition to that miracle, it would further require such shifts in intellect as might Andrew have demanded they equip themselves with professional competency of rocket engineering by Wednesday next.

Fully expecting these shirks of pessimism, the barometer of Andrew's action swung to the drastic. Concluding that kindness is a sweet juice best extracted by much pulping of cruelty, he made abrupt conversion from friend and manager to fiend and gaoler. The larder of Mapesbury Road being altogether ascetic, it was custom for Andrew to visit his mother's house for supper, returning with surplus victuals for the grateful consumption of his two flatmates. Deducing that the threat of severing this food chain should likely frighten them into tune, on the day of his next dinner engagement he sequestered Mick and Keith in the kitchen with a guitar, pen and paper with orders to prepare, for his approval, an original song by the time he returned; the consequence of their failing in that task being strict sanctions upon the share of any morsels courtesy of their intestines' very generous sponsor, Madame Celia Oldham.

The cell door slammed, Mick and Keith had no choice but to drown their gassy gurgles of stomach with nebulous strummings, an abundance of 'ooh!'s, a nursery of 'baby's, a convent-worth of 'girl's, an affirmative of 'yeah's and, when all other melodic vocabulary failed, an elocution of 'la, la, la's. The fruits of which Andrew heard when he returned, taking precaution to enter in quiet creeps so he could secretly hover outside their prison, heart soaring at the wails of labour. For this was a birth of glimmering twins, no less: Mick and Keith having discovered within them all along the magic spark of 'Jagger & Richards'.

The news of this delivery had yet to reach Brian when, that same week, he took temporary leave of his girl and his goat to visit the Piccadilly offices of Mr Easton. His humours, in any case, were unlikely to be improved by such intelligence, the temperature of his suspicions already sweltering the instant he learned his group's other manager and the main rival to his attentions were now as good as married by leasehold. Brian's only assuage to these qualms was his reassuring unity with the object of his sojourn; who not only shared concerns over Andrew's increasing intimacy with Mick and Keith, but was one of the few still astute enough to recognise him as their true commander in chief, so paid with according increment.

The purpose of Brian's visit was to accentuate these same benefits of rank with regard to news of their forthcoming excursion: soon to embark on a tour of their great nation as part of a revue featuring The Everly Brothers and their God of gods, The Lord Bo Diddley. Specifically, the accommodation arrangements which, Brian imagined, might possibly be of Spartan quality and, while sufficient for the repose of the others, would be an unacceptable imposition to inflict on the group leader. Therefore, with Mr Easton's blessing, he demanded that all lengths be taken to guarantee he be billeted in a superior class of hostel to his companions.

This proposal striking its audience as perfectly rational, the matter was agreed upon and the applicant immensely pleased, taking his leave with a reminder from Mr Easton that he mustn't err in forgetting to collect his fan mail from the secretary on his exit.

Acting on this advice, Brian approached the desk of Mr Easton's angel of administration and requested he be furnished with said unsolicited outpourings of desire. With efficiency of occupation, she twisted to a neighbouring shelf upon which stacks of letters of varying height and depth were aligned, retrieved one of the more modest bundles and handed it over with an inviting smile. Her pleasantry unnoticed, Brian's focus had since locked on the largest stack still sat on the shelf, being a paper sarsen twice the height of the comparative wedge he'd just received. So troubled, he felt compelled to inquire as to the identity of the recipient who had inspired such gluttony amongst the country's pillar boxes, and was duly updated: 'Those are for Mick.'

Her words unintentionally blowing the coals of his jealousy, Brian dropped his meagre correspondence upon the floor and, with the queerest of expressions inconveniencing his face, turned and bolted from the premises; those flames so overwhelming his soul that by the time he returned to Windsor he'd not even the will to walk Billy G.

CHAPTER

XVII

⟳

Records their first full excursion of their native islands
and sundry curious matters.

WITH THE FIRST conkers cascading from the boughs,
nature sounded its autumn bugle and the provinces
prepared themselves to resume costume of woollens
and waterproofs, oblivious to the squall of a kind that defies
meteorological divination heading their way. A tempest lasting
thirty-six days, first brewing in the south before tearing northwards,
across the border into Caledonia, then reversing with stealth to
the south coast. For such was the route of The Rolling Stones, as
plotted by the travelling variety show in which they'd secreted
themselves like five Greek soldiers in the wooden steed of Everly,
its headline siblings of American rock 'n' roll vintage.

Though pleased to make acquaintance of those tunesome
brothers, they were infinitely more enamoured of its second billing,
their Holy Father, Bo Diddley, whom they welcomed with the awe
of Israelites; making sacrifice of their finances by presenting him
with the sacred offering of a pair of monogrammed cufflinks cast
in gold. Mightily impressed, The Lord Diddley returned them
pleasure of his company, his divine tongue passing gospel that they
were 'good cats' and ordained to join him in ritual of holy water:
'Cos we is now jug buddies'. So blessed, the Stones frequently
partook of jug with the Lord Diddley and his saint of maracas, the

archangel Jerome, whose intake was of a proportion to his bloodstream as to be more jug than he was man – believing himself only ever in peak of performance when full to the brim.

No sooner had their young wits acclimatised to one God when they were again capsized into seas of ecstasy by the arrival of a second. The advance ticket sales being of a figure modest enough to wet the promoter's brow with the beady dew of panic, another star of the American stage was affixed at the last minute in hope of encouraging thunder of footfall towards idle box offices. The nominated saviour was a prince of wails whose signature vocal seizures were shrill father to those ubiquitous parson bleats of The Beatles Pop Group which, as even they would admit, were mere bastard mimicries of his worship, the shrieking pianist Little Richard. This addition to the bill proved of particular benefit to Mick, soon an eager pupil captivated by a master skilled in arts of tease and sensation. Little Richard, who was indeed a Richard and so exempt from this History's company of Dicks, was famed for regularly divesting himself of his habits amongst the audience and, in as close to a state of nature as the laws of that parish allowed, strutting circuits of the front row or, his special fancy, up the aisle.

While friction with these esteemed shoulders helped smooth the recent injury to Brian's humours, nothing could shift the indelible stain now tinting his affections for Mick. He chose to travel separately in his own car, a Humber Hawk as black as his temper, rather than share the confined japes aboard the group's new van. His prior accommodation arrangements only engorging the others' suspicions of management favouritism and fiscal artifice, by such pageants of greed and arrogance so Brian unwittingly prepared his own grave and, upon the fifth night in Southend-On-Sea, was fool enough to jump in.

The hour before their curtain call, Keith purchased himself a fresh supper of fried chicken, its consumption interrupted when he was called to conference in a nearby alleyway with a daughter of Essex famed for her hospitality to roving minstrels. That conference agreeably resolved, Keith returned to find his supper reduced to a collection of bones, simultaneously catching sight of Brian, retreating through the stage door, sucking his fingers in audible kisses of gratification. Not of such soft heart as to allow this liberty pass without reprisal, Keith waited until they next crossed paths – moments before the band were expected on stage – choosing that occasion as proper to swoop his fist deep into Brian's eye-socket, any confusion over his motives avoided by his explanatory garnish: "'Ere, you cunt! You ate me chicken!' Sympathy for the fowl-scoffing scoundrel in their midst being in such short supply, Keith was lauded for his efforts, which soon took colourful occupation of Brian's face as a badge of dishonour for all the world to see.

Having been thus humiliated and stripped of rank, Brian might well have taken hasty leave of the Stones were it not for the divine intervention of the Lord Diddley, who advised him to lay aside any grievances and persevere: his oracular estimation predicting rewards of fame and fortune to outlast even The Beatles Pop Group since, so sayeth his holy Diddleyship, 'You cats play like black dudes, ya dig?'

Consoled by this powerful sermon, Brian reaped further spiritual compensation from the damozel squeals that greeted the band's arrival on stage most nights, customarily followed by the sweet aroma of wet gymslips: it being the privilege of the theatre caretakers to hoist such laundry from their savoury rivulets at the end of each evening. That these demonstrative amities were occasionally reciprocated in more private quarters should come as no surprise to the Reader at this point in our story: with Keith having already been described pausing repast to satisfy hunger of trembling knees; Bill also discovered making heavy demands upon his joints in a coal cellar in Sheffield; and Mick so careful as to forbid the girl Chrissie from Windsor – now his steady article of amour back home – from accompanying him on tour lest her presence thwart any schemes he may enter necessitating similar orthopaedic strains.

Though Brian had allowed his own maid of Windsor, the teen Linda, to join him for the first few dates as guarantor of post-performance bareback reward, he quickly saw the prudence of Mick's prohibition and, following example, enjoyed immediate profit of coitus. While rich in this capacity, he became, in tandem, a miser of chivalry: his a regrettable habit that, once the song of his silent flute had concluded, he would vanish from the stage in a flurry of buckling, leaving his audience bereft of not only virtue, but often wherewithal; the poor child having been transported halfway across the country to be deflowered then abandoned in grizzling sin, dependent on the charity of his contrastingly gallant bandmates to donate them adequate return funds to the town of their henceforth scarlet reputation.

So The Rolling Stones raged across the British Isles, on stage and off, a gale of lust and long hair gathering force of stamina and bounty of adulation, twisting bough of heartstring and whistling howls of ecstasy, blowing back to London for the homecoming finale in early November, to a changed capital in a changed country.

Sapped of power, respect and health, Supermac had tended his resignation a fortnight earlier, the lost nation now forced to suckle from the breast of his pasty and doomed successor. London was not the same city, but nor were the Stones the same band who'd galloped beyond its boundaries five weeks earlier. Their ranks had realigned, their spirits been galvanised and their knee-caps toughened to feats of contorted union in all opportune crannies of alley and fuel store. They had begun their excursion dutiful mannequins to the matching jackets provided by Mr

Easton and ended it scarecrows of their own casual apparel. They
had been anointed by the light of Little Richard, and had drunk
from the jug of their Lord Diddley. And they had seen, and smelt,
the desire they inflicted, from the nether-mouths of Nottingham
to the tuzzy-muzzies of Taunton and the shady-springs of St
Albans: an elevation in acclamation not lost on the brothers
Everly, whose unfortunate task it remained to close every night;
by the last week through ireful showers of paper missiles and
harpy choruses beckoning the return of the five girdle-busters last
seen before the interval.

These scenes uppermost in Mick's mind, it was unfortunate
timing for the London School of Economics that he should return
home, thus metamorphosed by the road, to find his tutor's most
recent epistle inquiring if he intended to conclude the course of
study from which he had lately absented himself. Replying in the
courteous negative, Mick explained he had been presented with a
rare 'opportunity in the entertainment industry', which he now
felt duty-bound to pursue; otherwise refraining from supplying
them with unnecessary detail regarding its spectrum of benefits to
body and soul, against which their call to academia was but a
whisper of caution to a roar of joy.

'Requiem For A Rolling Stone'

fright and violent transports of evacuation, on second glance at its dimensions Bill's diarist's eye for detail speedily established more rational explanation, so choosing to exorcise the spectre from sight with the weary sigh: 'Go to bed, Brian.'

Thus unmasked, Brian ignored that directive, instead stripping himself of his amendments of linen, a guise he'd prepared with the meticulous help of Mick and Keith, all three disappointed by its lack of comic avail, and, resuming more conventional dress, slipped out of the hotel alone. Those first hours of Nineteen Sixty-Four he spent walking off his troubles in the deserted streets of Lincoln, lost in lengthy reflection on his change in fortunes over the past twelve months; in bank, in bareback, but most of all in band. So distracted by these examinations, his feet eventually led him to the summit of the town and the ancient cathedral; its Gothic enormity assuming an especially spooky character in the silence of night.

Sitting down to rest on its stone steps, and blowing on his hands for warmth, he suddenly heard its great organ stir from behind the locked doors: a single note, long and low, as if piped from the bottommost chamber in Hell. A trick of either the wind or his mind, but of a tone complementary to his present condition, as if the spirits had listened to his inner dialogue of troubles and composed a monotone requiem mass: in honour of the passing of young Brian Jones, who was once, until recently, the leader of The Rolling Stones.

CHAPTER

XIX

They welcome the New Year with open arms,
that sentiment sadly unrequited.

THAT THERE ARE, amongst the living, stranger apparitions than any which might be supposed to stalk the many cathedral cities of England in the dead of night was borne out the following day when the Stones travelled cross country from Lincoln to Manchester, to the television studios of a new popular music programme entitled *Top Of The Pops*, on which they were to appear as the opening band on its maiden New Year's Day broadcast. That bearer being the show's host: a blond goblin whose profile cast perfect silhouette of Mr Punch, whose unblinking eyes popped out of their cavities like a pair of half-peeled boiled eggs, and who spoke in the queerest fashion; reminiscent of some robot from science fiction attempting to yodel in a Yorkshire accent.

So grotesque was this medley of visage and voice that even Brian in extremity of Nanker was less unsettling a proposition than the blond goblin, whose every manner suggested recent escape from a story by the German siblings Grimm – in which he might be otherwise be engaged dancing jigs around forest fires, having deceived some queen into surrendering her firstborn.

The show finished, and their stomachs mercifully untainted by goblin acquaintance, they thus made the decision to run the risk of local cuisine and find appropriate repast prior to the two-hundred-mile-drive home to London. Options severely limited by New Year's Day closure, they eventually located the inviting light of a restaurant specialising in Oriental fare, parked their van and entered with hungry speed. Its few staff were all persons native to that same region of the globe who, having some difficulty with the consonants of the English tongue, directed the band to a table with stiff hand gestures; conversing amongst themselves in Mandarin which, as translated by facial rictus alone, seemed to express considerable disapproval of their guests' general deportment.

First ordering flagons of ale and quarts of wine, the Stones made brief survey of the glutamic delicacies on offer, furnished their scowling waiter with their chosen inventory of chows, foos and sueys, and so waited for the magic of pan and wok to silence their gaseous impatience. Two score minutes later, with not so much as a cracker of prawn having passed their lips – Mick's now wobbling in a monstrous pucker of malnutrition – they sang a chorus of irritation to their hosts, who thus relayed their concerns to the kitchen from whence echoed grand commotion of hissing steam and clanging copper. A full hour elapsed, their placemats yet to be blessed with hot crockery, they at last relinquished all hope of clattering chopsticks, dropped a consolatory sum for their drinks consumed, and made motion towards the exit.

To their surprise, their tyrants of appetite suddenly erupted in cries of foreign alarm, with clear purpose to communicate this cancellation of custom to the rear of the house; out of which an aproned Chinaman of bloody complexion now burst. That his intentions towards them were hostile was construed by all on account of the culinary hatchet swishing in his hand and his attending scream; taking pains to convey his opinion of their desertion in English as opposed to his Asian mother tongue, to the effect that they were 'Flucking blastards!' These words, and its orator's advancing cleaver, thus sped their heels to the safety of their van at an impressive velocity, managing to drive away, still famished, but nurtured by relief that their pursuer had failed to gain the satisfaction of amending his menu with a January chef's special of 'Sweet and Sour Flucking Blastard with Crispy Noodles'.

It was now an unfortunate symptom of life as a Rolling Stone that such incidents became increasingly less isolated, this reception amongst the catering professions, and its patrons, casting the die for myriad misadventures to come – the group having to wait only three days before their next serving of public disfavour. Though during the Christmas period they had tried to make merriment of frequent criticisms about the length of their locks, placing a festive advertisement in the press wishing a 'HAPPY CHRISTMAS TO THE STARVING HAIRDRESSERS AND THEIR FAMILIES', their fringe-faced renunciation of clippers was yet unacceptable to the majority of the population, some of whom channelled their offence into wild presumptions about the group's individual histories; sowing a rumour which presently blossomed in print that Mick had secretly begun life ready furnished with menstrual apparatus, owing his current façade of masculinity to the perversions of surgery.

These slanders, and lesser press witticisms likening them to 'refugees from a barber shop', 'hairy pudding basins' and 'gentlemen of the road' only calcified the prejudice which greeted them on excursion to Oxford that first week of January. Taking rest at a roadside service café, the Stones had not long sat down and ordered themselves a round of breakfasts when a lone voice piped 'get yer 'air cut!' Not unaccustomed to such jeers, they made deliberate point of avoiding any invitation of dialogue; the list of culprits being any one of the thickset fellows among the adjacent tables – all in working clothes of one sort or another – their faces conveying a mutual fascination with the group's table, in whose direction they curdled their lips into a vast repertoire of leers, with eyes distorted into most hideous obliquities of vision.

Only after supplementary bait of wolf-whistle, 'you breedin' a flea circus?', and 'go awn an' crawl back to yer cave' did their antagonisers secure a response. First requesting conference with their waiter as to the total quantity of diners present, Mick instructed him to prepare individual portions of a single fried egg to that same number, being forty, to be distributed accordingly and with paid compliments of the five hairy darlings of their affections. These cholesterol increments cooked and served, all verbal opposition to their company suddenly stopped amidst stares of vexation, apologetic mumbles of 'thank you' and the scraping of knife and fork through oily albumen, guiltily consumed by those who now looked upon the Stones as five Samsons whose tresses must be invested with divine powers of uncommon generosity.

Regrettably, this artful placation of hostilities was too big a strain upon their purses to execute with any security of habit, nor were there enough readily available missed pregnancies amongst the entire chicken kingdom to silence the outnumbering orifices burbling intimidations in their direction. The consequences of which were dramatically illustrated the following Tuesday in circumstances near identical, excepting this occasion being night instead of day, and these roadside services being the canteen of London airport, where the Stones made detour for supper on the way home from playing a concert in the Berkshire borough of Slough.

That supper spoiled by some spicy abuse of American flavour from an opposite table, Mick succumbed to the hot pulses of intolerance, stood up and walked over to confront his persecutor, announcing his noble intention to acquire a grovelling apology. The American, interpreting the situation from a different perspective, saw in that splendour of mouthpiece a safe bullseye and a soft knuckle cushion, highlighting those qualities in the briefest demonstration of pugilistic skill, thus encouraging Mick to adapt his attitude to the horizontal.

Keith was first to unfurl the standard of solidarity, leaping out of his seat in wild remonstrations, for which trouble he, too, was physically persuaded by that descendant of Pilgrim Fathers to join the camaraderie of floor. Neither Brian, Bill nor Charlie wishing to volunteer themselves as opportunity for a hat-trick and, deducing that the economy of peace would involve more than one sunny-side upper but a bankruptcy of omelettes, they gathered up their wounded soldiers and beat swift retreat. The hard lesson learned that, in defence of honour, though instinct might urge one to fight fire with fire, there are times when an egg is worth more than an 'oof!'

CHAPTER

XX

_In which they tamper with roses and learn to feign innocence
when fate casts the gardener into their midst._

THE BLOWS OF national indignation, whether printed or
punched, raining upon the heads of his five marionettes
of mischief were not lost on Andrew. Calculating the
recent increase of bombardment as directly proportionate to the
growth in sales, screams and suffocating urinary vapours, he finally
recognised their true potential in the pantomime of the popular
music business. In assuming the lead of its principal boys, The
Beatles Pop Group had thus created a corresponding vacancy for
villain: the hisses and boos from the general public now indicating
The Rolling Stones were ideally suited to that role.

This being the case, and so far a profitable one, Andrew realised
even he'd underestimated his own genius – having accidentally
cracked the secret formula to convert outrage into fortune – and
to that alchemical end set about provoking yet more slings and
arrows. Ever available to be quoted on record, he took pleasure in
upholding the prejudice of the press by telling its representatives
that the Stones 'didn't wash', nor could he deny they were, as a rule,
'horrible', and that the majority of people, as he perceived it,
regarded them to be no less than 'morons'. Actions being more
effective than mere words, to this campaign of deliberate ill repute
he added some fresh muscle, equipping himself with a gentleman's

gentleman named Reginald: a fellow of such indelicate persuasions that Keith granted him nickname of 'The Butcher' and whose main purpose, other than Andrew's chauffeur, was to cast potent suspicions amongst their professional associates that the Stones were now in rough society of malefactors. All of which succeeded in its tarnishing objective, much to the despair of Mr Easton, being of a generation who knew no glory in impropriety and who now regarded Andrew as a headmaster might an unruly menace bringing shame upon the school blazer – albeit one who had so infested the mind of their golden goose that he daren't expel him for fear it would never excrete again.

The goose itself had just been sent flapping back on the road in another touring variety package, originally booked as support to three Nefertitis of altitudinous pompadour named The Ronettes, but by virtue of their current infamy now moved to the top of the bill. After their recent quibble in the London airport cafeteria, of reductive influence upon their previous high opinion of their American cousins as raised by the jug of Lord Diddley, the Stones' faith in transatlantic relations was mercifully restored by their new dressing room companions. The three Ronettes – two sisters and a cousin from New York City – were as rich in pleasantries as they were pulchritude, being possessed of a natural ebony magnificence, while their shiny stage couture was so designed as to cling to their fundaments like a fondant ganache; in which fashion even the mildest tempo of hips accompanying their satin coos to 'Be My Baby' prompted violent arousal of the Stones' sweet appetites.

These salivations were all the more ferocious for the preventative enterprises of the young ladies' manager and producer: a Mr Spector who, in his chaperoning absence, telecommunicated a warning epistle at the outset of the tour to 'Keep away from my girls', thus elevating them to the status of forbidden fruit and so multiplying the pangs of illicit scrumpage.

Everything being fair in lust and war, both Mick and Keith focused their desire on the group's leader, Ronnie, and were thus forced to break the truce of friendship in a contest of seduction. Fortunately, Keith was as gracious in victory as Mick in defeat, the singer making virtue of that famous sporting adage that the race is sometimes less about the winning than the participation, refusing to lay vain waste to his energies of pursuit by directing them into the welcoming lap of Ronnie's older sister, Estelle. Brian was more tactical still: sparing himself the pain of such competition, his finite charms were successfully applied instead to young cousin Nedra. The sanctity of Mr Spector's harem thus violated, all three Stones were advised by their conquests to keep these sweet consumptions discreet for reasons they would soon appreciate when, the deeds still fresh, they found themselves in the disconcerting company of that same gentleman.

It so happened that Mr Spector was already an old acquaintance of Andrew, who had met him on his first visit to London, long before he began any association with the Stones; during which time he didn't so much befriend Mr Spector as fall under his spell. So besotted was he with that American gentleman's business wiles and brusque habits, Andrew adapted his personage accordingly into Mr Spector's English echo: even to the accessorising homage of ubiquitous sunglasses, worn night as in day and regardless of meteorological necessity. Such flattering imitation left favourable impression upon the original, who latterly had attempted to help Andrew licence the Stones to his American record label. This aim thwarted to the intense frustration of both parties by the contractual obfuscations of their prior arrangements with Sir Edward Lewis and the Decca organisation, their combined ire planted a seed for tuneful riposte which flourished hence, so bringing Mr Spector face to face with those guilty pluckers of his three wingless angels.

The Stones returned to London from their exertive excursion noticeably fatigued of spirit, in which condition they were under immediate obligation to produce yet more recordings. Their humours, already ragged from the road, were further tested by the spatial frugality of Andrew's chosen studio, Regent Sounds on Denmark Street: at full occupancy feeling no bigger than an outdoor privy, that intimacy serving to incubate the faintest whiff of antipathy into heavy stench of irritation in a thrice. Those odours fast brewing, Andrew sprang into life, placing a call to Mr Spector, currently on stopover in the capital with his friend, a young singer named Mr Pitney, and begged that they both come and assist his frantic fumigations of temper.

Mr Spector and Mr Pitney arrived within the hour by limousine, the latter entering first, a bottle of Napoleonic cognac in his hand, demanding the assembled help him drain it forthwith: it being his birthday and it being tradition amongst the Pitney lineage to anoint such anniversaries in congregative toast of that peppery spirit. Neither of these details having the slightest anchorage in fact, the Stones were sufficiently ignorant of Mr Pitney's temporal particulars of birth certificate, and sufficiently needy of enlivening their attitudes, that none refused their share of tonic; which, according to the embellished fictions of Pitneyism, they were instructed to savour in a single gulp, so flinching in violent shivers of visage from which they rapidly emerged, eyes streaming yet all humours otherwise instantaneously brightened by that magical perfume.

Mr Pitney's cordial was also a blessed anaesthetic to the scrutiny of Mr Spector, a fellow whose modest stature was of irrelevance to the scalding brilliance of his eyeballs, which didn't so much look at the world as lacerate it, and which at that present moment were threshing their gaze through the skin and bone of the five Stones; seeking the smallest blush, twitch or wibble that might suggest their culpability in compromising the honour of his Ronettes, as if his pupils might penetrate their most private carnal recollections and find damning photographic evidence to justify sentence of death, in which capacity he also seemed more than capable of fulfilling without assistance.

Their guilt successfully masked by more unnecessary birthday toasts to Mr Pitney, and Mr Spector's clairvoyant suspicions fogged by the same dizzying ingestions, all present were thus elevated to such supreme states of amicability that the Stones quite forgot their earlier grievances, resuming play with welcome assistance from their guests. Making maracas out of the emptied cognac bottle and some coinage of American mint, Mr Spector was thus encouraged to shake vigorously in rhythm to 'Not Fade Away', an old Buddy Holly hiccup which, refashioned in jigger of Lord Diddley, they'd chosen as their next disc.

The supply of creative lubricant replenished, guzzled, and replenished again, by late evening these joyous intoxications had so polluted Mr Spector's muse that he nominated Mr Pitney and the group to join him in improvising a tribute to the umpire of their fortuitous alliance – the honourable Andrew – in course of which they may also wish to pass comment on their Decca paymasters, with special regard to its semi-embalmed lord and master, Sir Edward Lewis.

All bingo belches saying 'Aye!', this gracious paean was eagerly concocted. Of predominant homage to Andrew and his love of nature's tufted treasures, it was seasoned with witty debate on the quality of The Rolling Stones – whom Mr Spector declared 'fuckin' shit!' – and with Mick in fine approximation of Decca's knight in chief, whom he also encouraged to follow Andrew's lead and dedicate his energies to the conjugal: or as he surmised, 'Get her cunt, Sir Edward!'

This masterpiece of wit consigned to posterity of tape, Andrew wept with gratitude, Mr Pitney proposed another toast, Mr

Spector sang praise to his hosts, the Stones returned that sentiment and all tumbled forward in mutual embrace with much singing of hoorahs, happy birthdays, and jolly good fellows until the last vessel was drained. And with it all residue of suspicion in Mr Spector that such fine young specimens of sensitive diction and moderate thirst would have dared pinch the petals of his most virtuous dark blooms.

CHAPTER

XXI

Is a Chapter of harmless flirtation, and may appear of no
great importance in its place. But it should be read
notwithstanding, as a Sequel to the last, and a Key to
one that will follow when its time arrives.

IT IS A regrettable irritant amongst the laws of chemistry that
the higher the liquor's acrobatics, the harder sobriety's landing:
and none plummeted so violently into the pits of crapulence
as Andrew, who awoke the next morning, his brain feeling like a
freshly landed mackerel flapping on the quarter deck in a sorry
dance of asphyxiation and only a fin's twitch from death.

These bodily distresses were multiplied to greater agonies still
as his memory slowly resuscitated to the tune of the previous
evening's zesty improvisation which, should it ever fall into the
wrong hands and find its way to tremble the ear-trumpet of Sir
Edward Lewis in the throne-room of Decca, would very likely set
in motion Andrew's swift and comprehensive ruin. Haunted by
these black presages, he allowed daylight's savage sabre to slash
apart his eyelids long enough to take store of his immediate
surroundings; spying a canister of tape containing the very same
jingle of japery which they'd so named, as written on the tin cover,
'Andrew's Blues', and which the group saw fit to credit both to Mr
Spector and to their composing doppelgangers, Messrs Nanker &
Phelge. The relief of which was just enough to hoist Andrew out

of his stewed brandy sewer and back to his former glories of intellect, which he wasted no time in re-employing.

To his extremities of annoyance, Mr Easton had attempted to undo Andrew's careful labours to vilify the Stones in the eyes of the nation's elders by cajoling their participation in a short television advertisement for the popular breakfast comestibles, Rice Krispies. Though sight of the Stones at the hour of the day when that cereal was commonly consumed would likely have adverse effect on the adult appetite, Mr Easton believed that mere sound of the Stones may yet endear them to the country's housewives; since no group, however unkempt, could pose any authentic degree of moral danger who were also willing to rhapsodise about Mr Kellogg's celebrated grains. The lyrics ready provided by an advertising agency, complement of tune was left to the fertility of the group, with Brian handed this honour after Mick and Keith declined on account he had long been murmuring about his melodic scope and original flair and was thus clearly born to that lofty task. In execution of which Brian exposed himself as but a mimic of narrow inspiration while, by contrast, Mick proved so unusually versatile in pronunciation of 'snap' and 'crackle' as to imbue those phrases with sufficient sentiment of bedcraft to safely pervert the course of Mr Easton's intentions.

The equilibrium of infamy restored, Andrew further embellished those characteristics with the aid of a journalist confrere, who placed in print nine words to the effect of: 'WOULD YOU LET YOUR DAUGHTER MARRY A ROLLING STONE?' The consensus of domestic opinion, as measured in a panic of polishing blunderbusses, overworked locksmiths and frantic applications to the conventual sisterhood, being firmly in the negative.

Rich in such ingloriousness, they were nevertheless still paupers of repertoire: the gestation of Mick and Keith into 'Jagger & Richards' taking longer than Andrew had first anticipated, and thus far productive of but a few ripened fruits, of which only one was fit to be recorded by the Stones themselves, being an exquisite ballad called 'Tell Me', reserved for their first long player; which otherwise consisted of predominantly borrowed fare and a couple of trifles relegated to the lowly authorship of Nanker & Phelge.

What scraps of staff paper bearing their initials remained, Andrew had donated to whichever artistes he could bait to record them: including the generous Mr Pitney, an obscure croaker named Bean, and – his latest catch – a teenage pipsqueak christened Adrienne Posta who agreed to puff and trill, as best she could, their saccharine potion 'Shang A Doo Lang'.

The release of Miss Posta's disc considered an occasion worth celebrating, Andrew had requested her father allow them use of the Posta dynasty's Marylebone apartment in which to stage due ceremony of commemoration. Mr Posta, by profession a manufacturer of furniture and thus of a salutary disposition to welcome compliment of his home décor, was delighted to accommodate Andrew's scheme; settling on the evening of Good Friday as an appropriate time to exhibit that hospitality and toast the phenomenon of his daughter's outstanding Doo Lang.

Andrew, Mick and Keith had not long arrived, shaken hands with old Mr Posta, paid compliments to young Miss Posta and taken their first swills of champagne when they were greeted by a face set in a familiar vulpine expression of astonishment: unmistakably that of Paul from The Beatles Pop Group, in company of his betrothed, one coppery Miss Asher, and a coterie of strangers.

It was then that they caught sight of the sublimity in that midst: a potentate of the fair sex possessed of such flummoxing beauty as to stir in them simultaneous paroxysms in jaw, pulse and groin. Had a goddess from the brush of Botticelli skipped free from her frame into the dreary sphere of mortals – choosing to mask her divine indecencies in a pair of blue jeans and a gentleman's overshirt – she would have been no less destructive to their Cyprian sensibilities, being a maddening confusion of matchgirl and dollymop with lips as pretty as any gulf of Venus. Or, as Andrew had already filed in his cerebral register, of remarkable similarity to 'the Virgin Mary with a cracking pair of tits'.

Unable to resist an audience with her endowed holiness, Mick and Andrew made quick pilgrimage across the room; in itself a blasphemy against their respective female companions, of whom Chrissie from Windsor was volubly traumatised to witness her beau desert her for the worship of another. Ignoring those shrieks of betrayal, Mick soon established that the buxom divinity was, alas, herself attached to the bespectacled bohemian fellow at her side, and seemingly immune to the invasive advances of rival suitors. Even those who chose, as he did, to orchestrate conversation by deliberate ejaculation of fluid upon those very same hillocks of heaven in vain hope that clumsy spillage of fizz would force an agreeably skittish dialogue; not only failing in that objective but damning himself by castigation in her private thoughts as displaying all the symptoms of 'a cheeky little yob'.

Having sense to waste neither a word nor a drop of catlap, Andrew made more artful approach through her squire, who introduced himself as a Mr Dunbar and enlightened him as to the identity of the newly dampened Aphrodite, one 'Marianne Faithfull'. This title striking Andrew as a tease of fabrication, he was assured by that gentleman there were deeds of birth, seventeen years old, to qualify these claims.

The revelation of this perfect christening illuminating his faculties to their utmost brilliance, Andrew next asked Mr Dunbar, 'Can she sing?' The young lady herself – thinking this a suitable point to enter the discussion in which she had so far remained silent – replied that she was sadly not well practised in the melodic arts, though neither had she considered them beyond reach of her vocal capabilities, which in speech alone were of such distracted delicacy that the words drifted from her mouth like so many dandelion seeds in a summer wind. These brief interchanges all Andrew required by way of audition, he furnished Mr Dunbar with his card, declared that he and Marianne were a pair of 'darlings', and implored liberty to measure her choral credentials in a recording studio at the earliest convenient opportunity, so agreed.

By the late hour the three residents of Mapesbury Road returned home – Mick having since made tender amends to Chrissie, while Keith had spent the evening engaged in pleasant intimacy with a young model – the fate of Miss Posta's Shanging had entirely vanished from Andrew's concerns, replaced by fresh Hallelujahs both for the Blessed Marianne, and the foresight of his own twitchy genius. For, only a few months earlier, during his initial husbandry of Mick and Keith, he had challenged them to resist all instincts of Rhythm and Blues by constructing a song sympathetic to the domicile of that tressed temptress Rapunzel: 'with bricked walls around it, high windows and no sex'.

Their response was, indeed, so fortified against convivial society that Mick feared for the damage it may pose to his reputation as a champion hornpiper, and so consigned it to their sorry litter of unsingables, never expecting Andrew to retrieve it for his new Madonna in the hope its vibrations sat comfortably upon, and within, that majestic décolletage.

And so, by these vicissitudes of fate, Miss Marianne Faithfull was granted her own contract with the Decca recording company, and the privilege of wobbling her ghostly young gizzard through Mick and Keith's 'As Tears Go By', which Andrew recorded with orchestral accompaniment and at such costs that he was obliged to request conference with Sir Edward Lewis to press for extra funds. His triumph in that venture being all the more remarkable for his barely concealed terror that this fossilised knight of the gramophone trade may possess gift of telepathy, and so question why it was young Mr Oldham's train of thought throughout that interview was thus preoccupied with profane shanties requesting that he, Sir Edward, at such an advanced stage of life should yet hound after some 'cunt' of unspecified ownership.

CHAPTER

XXII

⤜⤛

Our heroes hit the road again; and it finds
ample occasion to clobber them back.

ITH THEIR FIRST album ready by April to cause
ructions in the nation's living rooms – whether from
its ugly bombinations befouling the family radiogram,
or the offensive display of its sleeve, being a portrait of the group in
chiaroscuro; all five grimacing in such confrontational aspects as
might only ever be seen with typeset particulars of the reward sum
for capturing such persons dead or alive – the Stones prepared for
another exhaustive peregrination of the country's music halls.

None of them, however, were prepared for the teenage
apocalypse which greeted them on the eve of the record's release
in the northern milltown of Rochdale, where they'd been
requisitioned for the launch night of a new palace of entertainment,
so named the 'Cubi Klub'. The demand for tickets outnumbering
available supply triplefold, those unlucky applicants had
instinctually decided to surround the premises in a two-thousand
strong fever optimistic of entry: a number which placed no undue
strain upon the local constabulary, whose attempts at dispersal
were causative to a great many projectiles of worrying solidity; as
well as the Greater Manchester ambulance service, their stretchers
buckling with the weight of damsels so throttled by the brewing
excitement inside the hall that they'd surrendered all efforts to the

vertical. These disturbances already occurring before the Stones had even arrived on site, itself an impossible feat on account of this impermeable human cordon, they were thus advised to abandon their commitment, and so leave their Lancashire desirers in tearful fury of unconsummation.

Such scenes of civil bedlam were to become the exasperating substance of normality in the lives of the Rolling Stones throughout the late spring and early summer, as their debut long player swung into the charts like a wrecking ball to displace The Beatles Pop Group from the top spot. This, only a year to the month since the Stones meekly handled their Mersey tackle at the Royal Albert Hall; and yet the misdirected gropes and pecks they'd accidentally braced that night seemed but timid caresses compared with those of the lipsticked vampires now crouching in wait wherever their Chelsea boots trod.

In Coventry, the Locarno manager took the desperate measure of employing a fire extinguisher to halt the drive of vixens rushing the stage. In Chester, the group were forced to flee the theatre over the neighbouring roofs and gables so as to avoid certain terrestrial ambuscade. And, closer to home in Catford, the floods of female want left the stalls resembling a sinking galley, pants and scanties floating between the aisles like flotsam in a urinary ocean from which limp and sodden bodies were dredged by the score.

In all instances the penalty for any Stone less than mercurial of heel in passage betwixt vehicle and venue was: certain loss of clothing; likely abrasions to skin; probable violation of scalp; potential loss of eyesight; conceivable disfigurement to the tools of generation; and the faint if not impossible prospect of strangulation, amputation and – pending circumstance – decapitation. Thus, by necessity, all developed the agility of weasels as essential impediment to permanent scarring, not to mention continuance of life; with the exception of Brian, whose smiling flights were of such casual acceleration as to appear wilfully indulging of those frenzied fingernails, every scratch and bite received as thrilling affirmation of his evident godliness.

That their amorous pests prized no spoil of contact so dear as a tuft of hair, however bloody its extraction, and to the wholly uneven reduction of the victim's style, would have been of petty consolation to the National Federation of Hairdressers, whose president had that week given address at their spring conference, upbraiding the menace of young men with 'slovenly, dirty and downright ragged hair-dos of which there were too many about'; naming the Stones as the instrumental epitome of this fashion, since one of them looked as if they sported 'a feather-duster on his head'.

The president was far from isolated in his disgust, which extended countrywide to the headmaster of a Midlands comprehensive school, who subjected eleven of his boys to suspension for fostering their follicles in unacceptable Stones shape, the conditions of clemency being immediate shearing to an acceptable length 'like The Beatles Pop Group'; and to the readership of London's *Evening Standard*, among them a young girl roused to such emotion of outrage she made pledge of correspondence to target Charlie, for reasons she never disclosed, and lace his tea 'with weed-killer'.

Adding to this list of printed damnations, all grist to Andrew's lucrative mill of pantomime villainy, were reports of their next engagement in the city of Bristol, where they'd arranged bed and board in the Italianate splendour of the Grand Hotel. Assuming their guest privileges included luncheon, the Stones took their custom to the restaurant of that fine establishment, whereupon their entry was obstructed by a starched maître d', whose visage was contorted in the most hateful rigor mortis. This paralysis of loathing he soon explained as consequence of the group's chosen vestments: being casual sweaters above, and denim and corduroy below and, in lieu of blazer and tie, therefore of a habit entirely unacceptable to their fellow patrons, unaccustomed as they were to common company of ragamuffins. Unless, of course, they disembarrass their appearance with those mandatory garments, as may be provided by the hotel management upon request.

After quick digest of these conditions, Mick replied on behalf of all, that their purses were as good as any, that no person other than themselves was in any position to dictate their dress, and that, in any case, they abstained from wearing ties as a precaution against it dangling in their soups; the sum total of these protests yet failing to win them exception.

The following week rampaged by, rich with incident: audiences sent berserk in Bournemouth, nutty in Newcastle, brainsick in Bradford, screwy in Stoke and frenzied in Folkestone; until thundering northwards, across the Pictish border into lawless Lanarkshire, where the limits of hysteria were again redefined by goings on inside, and outside, Hamilton's Chantinghall Hotel.

It was, by now, a routine irregularity that there were more persons wishing to see the Stones in each town than there were available tickets: a conundrum which one local entrepreneur sought to exploit with the printing of some thousand counterfeits, sold at a pretty penny, and with significant inconvenience to those who'd purchased the genuine article; as by the time the box office was alerted to this forgery, the venue had already filled beyond capacity with interlopers. Those now unfortunately exiled expressed their disappointment in such means as necessitated call for additional police reinforcements from the neighbouring settlements of Motherwell and Wishaw; while those boxed within were subject to degrees of heat and moisture as might only be expected during the intense cultivation of tropical orchids, conditions inductive to an epidemic of swoons in both sexes which bewildered the competence of the attendant medical officers.

Order was no better restored by the stage arrangements, the group's nerves propelled to immediate jangles of panic on taking first sight of the mesh fence, eight foot in height, erected between themselves and the asylum beyond. Far from dissuasive to the assembled lunatics, its construction offered them opportune stirrups to scale its façade in eager hope of stupration: those objectives only impeded by the regular buckets of water hurled in their direction by the bouncers, whose grasp of chemical law clearly hadn't yet encompassed the relative problems of so much liquid in the vicinity of so much electricity.

This carnage set the standard for their remaining Scottish fixtures: the next in Aberdeen on a bill of variety headlined by a confederacy of pudding-heads called Freddie And The Dreamers, whose singer – the eponymous Frederick – bore a permanent mask of inanity, exhibited all the muscular delicacy of a court eunuch, and was cursed with traumatic epilepsies of movement lending him the air of a wretch in permanent agony of bladder desperately scouting for the nearest public convenience. His fellow Dreamers were no less unsightly, predisposed to preposterous elevations of leg in rhythm to their asinine yodels about romance and botany which, until recently, had proven popular enough to furnish them with a clutch of hits beloved of all ages deceased from the neck upwards.

While respectful to the scheduled order lending Freddie prominence, the Stones nevertheless made polite suggestion that recent scenes in Hamilton were indicative of potential grievance to any band who might attempt to follow them on stage – let alone one of such sapless constitution – and that it would be in the interests of peace to instead let them close proceedings as guarantee against strife and skirmish. There being no greater confirmation of Freddie's imbecility than his blunt refusal of this offer, the evening took inevitable course of doom. The Stones relegated to the position before the interval, the grand finale witnessed the Dreamers' feeble din drowned by a fierce halloo of 'We want The Stones!', the improvisational timpani of breaking seats and the severest of demands upon the patience of the Aberdonian police; all the while that capering buffoon engaged in vain attempts to quell anger with diversion of his increasingly desperate hops and skips, provocative of a volley of missiles yet exacerbating the elasticity of his deranged saltations.

These disturbances largely confined to the local periodicals of the parishes concerned, there was therefore minimum risk of their riotous reputation travelling across the Atlantic and troubling the breakfast tables of the North Americas. Where, to their immense excitement, the Stones were soon engaged to arrive, that visit contributing to fresh scenes of havoc, an account of which is deserved of its own chapter, being the very next.

CHAPTER

XXIII

❧

Descriptive of adventures abroad.

SOME TRIFLING EXCITEMENT prevailed upon the very brink and margin of the land of liberty the day Andrew and the Stones landed there by aircraft in the first week of June, Nineteen Sixty-Four. Only a few months earlier The Beatles Pop Group had undertaken a similar voyage of historic impact upon the sanity of the young American female; the majority of whom succumbed to the vapours at the briefest glimpse of their waggling mops, and so laying foundations for worship of any English band who may follow in their wake, especially those so tantalisingly woolly of temple.

The Stones were thus immediate beneficiaries of their peers' charitable preliminaries, greeted at New York City's Kennedy Airport – only recently renamed in honour of that slain president hitherto discussed in this History – by several hundred baying foxtrels; the inky bayonets of the popular press; bouquets of flowers, organised as a precautionary masking scent lest the unflattering hearsay regarding their daily toilet be proved valid; and the company of two English sheepdogs, there as an intended jape of juxtaposition with their own superfluity of locks – a subject which dominated interrogations from the welcoming representatives of the *New York Stabber*, the *New York Family Spy*, the *New York Private Listener*, the *New York Peeper*, the *New York*

Plunderer, the *New York Keyhole Reporter*, the *New York Rowdy Journal*, and other publications of their New York ilk. In course of which Mick made jest of their follicular homage to the regal styling of King Charles the First, Brian countered a query about personal hygiene by inviting that inquisitor to savour his armpit at close quarters, and Charlie mastered such mute grimaces of hostility to the monotony of questions about hair-scissors as to safely annul need of verbal reply.

These charades of hospitality concluded, the officers of law enforcement abandoned restraint of the slavering minxes who impulsively tore towards the Stones in a terrifying tide of shrieks and pincers, instigating urgent retreat into five separate limousines. Each member was thus brusquely parcelled inside, joined by reporters from whichever *Peeper*, *Plunderer* or *Rowdy Journal* were flighty of foot enough to join them, their ensuing journey into Manhattan hotly pursued by a convoy of vulpettes pelting them with flora and various other fluffy tokens of affection.

Their girlish appetites for pandemonium, unabated by the lengthy chase, were regurgitated with redoubled violence when the group reached their destined hotel in Times Square; the entrance of which was already besieged by an even greater lipsticked armada, who proceeded to overwhelm the flimsy barricades of police and porters. Stepping from their vehicles into this maelstrom of drizzling mascara, the Stones hurtled through reception like fleeing banditti, their lightning reflexes guiding them to the first available door tempting refuge and slamming it firm behind them. Finding themselves cocooned by linen, their combined wits readily deduced they had foolishly erred in taking unknowing sanctuary of the hotel's laundry cupboard, where they would have to remain, sweating in a cell of fabric with no other means of exit, until eventual escort of fortified law conducted them safely to their proper chambers.

In due course, the warm embrace of the East Coast – its Manhattan streets so handsome the city fathers swore they 'whipped the universe', to say nothing of their delectable daughters whose hip-ricochet-heels polished its pavements to a shine – was tempered by the chill of the West when, two days later, they flew on to Los Angeles for their first American television broadcast.

Compared with the Houses of Buckingham and Versailles, the *Hollywood Palace* was noticeably lacking in rococo splendour being – like most concerns to trouble that region of sunburnt narcissi – the very essence of nonsense and fantasy; their fellow guests including a mother and daughter elephant act, two generations of singing Mormons, and a trampolinist. The host was a Mr Martin, popularly known as 'Dino': a singing prankster who prided himself on affectations of insobriety and who took unnatural pleasure in ridiculing the Stones' appearance in order to titillate an audience whose vaudeville preferences were typically more sympathetic to elephant, Mormon and acrobat. These japes comprised the following: repeated sarcastic tumbles of eyeball; the false intelligence that they were due to return to London post-haste for an imminent 'hair-pulling contest' with The Beatles Pop Group; dumb show of terror at the prospect of being left alone in their company; and a final slur at the expense of the trampolinist, who was accused of fathering all five Stones, and whose lethal gymnastics were therefore the means he'd chosen to end his shame by committing suicide.

The sum of these defamations ordinarily deserving of retribution – with Brian suggesting a novel amendment of Mr Martin's dressing quarters using the generous backstage evacuations of Bertha the elephant, and her daughter Tina – they nevertheless exhibited discipline against those instincts which, alas, would be tested yet again during their subsequent engagement in the southern state of Texas.

What high expectations Keith entertained, based on his boyhood fantasies of Roy Rogers, were lassoed into the dust by their ordeal at the San Antonio Teen Fair: theirs the ignominious privilege of following the much admired trio of Candy, Charlie and Enoch, whose efforts of musical recitation, dance and general dressage gave rise to happy agonies of ribcage amongst the gathered crowd as consequence of those three named individuals being born chimpanzees.

While the Stones were no strangers to primate comparisons from those excited enough to pass comment on their prominent barbering, this in no way endeared their skills to the Stetsoned assembly; largely comprised of those employed in bovine occupations, whose affinity with the beasts of their trade extended to laconic, horizontal gyrations of jaw in ceaseless mastication of tobacco, and whose annoyance took appropriate chorus of moos rather than boos, and the flinging of enough loose vegetables as might later be washed and prepared to configure a hearty casserole. Texas would, however, leave at least some contrastingly pleasant imprints upon their character, all acquiring souvenir of ten-gallon hats, while Charlie – the Stone, that is, as opposed to his monkey namesake mentioned afore – amassed a fine armoury of vintage pistols and several bound volumes relating to the American Civil War, a topic in which he was fast becoming as conversant a scholar as he was of handkerchiefs.

To these physical mementos of that home of the brave were, of course, added various fleeting intimacies which, at this near halfway stage of these much too scrofulous adventures the Reader must have surely already supposed, and which therefore needn't be catalogued in gratuitous detail of every blonde and brunette, their tender Southern strokes and all attendant 'yee-haw!' of shakedown rodeo. And so, bypassing those crude unnecessaries, which though on occasion crude were, in point of fact, very necessary in maintaining group morale – notwithstanding contributory to transatlantic goodwill – we shall jump to the single most important incident of that inaugural sally to the Americas.

Nearly all religions of this Earth – regardless of whichever fearfully obtuse human mind invented their infinite rules and restrictions – select some ancient edifice in which to invest all focus of prayer, wailing, bowing and curses of vengeance against the debunking wisdom of blasphemy. So it was with our five pilgrims of the Lord Diddley, for whom there was no more a sacred spot on our insignificant globe than an address in the Midwest city of Chicago: being number Twenty-One-Twenty South Michigan Avenue, headquarters of the Chess recording company, musical Mount Olympus of Chuck Berry, Muddy Waters and – hail! hail! – his Diddleyship.

Through a combination of Andrew's princely coercions and persuasive connections, he had succeeded in gaining them, not merely a visit to this holiest of temples, but use of its recording cella: the very same where Mr Berry executed his *Rockin' At The Hops*, the talisman which first bound Mick and Keith together and for whom this occasion was therefore tantamount to crawling in mutual embrace back into the foetal sack of their union. Their fervour rippled awe through the rest of the group – even Charlie, otherwise occupied in thoughts of jazz, jacket linings and the caps of Stonewall Jackson – who all strode through the side entrance from the parking lot in ecstasies of saved sinners passing under the pearly gates.

Carrying their instruments inside, they trod along a thin corridor, tiptoed around a ladder atop of which a negro gentleman in dark overalls was coating the ceiling with brush and paint, and were welcomed within the principal studio womb by Mr Chess himself; that gentleman forewarned by their mutual friend, the Lord Diddley, that they were 'good cats', if still taken aback that he'd somehow agreed to show hospitality to, as first appearances indicated, a quintet of 'strange white English motherfuckers'.

Mick and Keith's senses already out at elbows with reality, it was then that the decorator descended from his steps and exchanged brief words with Mr Chess: in course of which he was addressed as 'Muddy', as in the esteemed Mr Waters, being the very same Messiah, one who apparently preferred whitewashing above the heads of his disciples to cleaning their feet, and whose unveiled identity sent them into yet queerer gibbers of goggling eyes and sagging mandibles.

In the same zenith of reverence, the Stones occupied the next two days brewing music of a dark sweetness such as they had never brewed before: as if the tiniest particles of past magic hung in the atmosphere like lingering gun smoke to be sucked in their lungs, vibrated through their veins, guiding throats, feet and fingers. In these remarkable feats, of a genre which called for definition as Blues 'n' Witchcraft or Rhythm 'n' Voodoo, oft times with an audience of Messrs Berry and Waters murmuring blessings of approval, never were they more sublimely necromantic than on a song they'd been handed by a New York disc jockey by a group new to their attentions called The Valentinos. The Stones instinctively unstitched and refashioned the tune's Pacific Coast shindig into a Dartford rave, crowned with Brian's closing thunderclap chords; as magnificent a use of that electrified instrument as its earliest inventor could have ever dreamed feasible. Its title: 'It's All Over Now'.

Yet, contrary to all sentiment of chorus, this syncopated orgy of obscure origin would become the record to affect new beginnings of fortune when they eventually returned home to the darkened chimney stacks of England. And, once there, lost no time in replenishing any credit of disgrace which might have shrunk from the purse of public offence during their three week absence, as the Reader will soon discover in the course of the following pages, should they yet be of leisure to peruse them.

XXIV

A brief one, in which they accept responsibility of jury service,
and themselves are unanimously judged to be guilty.

THEY CAME HOME to screams, to tears, to flashing camera
bulbs and police helmets knocked rolling off their owners'
ruddy domes by a swarm of perfumed uncontainables; to
the expectant gnashing for a general election and cries of corruption
in The Yard; to the first feature film by The Beatles Pop Group
and a newly completed Post Office Tower; to a customs crisis in
meat thefts and a schoolboy savaged by a panda in London Zoo;
to mud slides of creeping clay in Lewisham and dozing lineswomen
in Wimbledon; to warring mods, marauding rockers and the
number one sound of an optically delicate American named Mr
Orbison. And to an offer from the British Safety Council to
present the group with five golden hairnets, thus highlighting the
dangers posed to all young men of their shaggy inclination who
may find themselves fatally ensnared in factory machinery, much
like the ancient fable of the Israelite King caught in the oak tree,
and so named in his honour, the Absalom Award. Which, to the
surprise of nobody other than the puffing Council controller, they
chose to ignore.

They came home to a country whose television service had not
long multiplied to three channels only to suddenly reduce to two;
that subtraction the result of fiscal ingratitude amongst the

technicians of the ITV network who had downed tools, so plunging the further perils of Little Joe Cartwright and Ena Sharples into darkness until their pay packets were amended with agreeable increment of pounds and shillings more worthy of their artistry. And so, upon the evening of Saturday the fourth of July, the Great British viewing public were limited to a primetime choice of a review of the day's news on BBC Two, or the popular panel show *Juke Box Jury*, in which a selection of the latest discs hopeful of ascending the Hit Parade were subject to the critical appraisals of invited guests from the many spheres of entertainment: the majority of households settling on the latter at ten minutes past seven on BBC One.

That hour arriving, in all corners of this demi-paradise its greying happy breed sat in their favourite chairs – wearing their favourite slippers, their intestines grumbling from recent digestion of starch, sugar and fat, their buttocks blowing with putrid gases, nuggets of gristle lodged in their teeth, sloshing milky tea and Bass beer down their throats at such speeds as to repeat on them in amphibian belches – and stared at the small flickering oblong which was so effortlessly the master of their attentions.

They sat and they stared and they slurped and they belched as *Juke Box Jury*'s familiar host, Mr Jacobs, welcomed them to 'a special edition' of the programme. The studio audience screaming uncontrollably, the riddle of this specialness was solved when the panel was revealed to be five members, one juror more than normal. And they sat and they stared and their bowels growled and their sphincters spluttered as they realised the five panellists were, in point of fact and indigestion, those reviled abstainers of the prize of Absalom: The Rolling Stones.

For the next twenty-seven minutes, the British minions felt their organs pump with rage, their various orifices bubble in chorus of disgust and their eyes screw and pop in disbelief as, from left to right, Mick, Charlie, Brian, Keith and Bill puffed on their

'The Jury Sworn In'

cigarettes, chewed on their gum, grunting, giggling and half-Nankering through the selected offerings: mumbling apathetic verdicts in shape of 'awful', 'innit', 'erm', 'boring', 'nah', 'crummy', 'dunno', 'who cares?', 'rubbish', 'you're joking?', 'uh?', 'what?' and 'eh?' Scant mercy was spared their old adversaries Freddie And The Dreamers, whose submission involved a piece of film in which their leapfrogging dunce assumed the dress of a medieval jester, a role to which his talents were, for once, properly employed; nor Elvis Presley, shown in a clip from his latest cinematic *tour de force* frolicking in a haystack with two young ladies competing for his affections, his accompanying sonnet to the virtues of women from the countryside heretically dismissed by Keith as 'dated' and Charlie as 'cobblers'. And having been less than charitable about a new disc from a seventeen-year-old chanteuse from Solihull, Miss Christine Holmes, they were duly informed that Miss Holmes was there in person, and so had to suffer the disgrace of shaking hands with her five flagellators as their darting eyes made shifty inspection of her more redeeming attributes.

All these horrors ending at thirty-seven minutes past seven, some million hands at once began rummaging through some million sideboards in quest of stationery with which to bleed their outrage in ballpoint puddles of nervous complaint to soak the mail rooms of Newspaper, Church and Parliament, and altogether flood the British Broadcasting Corporation. By the following Monday morning the first of these salty stains were hot print, steaming with the conviction that the Stones were 'a grotesque parody of incoherent youth', despair that 'none of the ill-mannered louts had the courtesy to stand when shaking hands with a young lady' and bewildered pleas for 'Charlie Watts to have elocution lessons – it was an agony to understand him.'

The doubtful prospect of these suggestions having the desired effect upon our rogue of rhythm to oblige and seek professional aid to improve his diction notwithstanding, Charlie was blissfully unaware of their existence, having already removed himself to the Balearics for a week's holiday with Mick and their respective girl-friends; though not so unaware of their agents of propagation. For they had been pursued to their Ibizan retreat by one especially persistent correspondent, who managed to coax from Mick a few pithy quotations on the subject of their accommodation, of a calibre no less pejorative than those expressed in company of Mr Jacobs. Foremost, his disappointment that, having flown in excess of one thousand miles to escape the hullaballoo of Albion, their chosen Palmyra Hotel was infested with their fellow countrymen, who entertained themselves the whole day in the swimming pool, an urge they could have easily addressed in the chlorinated baths of home. And that the same bulldog breed had perverted his hopes of sampling foreign fare of distinct character, since the caterers of that establishment had adapted their menu to the blandest of English palettes for fear that their abundance of guests from that region might otherwise reject the cuisine as being 'too Spanishy'.

The happy reporter thus furnished with this scabrous critique filed their account, the flames of the lynch mob still bloodlusting after *Juke Box Jury* fanned yet higher by Mick's unpatriotic bugles, which appeared in the press the same day as photographs of The Beatles Pop Group shaking the regal fingers of her juniper-breathed highness, Princess Margaret.

In plain language, the Stones' behavioural predilections during that first week of July could not have been more engendering to nationwide dreams of their heads placed upon pikes the length of London Bridge – no doubt as their distinguished Liverpudlian forebears trundled past as inspective passengers in Her Majesty's horse-drawn carriage – had they deliberately set out to do so. And those blistering injuries to the morals of her subjects now all the worse, thanks to the criminally affinitive adolescents who purchased their latest antagonism in such quantities as to reward them with their first number one: the new national anthem for the slaughtered pride of the once glorious Empire of genteel manners and short back and sides. It was *all* over now.

CHAPTER

XXV

‿ℰꝏ

*Is wholly devoted to a reception that poses more than
modest threat to the mortality of our subjects.*

THE ALERT READER, blessed with such cerebral machinery
as to have no shortage of supply of memory, and who has
not merely gazed upon these pages in sorry trances of
confusion from which they regularly emerge dizzily oblivious to
the improving information encrypted within, will recall that,
among the many concerts by The Rolling Stones so far described,
none were as wild as that over the Scottish border in Hamilton,
just south of the ash clouds pumping from the metropolis of
Glasgow.

Those same clouds, black and sooty with sulphuric pollen,
bellowed from that city's myriad funnels of industry; their furnaces
stoked by sweating devils whose unenviable toils were rewarded
with one week's respite, when the flames died, the smoke cleared
and the smelters temporarily closed their gates. Seven days in
which to make amends for a whole year's inhalation of charcoal
and seek appropriate diversion of maritime climate for rest,
recreation and the replacement of all bodily fluids with the most
toxic potions as could ever be distilled from grain. By tradition,
around the third week of July, when all such devils made pilgrimage
by railway to the same paradise of embalmment. By tradition,
Blackpool, on the Lancashire coast. And, by tradition, christened

by the locals who admitted the thirsty terrors of Strathclyde into their hospitable midst, 'Scottish Weekend'.

It was Bill, ever the observant diarist, who first noted aloud to his fellow Stones that, for an English seaside retreat, there seemed to be 'a bloody lot of Scots around' as they arrived in Blackpool the Friday afternoon of Scottish Weekend; a cultural phenomenon none of the group could swear to possessing any prior knowledge of, and thus were unprepared for the scenes of frightening aspect which greeted them through the windows of their vehicle.

That long dead Jacobite midget prince of 'Bonnie' legend would have been none prouder to see such a formidable congregation of Picts and Gaels upon King George's soil, in such number as would petrify the old turnpikes of London into dire urgencies of barricade against Stuart invasion. An army that did not require arms other than those they were born with, and which they happily employed upon one another, in broad daylight, with brutal pugnacity; their talents for crushing facial cartilage miraculously unimpeded by their startling states of intoxication multiplying their duellist from singular to plural and rendering the accuracy of plant all the more impressive. This lustiness of spirit was not merely contained among the male Scotch species: their womenfolk no less ascetic in consumption of liquid bliss, no less timid in the shrieking of vulgar phrase, and no more diplomatic when resolving their differences with the blunt vocabulary of hands and feet. Such was the vista of Scottish Weekend, and such were the pangs of regret in every gentleperson of Anglo-Saxon blood, the Stones included, that the late Emperor Hadrian's famous erection couldn't withstand the test of time and deter these savages from straying so much as a yard south of Gretna Green.

The sum of these fierce sights effected an atmosphere of inevitable ruin pressing down on their heads when, later that evening, they took their places under the lights in the Empress Ballroom and discovered their audience to consist of those very same immigrants – several thousand strong – with only a dozen trembling valets to feign authority of order, none of them remotely capable in that task, and not a single law enforcement officer in the room on account of the entire Blackpool constabulary being destitute of the necessary pluck to risk beheading by the rabid Rabs of Caledonia.

The group's only grace was the dimension of the stage itself, a clear six-foot from the ground, placing them above the heads of the majority of these brutes, being of almost universally squat proportions suggestive of ancestries associated with the circus trades in which they also might excel had circumstance not cursed them to a fate of lathe, press and welding torch. The Stones commencing their entertainment, their habitual effect on the female contingency, collectively referred to by their male counterparts as 'the lassies', was typically pronounced and especially gratifying to Brian who, considering himself the primary focus of their howling desire, responded with exaggerated pouts and preens intended to sustain full volume of lust. While successful in his objective, his antics also garnered the unfortunate attentions of the rowdier winebibbers present, for whom the five men on stage blurred into fifteen, all representative of Sassenach menace to the fertile furrows of lassiedom, to be repelled accordingly.

That accord first expressed in boos and jeers, Keith was irritated to reply by locking eyes on the chanting culprits and, ensuring he had their full concentration, mouthing two words with such precision of lips as they might easily understand: the first being a verb, the second a preposition, their union an instruction to exit the premises of the most expressive discourtesy. The consequences of these actions were to be felt by the rest of the group, all of whose hair, clothing, skin and instruments soon became damp with sputum, rapidly discharged from the barley-sore throats of the Scotch hobgoblins, in remarkable trajectories from pit to stage as would easily ruffle envy in the soul of their old friend, sadly since vanished from this History but for ever, affectionately, the illustrious Mr Phelge.

Among these sputumites was one so bold they adopted such close quarters as to be physically dangling from the edge of the performance rostrum, clinging by their porky digits, evidently immune to the pressure of Keith's boot crunching down on metacarpals which only agitated yet more violent squirts of spittle. Having thus failed to eradicate this grochelling fiend from his immediate vicinity, Keith resorted to yet more dramatic means of abolition. Further exploiting his elevated position, which placed his feet on a parallel horizon with his foe's head, he made handsome demonstration of his long neglected skills on the sports field: substituting Glaswegian skull for football, kicked with such force as ought to have dispatched it to the opposite side of the ballroom were it not for the knotted sinews which held it atop of the vertebrae where, defying all probability of decapitation, it oscillated like the hammer of an alarm clock blurring between invisible bells; and so rang out the signal for 'Attack!'

A cluster of hands now swarmed the length of the stage, each a meaty grappling hook glinting with knotted jewellery pulling their hideous owners into plain sight: scarred of forehead, crimson of cheek, mutilated of ear, smashed of teeth and noxious of breath. To Keith and his kinsmen, it looked like Hell had just spewed its foulest cavalry of undesirables through the floorboards in a Satanic lava flow; hissing with the sound of garbled promises to maim and torture, pumping towards them at a speed to send all instruments tumbling, all amplifiers squealing, and all Stones off through the wings and into the dressing room, where their prayers converged on the durability of the bolted doors of unknown alloy: being all that separated them from the molten riot and, ergo, the following day's obituary columns.

What they could not see with their eyes, their imaginations painted in vivid detail according to the percussive echoes beyond, each adding another brushstroke to the ginormous tableau of destruction, of a scale as would rival the most humbling frescoes ever commissioned by popery: guitars reduced to wood, wires and string; drums and cymbals crushed like taffeta and tissue; microphone stands snapped like sparrow legs; speaker cabinets collapsing like packets of Woodbines; the very wooden boards beneath their feet pounded into matchsticks; the velvet curtains clawed to confetti of red and gold rags; the chandeliers disintegrating from the strikes of chairs and bottles buzzing overhead like flies; the curdling chorus of the trapped and trampled; the triumphant roar of the vicious and vandalising; knuckles into flesh; ring ripping skin; blade piercing blubber; blood and vomitus; tears and urine; broken glass, lost shoes, loose coins, lipsticks, cigarette butts and spilled beer; and the ceaseless tribal chants of so many demented patriots, repetitive of two syllables elongated in tuneless booms, yet of proud lucidity: 'SCOT-LAND!'

These sounds developing that mental picture to degrees of detail placing demands upon their nerves of unbearable severity, a shiver of policemen displaying symptoms of anxiety in no way relieving to that condition finally arrived to escort them to safety; a status achieved by the most laborious exodus over the roofs of several buildings, their shaky progress serenaded by the incessant rumble and holler of Armageddon raging beneath.

It raged still, long after their vehicle had sped beyond the farthest outskirts of the town, which awoke the next morning to another day of that noble tradition, Scottish Weekend, and the birth of a brand new local custom – one the district councillors set in legislation during an emergency assembly held the following Monday when the estimate of damages was properly totalised.

That never, not in Scottish Weekend, not in any weekend, nor any weekday whatever the month, whatever the season, would Blackpool again play host to those five shameless London lobbyists of northern civic sabotage – an invoice for thousands upon their purse and as many curses upon their heads!

CHAPTER

XXVI

A midway retrospect.

POILED, AS I am, in my capacity as the Author who has
undertaken to relate this History with the most shameful
particulars regarding the antics of our subjects, I am
conscious that there may be some readers for whom the gravity
of their impact upon our ill-omened isle during the year Nineteen
Sixty-Four has already sunk in enough; and that to emphasise
this situation, fully understood, with supplementary description
of every occasion their presence in some parochial district ended
in scenes of sirens and stretchers would make very heavy and
very repetitious labour of reading. So let me merely surmise by
stating that what happened in Blackpool would, in lesser varying
degrees of physical destruction and mental dementia, happen
again and again, across autumn and into winter, wherever and
whenever The Rolling Stones presented themselves before a
paying public. Therefore, with the greatest of apologies to those
of inexhaustibly anarchic appetites who feel in any sense robbed
of sensation, we must bypass all superfluity of knickers and
bloodshed, zip through the days at lightning speed and leap to
that year's end, to review how these events left their mark upon
the individual perpetrators.

The trinity of Mapesbury Road had amicably disintegrated some
months previous, with Andrew taking refuge in matrimony and

temporary leave of his senses; announcing to the press that, at the age of twenty, he had decided to retire from the music industry, unfasten his cart and relax his whip hand upon the Stones, who were now free to canter into the future dragging their loose reins behind them. This brief recess of lunacy was to last all of seven days, after which he was soon yanking on their bridles wilder than ever before, angered that they had chosen for their next release an old blues tune about a 'Little Red Rooster', of a drowsy design he considered altogether crippled in its chances of repeating the number one success of its predecessor. Only when it did, indeed, top the Hit Parade for one week that December did Andrew happily admit he had underestimated his quintet of Midases, able to sell obscure odes about slumberous poultry by the hundreds of thousands: also adding another stripe of notoriety to their sleeves when the same disc's release was vetoed in the United States; their corresponding label deciding that its words, as borrowed from another of their Chess Records saints, Mr Howlin' Wolf, were not the innocent preoccupation with farmyard morale they first appeared but concerned with coloured cocks of a quite different kind.

His two former flatmates remained as one, relocating to the quiet of Hampstead village, where its gentrified revellers staggering up and down the hill to and from The Holly Bush inn may, occasionally, have paused to savour the firm of Jagger & Richards in full volume of business, tabling motions of verse and chorus with yodel and guitar, interrupted by the random pines of 'Ratbag': a young collie Keith received as a gift from a fan while touring the Americas, which he decided to transport home to England in such a manner as would avoid the painful separation of man and beast for purpose of quarantine, smuggling the affectionate mutt, and whatever rabid foreign pestilence may be incubating within its jowls, through customs under his overcoat. And with that image of sweet Ratbag nuzzling tight to his master's chest forever etched in our hearts, we take leave of Keith and shift focus to his lardaceous-lipped persona grata.

For Mick, the year's fruits of celebrity weren't without their bruises. His romance with Chrissie was now public knowledge, to the compromise of that young woman's public safety when recognised by those regarding her situation with uncontrollable envy, of whom there were a terrifying multitude, each capable of the most shocking reproaches of tongue and hairpin. His gender status was still inflammatory to rumours of medical jiggery-pokery, as was his mortality: being an alleged sufferer of leukaemia, a condition it was believed he shared with Brian, the pair of them having approximately less than six months before their full birth names provided stonemason's chisel with happy employment. His purported predilection for yellow socks had also instigated a minor crisis in the postal service, burdened with delivery of those garments from ingratiating coquettes from every shire in the kingdom to the spatial inconvenience of the group's management and record company, and to the added dismay of Chrissie; now employed by the latter in a secretarial position, hers the responsibility to open each parcel and read the explicit appeals to her lover's debauchery, all requesting it be administered *au naturel* bar decorative trim of lemon bootikins.

And so, very briefly, to Bill, whose marital status had earlier been exposed in the papers, though to his great relief this information failed to deter the abundance of candidates seeking conference with his glister-pipe, and with it due fame of posterity in the pages of his diary which, by the year's end, were embarrassingly rich in annotated conquests.

And to Charlie, who had also joined Bill and Andrew in matrimonial society, making an honest woman of his long-term sweetheart, an art student named Shirley, and setting up home in a mansion flat near Regent's Park; where, when not in active service of the Stones, he liked to spend an evening listening to jazz recordings, browsing his library of American military history, inspecting his collection of vintage pistols and quietly polishing his undiminished enigma to an unfathomably handsome shine.

Which leaves only Brian as the last to be accounted for and – as those who would rather be equipped with as much good news before bad might appreciate – his placement at the end of this retrospect is altogether intentional. For where the raging flames of fame had brought warmth to the lives of his fellow Stones, Brian had strayed a little too close to its glare: his eyes blinded, his heart scorched in the heat of adulation until his veins pumped cinders, polluting mind and body with black thoughts and blacker deeds.

The domestic paradise he'd established in Windsor proved an ephemeral fancy: his devotion for young Linda, her parents and the malodorous Billy G perishing with the announcement that his virility had once again reaped unexpected consequence of son, born that summer when the mother was but seventeen, and christened by its father – with alarming vacuity of imagination – the same as his previous folly of procreation, 'Julian'. Or, as Brian otherwise preferred, 'Broad Bean Head', on account of its striking cranial resemblance to that misshapen legume.

To this unfortunate victim of illegitimacy he added yet another, the result of his regular investment of energy on a girl of appropriate youth to merit that expenditure, yet who was similarly denied not only prestige of wedlock but, all the wickeder, dignity of provision. Her attempts to infiltrate Brian's obligations in that respect were obstructed by Andrew, who encouraged her to sign a docket agreeing never to pester that culpable advocate of bareback bastardy ever again, nor divulge his paternity; for which she received a single payment of seven hundred pounds, that figure deducted from Brian's earnings through the most fiendish artifices of accountancy as he himself would never suspect.

This is not to say Brian was entirely devoid of suspicions – which were, indeed, countless in number and identical in temper – concerning the other members of the group, now convinced that his character occupied their every devious colloquy. His train thus obsessed with conspiracy and guile, he had recently taken to hovering outside the doors of dressing rooms, ears pricked for one syllable of slander to justify this permanence of anxiety, itself only serving to weaken his spirit and warp his moods, so irritating Mick, Keith, Bill and Charlie into private analysis of his inexplicable conduct, and so fulfil all prophecy of Brian's persecution of conscience.

These, our five picaros, each in their chosen indulgences of infamy. Mick in his yellow socks. Keith with his Ratbag. Bill with his diary. Charlie with his pistols. Brian with his ear pressed against a hotel bedroom, his face contorted in icy creeps – like those of so many at the close of Nineteen Sixty-Four.

Outside, in the streets and hillsides, a Moorish whisper in the howl of the December wind. *'Chaos is come again.'*

Young gentlemen's hair hanging in dishevelled parcels indistinguishable from women's. Hemlines a peepshow to premarital obscenities. Disorder in the workplace and despair in the homestead. The repeal of the death penalty and a crack in the crown.

All sweet memories of once glorious Empire faded. All values in bankruptcy. All tradition in tatters. All taxable blood boiling in search of the root of this national rot. All eyes spying. All fingers pointing. All Lionhearts uniting, their tongues together crying.

'Will no one rid us of The Rolling Stones?'

BOOK *the* THIRD

GAMING

XXVII

Our principals scatter their seed across
the Southern hemisphere.

DELUDED ARE THOSE who, in all innocence and wonder, liken life to a tapestry. For if the passage of time was merely a matter of cloth, at the close of each calendar year it could be gently assaulted with wicker paddles so as to thump all filth and grit loose from the crevices of its fabric and commence the next afresh. But life is no tapestry, time is no cloth, and the past blemishes of Nineteen Sixty-Four – as portrayed in the woeful resolution to our previous instalment – were as hideously indelible on the first stitch of Nineteen Sixty-Five as the stains upon the vendibles of an Irish shopkeeper who, seven days into January, had refused service to five travelling Englishmen; the identity of whom will engender surprise in the breasts of few but the Reader of most pitiable memory.

That refusal, as the bog-trotter tradesman took liberty to explain, was planted in a historical grievance involving the campaign of Oliver Cromwell against his homeland, the scars of which were still visible in the concave imprints of cannonballs upon his parish church. The balls being English, he had therefore operated his business as vendor of military surplus clothing avowing to repudiate benefaction from all persons spawned from the same nation as those antique armaments. Alas, his patriotism, though noble of heart, was expressed with such syllables of hostility, during which his zeal on the issue of Anglo-Saxon balls excited him to idle threats of retaliatory castration, that our five sons of Saint George were moved to vacate his concession in such a fashion as elevated his position regarding want of their custom to the highest planes of revulsion. That is, with fountaining riposte of Brian's bladder discharging steaming-hot egesta upon his precious articles of commerce.

So The Rolling Stones – the shiftless stain of Sixty-Four already discolouring the threads of Sixty-Five – christened the New Year en route to a concert in the Irish city of Cork, with symbolic foresight, their *annus urinus*, as shall become apparent in due season.

For England, that country so nourishing to apoplexies in the unfortunate merchant hitherto described – now cursed to sleepless fits punctuated by torture of nightmares, all involving his choicest jerkins as drenched by the waste waters of Cromwell – the New Year was instead branded with depressing haste an *annus horribilis*. The grim circumstances casting this pall – though in no way directly attributable to our abhorred quintet – only exaggerated the emotions of its abundance of citizens convinced that every bullet of the last war had been fired in vain if the price of victory entailed accepting their children's gay deliriums over the sight of these tatty-tressed ruffians, now that the father of their freedom, Sir Winston Leonard Spencer Churchill, godfather to Miss Bunty and her shorts of society renown, lay dying. Worse, that he should suffer the fatal stroke on the very day that The Rolling Stones departed these shores for the opposite side of the globe; as if the improbable whim that they might never return disordered his fancy with unbearable glee, so blowing the last valve of his many-sided genius and finalising his exit from the mortal stage before the month of January was out.

Consequently, in their absence from home our cavaliers of upset would never witness the headlines of bedside vigil, the steady ebbing of his tide, the last breath, the flags at half-mast, the royal tributes, the sobs in the saloon bar and the blubs on the buses, and a state funereal the likes of which London – *'like a great rhinoceros, like a great hippopotamus!'* – had never seen; as if the entire city shuddered as one beneath a billowing black veil, the Thames their gutter overflowing with tears. For by then they were comfortably hostelled as far away from their black-arm-banded countrymen as was possible by magic of aviation: travelling such longitudes in contrary motion to the planet's spin that between departing on a Tuesday and arriving on a Thursday they had somehow misplaced an entire Wednesday; its whereabouts, despite all arithmetic of wristwatches, pocket diaries and the confused assistance of baggage handlers requested to help seek this infernal diurnal, seemingly inexplicable.

Their destination was that large aboriginal kingdom of the south Pacific, once an insignificant desert populated by tribesmen belching into sticks of eucalyptus and a curious spectrum of marsupials, until mercifully improved by the arrival of ships bursting at the hull with a great many British miscreants, who since propagated into a friendly if obtuse society of lager-drinkers and livestock-griddlers. This, too, the nation where Mick's mother happened to have gasped her first breath beyond the womb, even if her blood, and his, being pure Kentish lineage luckily owed nothing to the generational dilutions of that criminal gene pool. The daughters of which greeted the Stones at Sydney airport in their thousands, shewing such boisterous transports of excitement as disoriented the attendant police; themselves baffled as to why they should be charged with protective custody of unsightly specimens who, according to their similarly diluted intellectual assessment, in times of old would have been condemned for felony of female impersonation and sentenced to the same shackled labour of rock and pickaxe as their great, great, grandfathers; or as expressed in their chosen mutation of their ancestral tongue: 'Five long-haired pommie poofters'.

While clearly five, while undeniably profuse of hair, the presumption of jaspery was never more foolishly applied than in the case of our subjects, whose carnal proclivities, as already imparted herein with all necessary gratuity, were exclusively concerned with wickets as opposed to stumps. Indeed, had those antipodean law enforcers the privilege of standing sentinel over the band's bedchambers they would have immediately revised those rash opinions after witnessing powers of industry in Australia's central furrows which, even in strictest understatement, might only be described as ferocious.

Of this dynamic and diabolic cabal, none were more vigorous of plough and needy of toil than Bill and Brian who, combining their debased geniuses, devised a novel system of selection in coalescence with the porters of each hotel: so named their 'laundry service'. The crowds of alacritous honeypots expectantly gathered outside the foyer being visible from the safe vantage of their upper-storey windows, after selecting whichever article they considered worthy of their labours, instructions would be telephoned to the concierge whose obligation it was to venture outside into the street where, armed with adequate sartorial description they would locate the specified laundry, chaperone them to the elevator and dispatch to the correct floor to be scrubbed, tumbled, pressed and steamed as their respective host desired. Only occasionally would this cunning procedure fail if, whether through lapse of diligence or colour-blindness, the porter mistook pink jacket for puce or auburn hair for ginger; taxing the worn limits of Bill and Brian's chivalry, reduced as it was to returning these unwanted supplies of insufficient charms back from whence they came in dismal weeps.

Ay, Reader! You may well retch at these serial indignities against the paradise of womanhood, from which I gain no pleasure in

communicating. Indeed, this is but a spoonful of disgust compared
to the feast of vulgarity I could easily embellish from the contest of
conquest between Bill and Brian throughout their travels in
Australasia; how each employed devious strategies to steal one
another's nubile quarry; how they sometimes shared the same prize
of passion in succession of relay; and how Bill ultimately triumphed
by coaxing one pearl of Perth out from Brian's bed moments before
his first shuck of the oyster, thus humiliating that bareback hussar
whose cuckolding provided topic of immense levity to his travelling
companions and renewed complex of conspiracy within the wits of
the hussar himself. And so, accepting that I have shone only what
minimal light I believe essential upon the exploits of these men of
oft despicable hankers regarding their welcome in that province (and
carefully leaving in the gloom of unwanted digression any attempt
to relay which Stone spent an evening imbedded in a sweet Victoria
nonesuch before repeating that feat in the maternal nonesuch from
whence the first had sprung not two decades earlier – the procreative
possibilities of which might have horrified the annals of midwifery
in simultaneous delivery of two sons being variously grandson, step-
brother, uncle and nephew), we buckle up all belts and, bypassing a
visit to New Zealand of trifling significance, advance to the Orient.

The calendar had not long flipped over to February when they
landed in the city of Singapore; and yet the locals being
predominantly Chinese, a funny breed with funny customs –
notwithstanding the funny pursuit of roving musicians from their
restaurants with funny threat of kitchen utensils, as the Reader
may recall, whether humorously or not – were only now celebrating
what, according to their funny zodiac, which swapped scales and
archers for rats and snakes, constituted the start of the New Year.
A funny breed, yet not so different from their Caucasian cousins
in their abolition of female reason in presence of the Rolling
Stones; who in performance struggled for their efforts to be

appreciated above the Singapore Slingers, whose cawing chants, though interpreted through Brian's vortex of vanity to be some indistinct foreign gibberish expressive of admiration towards his vicinity of the stage, were to every other ear easily translatable – even amidst the incessant din of festive firecrackers ricocheting inside and outside the hall – as 'Wee-won-Mick!'

The hospitality of their Singaporean hosts was of a correspondingly funny if exceptional nature: inviting the group to a banquet following their concert at which were provided not only beverages and exotic foods, both sweet and savoury, but also the companionship of professional concubines, thus eliminating any need to exercise all usual schemes of laundry.

Whilst this gesture of generosity was received with grateful enthusiasm, the absence of the chase took unexpectedly adverse effect upon Bill's fondness for the thrill which, to the panic of his pride and the shame of his sex, refused to stand. Fortunately, this crisis was not beyond the patience of his designated pleasurer, whose skills of resuscitation were inexhaustible, and who, after many laborious jousts against flaccidity, demonstrated the most enterprising use of mentholated toothpaste: so restoring him to a suitable state to appreciate her services, also instigating one of his lengthier digressions on commercial toiletries in the appropriate page of his diary – if coded in such a manner as his wife, should she ever find leisure to browse its catalogue of extramarital abominations, would be at pains of intellect to properly decipher.

And so, having soiled these foreign kingdoms with their fluids, in much the same manner as they had the wares of our lamentable military outfitter from County Cork – sleep still stalled from visiting his eyelids by the haunting memory of Brian's piquant spurts – we can now withdraw from this Asiatic episode, haste over the Tropic of Cancer, and progress our History in a more familiar climate.

CHAPTER

XXVIII

Their notoriety at home is enhanced and their foes multiply.

THAT CLIMATE, AS measured by the barometer of March, Nineteen Sixty-Five, was unexpectedly cold on account of the snow suffocating the south of England; the streets as white as the hesitant sticks of the unseeing, who that month had fresh terrors to contend with as they tapped and groped through the cruel darkness life had bestowed upon them. Notwithstanding the risk that, at any moment, they may be rendered parallel to the frozen ground through the calamitous if highly probable surrender of shoe to sheen of ice, they were now at the mercy of the impoverished apostles of our five rakes, courtesy of the printed instructions upon the reverse sleeve of their latest long player; which, being their second, they so christened with minimum ceremony and appropriate chronology *The Rolling Stones No. 2*. These instructions being the proud prose of Andrew, composed whilst he was happily languishing in his bath tub, body soaking in soapy bliss, brain soaking in the violent gibberish of a recent novel by a certain Mr Burgess called *A Clockwork Orange*: that any person happening upon the disc who lacked the necessary 'bread' to make a purchase might consider redressing their financial embarrassment by approaching the nearest available gentleman of optically destitute aspect, bludgeoning them across the head and relieving them of their monies.

While that author considered this licence to brigandage a mere 'satire on life', incapable of offending the suggested victims since, as he reasoned aloud, 'blind people can't read', after six weeks of being on sale – during which time no such assaults on the disabled for want of Stones albums were reported; the closest being the passive yet preposterous crime of a fourteen-year-old paper boy from Wigan who, over the course of a year, had succeeded in swindling his employers of nearly a thousand pounds, that entire fortune expended on 'pop records' and, scarce imagine what quantities, 'crisps' – the charitably sighted who employed themselves in the services of their eyeless dependents were at last alerted to its existence and made passionate protest on their behalf.

None was more passionate than the secretary of the Bournemouth Blind Aid Society – a Mrs Matthews – who, having borne and thought about it at considerable length, was moved to lament to the press: 'It doesn't bear thinking about.' The London headquarters of the National Institute of the Blind concurred with Mrs Matthews that the sleeve was medical evidence of 'a sick mind', exemplifying 'sheer damned bad taste', adding they considered it 'extraordinary' that such a reputable bastion of the domestic gramophone as Decca could advocate vindictive land-piracy as a fitting recreation for youth.

These grievances in due course trembled the ear trumpet of that bastion's commander, Sir Edward, who was forced to admit that, despite Andrew's humorous intentions, the contentious paragraph was of an unintelligible 'jargon' beyond the grasp of his sagacity, and so instructed his printers to remove it from further pressings; thus discouraging felony of teenage footpadding, restoring Mrs Matthews' thoughts to their previous vacuum of concern and, moreover, reducing the nervous shivers of the nation's white sticks to their normal frequency.

Normality for The Rolling Stones, in the strange frequencies with which they'd become accustomed, meant that, within a week of returning from the land of mentholated felicity, they were once more travelling up and down the highways of England, enflaming female devotions to the very precipice of suicide, as marked by the upper balconies from which several wobbling Juliets tumbled head first: all remarkably avoiding fatality by mercy of their stall-bound sistren, whose bodies provided adequate, if painful, cushion of landing, the twain suffering nothing worse than cracked teeth, black eyes and a farrago of easily treatable fractures.

Others more sensitive to the perils of altitude forewent such physical danger, preferring to demonstrate their piety by abscondence, pneumonia and malnutrition. This being the fate of three young girls from Lancashire who spent as many days traversing the Pennines in chase of their hairy idols, hitching passage, sleeping in telephone boxes, and subsisting on the communal larder of a single chocolate bar: all to the torment of their anxious parents none the wiser of their whereabouts, and for which, to the torment of their own equally anxious loins, they didn't once enjoy hosanna of laundry.

Normality, too, meant that, regardless of their status having again topped the Hit Parade with their new disc, 'The Last Time' – of no small significance in that it was their first number one bearing the composer credit of Jagger & Richards who had, indeed, written it themselves over the top of an old negro spiritual, much as an idle child given a box of crayons commits ingenious revision of the portrait of a family elder with the adornment of facial hair, acne and spectacles – they were still barred from the restaurants of the lavish establishments in which they bedded, by reason of their abstinence regarding respectable neckwear. Often to the great amusement of the popular press, who took pleasure in granting tiny paragraphs of celebrity to those such as Mr Harold Sparrow, head waiter at the Grill Room of Manchester's Midland Hotel, whose inflexible vocational beliefs were duly immortalised in hot metal.

The estimable Sparrow was immediately applauded for his defence of the knotted realm by the editorial of *Tailor & Cutter* – trade periodical for those in the professions of gentleman's cloth – who published an open letter to The Rolling Stones beseeching them to cease their 'disregard of proper clothes for the proper occasion' and lasso their collars accordingly. As an additional enticement, the magazine referred them to the latest innovation in tie technology, being those with purses attached to the end so as to bridge that previously unthinkable sartorial chasm betwixt noose and wallet. To which Mick was obliged to respond through the conduit of the *Daily Mirror* that they were not at liberty to promote that particular advent in couture for fear it would serve no purpose other than 'produce a nation of rich hunchbacks'.

But normality, as all who dally with her at such lengths will know, is but a dangerous minx, one whose familiar corset is all too easily unlaced by the tug of tedium, thus exposing the insatiable flesh of hot mischief. So it was for our jaded five as they repaired to their roadside hotel after a concert in Sunderland, in want of sweet supper and a little mirth, those two combined once Mick's room had been furnished with a sorry assortment of biscuits with which to gratify their savage appetites. Though supplied by the night porter on the assumption of a digestive destiny, these raw materials were instead consigned to ritual execution by heel and toe. The slaughter commenced with Brian, decimating some dozen rich teas whilst in full jubilance of Nanker, swiftly followed by Mick, who subjected a handful of fruit shortcake to the same fate of smithereens. Keith confined his trampling cruelties to a couple of fig rolls, while Bill danced the briefest of Chelsea boot boleros, obliterating the best intentions of the manufacturers responsible for the packet of bourbon crèmes now taking occupancy of the carpet in an apocalypse of crumb.

Long after they had vacated the scene, the sum of their pulverisations remained the following morning for the discovery of the chambermaid, whose shriek was of a pitch no more startling to those within earshot than had she opened the bedroom door and tripped over the cooling corpse of a prostrate vicar skewered through the heart by an ornamental Tunisian dagger. Seizing his moment of public distinction alongside those legends of inky censure Matthews and Sparrow, the hotel manager, a Mr Jones, immediately sought the confidence of the gentlefolk in employ of a popular tabloid; to whom he furnished detailed inventory of this bloodbath of baked sugar, in conjunction with his announcement that he would be pursuing the Rolling Stones for reimbursement totalling five guineas for their ungodly havoc wrought in the good name of Peek Freans. And, furthermore, that they ought to consider themselves banned from his premises for the rest of their lives which, if their Maker entertained any appreciation for the sanctity of the humble garibaldi, would be very short indeed.

And yet! A quick turn of the tabloid page and the outrage of Mr Jones is forgotten in a trice. A photograph of a smiling young woman of immense beauty. A story involving a Georgian engagement ring with diamond clusters and a secret proposal backstage. Three words above in block capitals: 'MARIANNE TO WED.' The fluttering Miss Faithfull to become Mrs Dunbar! And a neglected thread of our plot thickens with carnal foreboding – at which point we again lay it aside to fatten and fester until ripe for dramatic resumption.

CHAPTER

XXIX

⁓

The chief features of which will be found to be an
authentic version of a battle of wills.

I F THIS HISTORY has, thus far, contained anything of note
about the masculine psyche, beyond the unbreakable connexion
between unruly mind and unruly member resulting in some
of the cruder diversions of entertainment to leak from this Author's
pen (with apologies for all such titillating spillages included in the
vain hope of trembling even the thickest-woven of dunce caps
with some spasm of mirth), then it is that their society can be very
broadly divided into the makers and the breakers of rules. That
some gentlemen are born to be estimable Sparrows and set their
store in etiquette and epaulettes, shiny buttons and shoe polish,
white collars and whiter gloves, 'Please, Sir' and 'Thank you,
Madam', strict codes and unbreakable conditions. And others are
born to be Rolling Stones and grant nature liberty to curl their
hair, scuff their heels, loosen their collar, wet their whistle and
bulge their breeches with blissful disregard for all stipulations as
might be printed, displayed and brought to their attentions by the
scowling sentries of enforced decorum.

Of these two guilds, Mr Charles Keeley of Forest Gate belonged
to that former class. Much like the noble Sparrow was king to the
castle of the Manchester Midland Hotel Grill Room, lord of
crockery and master of napkin, so Mr Keeley reigned in parallel

supremacy over four petrol pumps and a modest cabin selling refreshments, together forming a welcoming bump to drowsy drivers and their draining tanks on the artery of the Romford Road connecting London with the county of Essex. That bump, by name, the Francis Service Station, where one particular evening the same Mr Keeley commenced his shift in the fading dusk of Thursday: readying his nocturnal stamina to parade his highly flammable ramparts with due care, keeping his wits sharp, his till tidy and his pumps pristine until the first light of Friday.

Beyond the sacred kerb of his forecourt the city was fast falling asleep; the workers dreaming of the weekend, the public houses all closed, the cinemas silent and the last trains to the suburbs whistling out of metropolitan earshot towards less exciting pastures of semi-detached tedium. On the streets and buses, the late-shifters, the lost and the lonely scattered themselves at generous intervals of private isolation. In the shadows of the alleyways, burglars scaled walls and guttering, their soft tread unheard between the yowl of a tom cat and the echo of lovers: fingertips pressing into fabric, fiddling with buttons, the rhythm of their wet kisses smacking in the dark like the steady dripping of a tap. From inside warehouses, beams of night-watchmen's torches swung against window panes, casting giant silhouettes on the opposite side of the street while policemen on bicycles stopped pedalling to assist pitiful drunkards bouncing off bins and lampposts like ball-bearings in a poorly played bagatelle. And, in his small fortress of fossil fuel, Mr Keeley glanced at the single customer attending their vehicle at one of the four pumps of his empire, consulted his watch and noted that Thursday, the eighteenth of March, Nineteen Sixty-Five, would very soon be gaoled into the past with the stroke of midnight just thirty minutes hence.

The single customer was a young motorist of twenty-two summers, whose automobile was as sensible as his haircut and as orderly as the cellular-matter bubbling beneath: belonging to a Mr Eric Lavender, happily employed in the guidance of the youth of that parish, whose pliable minds he attempted to steer away from thoughts salacious and criminal towards wholesome and holier persuasions. That is to say that Mr Lavender, like Mr Keeley, was of the same Sparrowish calibre, and as such no two men were more unfortunately stationed in time and place to witness the sudden arrival of a large black Daimler into the tarmacked square of the Francis Service Station, halting with a violent screech akin to the mating call of an absurdly libidinous jungle primate.

Had such a deputation of wild and wanton apes emerged from that vehicle once the doors either side swung open, they still could not have been eyed with more earnest attention by Mr Lavender, nor with more solemn presages by Mr Keeley, whose heart picked up pace as one of their number approached his cabin in a gait exhibiting great urgencies of internal function. The jury of Mr Keeley's humour still deliberating as to whether this hairy creature was human, simian or the cloven-hoofed Beelzebub incarnate, upon reaching the cabin window it proceeded to address him in these words:

'Oi, where can we have a piss here?'

Such an expostulation, when directed towards a man of Mr Keeley's quality, keeper of the sacrosanct plumbing of the Francis Service Station and all its drainage, was not only unseasonable but fruitless; his being a temper not to be ruffled and a toilet not to be ruined, replying in such terms as highlighted that position in as dictatorial a negative as even the mighty Sparrow may have employed when obstructing another shabby interloper of insufficient apparel from his elite realm of grilled suppers. To which the malingering abomination merely stood its ground to beg a second question:

'Where do you go to take a piss, then?'

That query demanding of an answer, it was nevertheless doomed to remain in rhetorical suspension; Mr Keeley's attentions since swallowed by the advance of two further hairy accomplices, one of exceptional spouting lips, the other distorting their visage with the fingers of both hands in a ghastly expression deliberately designed to discompose the constitutions of the most hardy and robust. Polite conversation having disintegrated moments earlier, the clear-thinking Mr Keeley raised his chin, puffed his chest and stamped this unfortunate scene with the might of due authority, as emitted:

'Get off my forecourt!'

The distorted visage, undistorting itself by removing all scaffolding of fingers, replied in alike fashion:

'Get off my foreskin!'

This lightning riposte conducting hearty peals of laughter amongst his fellow passengers, their gay gurgles were sadly denied supplementary vibrations from the ribcage of Mr Lavender, whose eyes were still transfixed in incomprehensible repulsion. Nor that of Mr Keeley, who stepped from his cabin intent on herding these hispid demons off his premises until his carriage was stopped by the placing of an arm across his throat, belonging to the face with the spouting lips, which duly ejaculated:

'We'll piss anywhere, man.'

These words prompted immediate chorus, light on melody but strong on repetition, accompanied by such clicking of heels and flapping of arms as an Irishman might generously consider the basis of a 'jig', in which deportment the three antagonists of Mr Keeley strolled to the far wall on the other side of the garage. Their intentions in that quarter already clearly vocalised in song, the percussive jingle of belt-buckle and whirr of zip rallied them to the hissing crescendo: baptising the brickwork in a triptych of streaks which together formed a bubbling tributary upon the ground, trickling in the vague direction of Plaistow.

'We'll piss anywhere, man!'

Having marked their territory, the three relieved brutes commenced casual steps back to their transportation, where young Mr Lavender was presently stood with jotter and pencil in blatant state of reportage; making note of its licence plate, and broadcasting his mortal offence in clear if quivering tones. For which effort he was attended by a lone cry of retaliation from another of their tribe who'd remained within the car:

'If anything comes of this, I will personally come back and do you!'

All the larrikins seated back in their mobile monkey house, as its engine snarled awake its windows descended, allowing room enough for a clutch of arms to poke forth like cannons from a Spanish galleon, the hands at each end shaped in two-fingered salutes, all shaking vigorously in the general direction of Messrs Keeley and Lavender, whose faces remained frozen in severe rictus of abused astonishment as the song and its singers, the flapping arms and their flicking fingers, vanished into the night.

Mr Lavender, having at last remembered to close his jaw, turned to Mr Keeley who checked his watch, its hands reading forty minutes past eleven. Thursday, still, but fast sinking into Friday. The streets and buses were a little emptier. The alleyways were a little darker. The far wall of the Francis Service Station was a little wetter. And, another minute passing, somewhere on the front desk of a nearby police station a telephone began to ring.

XXX

Which is all about the Law, fleas and other pests.

FAME, AS A great poet once said, is 'like a leprosy that starts and never ceases: a few survive its cruel curse; but most just fall to pieces'. That is, not all who find their egos molested by that damnable pox of vainglory, whether by choice or accident, are born with the mettle to bear it. A mettle such as that possessed by our Rolling Stones, who awoke on Saturday, the twentieth of March, Nineteen Sixty-Five, to discover their particular leprosy had, again, made the pages of a national newspaper. The front page, no less; beside a photograph of the Queen Mother, captured celebrating another week's systematic abuse of the equine kingdom upon the turf of Sandown, against which sat another column, headed by the mysterious announcement in striking Roman type: 'ROLLING STONES UPSET MR LAVENDER.' Mysterious, for not one of the Rolling Stones had the faintest recollection of ever encountering any person introducing themselves by name of that pungent flora, let alone upsetting them to such a degree as would excite the printers of the *Daily Express*.

In this ignorance of the Lavender ancestry they were far from alone: the thoughts of all persons glancing at that headline amounting to the same void of knowledge as to this enigma of sudden legend who, to the bewilderment of the entire populace, had jumped the queue of domestic obscurity to find himself in bold print; parallel to The Queen Mother's hat, and in company of those reviled villains to the silk and grooming trades.

Dare we imagine what gusts of jealousy must have whistled down the nostrils of Matthews of Bournemouth, Sparrow of Manchester and Jones of Scotch Corner, upon seeing this triumph of royal proximity afforded to Lavender of Forest Gate; when their own celebrity in duel with those same adversaries was but a smudge on pages seven, twelve and twenty-two, destined for obsolescence of chip fat and vinegar.* Nor what pride must have swollen the glands of this newly revered David, whose fracas with pop's boorish Goliaths at the Francis Service Station, Romford Road on Thursday past, had been generously allowed such prolific status. Mr Lavender, 'upset' by the 'disgusting' behaviour of the Rolling Stones, to such obscene degrees: 'If the police do not prosecute, I will!'

The article digested, the memories of our subjects now bubbled backwards to their journey home after the previous week's concert at the Romford Odeon, during which Bill, Brian and Mick had cause to relieve their bladders and so directed their car to stop at a garage somewhere in the vague vicinity of West Ham; whereupon they were forbade use of the proper facilities and so took matters into their own hands, along with their sweetmeats, which found alternative quarters for waste disposal in an alfresco setting; that ingenuity clearly unsettling the proprietor and an attendant motorist – and therein the perplexing identity of 'Mr Lavender' was solved.

The sword of prosecution now unsheathed, it would cut and thrust through the corridors of wig and cape, gaining ink and affidavit until ready to plunge in those bleak chambers of old wood and horsehair, bench and bar, sweaty palms and dry coughs, flap collars and *functus officios*, banging 'order', 'yes, m'Lud', and other arcane ceremonies which reduce those of the stoutest and most

---

* Ah! Fear not, well-remembered Reader, that ogress shall never again occur!

innocent hearts to shivering palpitations of doom. For strange indeed must be those feudal minds, marbled with gout and privilege, which gravitate towards the legal profession; who moralise, terrorise and catastrophise; who sow fear and panic upon the calmest of soils and so profit from its crops of confusion; who make art of hectoring, truculence and intimidation; who look down upon their fellow humans as but draughts upon a backgammon board, their lives to be toyed and gambled with for sport of competition and a king's ransom; who, if as Mr Dickens insists the Law is an ass, are thus the flies buzzing around its rear dilberry maker.

The ensuing trial redressing the now infamous Mr Lavender's upset occurring several months hence, and thus by default of chronology occupying a later chapter in this History, it would not, however, be the first occasion that a Rolling Stone was summoned to bow before *corpus juris*; that event taking place several months previous, having slipped between the paragraphs of our preceding chapters concerning the autumn of Nineteen Sixty-Four, to be retrieved here as due occasion to throw the shadow of a noose upon these pages. A noose braided from every barber's bib cherished by the National Federation of Hairdressers, every tie that ever dangled in the soup of every grand hotel from Bristol to Manchester, all cloth at command of Her Majesty's flag sergeant, every black arm-band for Sir Winston Churchill; weaving together until of appropriate thickness of oakum for whichever magistrate saw fit to start tightening its coil around their Adam's apples.

It was the misfortune of Mick to feel the first such tug, falling foul of the codes governing the nation's highways when caught cruising in the Midlands without possession of valid licence or insurance, for which he was forced to adopt dark suit and tie and step into a dock in Staffordshire. Ritual dictating that he be accompanied by his own dilberry fly, those buzzes in his defence were provided by a certain Mr Parkinson; that gentleman

'The Client Without Fleas'

volunteering a fine speech to the court requesting they ignore the prejudices of the media with regard to Mick's hirsute aspect and judge him accordingly: arguing that no less honourable a Titan of English history than the Duke of Marlborough possessed longer hair than his client, which he powdered due to infestation of fleas, a symptom which Mick was mercifully immune from and therefore worthy of their preferential esteem. In response to which His Honour, maintaining a watchful eye on Mick to ensure he was not yet secretly engaged in frictions of scalp as might render this plea contemptible, banged his gavel to the figure of sixteen pounds as an appropriate fine for reckless motoring, lice or no lice.

That judge must have assumed that some influence of this verdict would rub off upon the other Stones like a corrective scent; its perfume encouraging them to conduct their automobile affairs in possession of the proper paperwork, thus avoiding the shame of quaking before 'm'Lud' pleading all guilt of irresponsibility, if all innocence of nits. But, as the lay person if not the Law person knows, assumption is the mother of all unprintables, and so Mick's day in court was of negligible deterrent: its warning fetor so feeble it troubled not even the facial rostrum of his fellow occupant of the basement maisonette of Number Ten, Holly Hill; an address now under siege by those enterprising females whose economy of desire and itch of jenny had maddened their powers of investigation so far as to locate said Hampstead domicile he shared with Keith.

Perchance it was the distraction of these lusty sleuths which prevented Keith benefiting from the lesson of his cohabitant's violation of driving decorum and so obliging him to adopt his own sober dress, affix his top button and strangle his collar with such woven threads as would have vibrated the bugles of *Tailor & Cutter* magazine with fanfares of victory; in which condition he was ordered to tread in the footsteps of Oscar Wilde in as penitent path as he could to Bow Street Magistrates' Court. There, with the same fence of Parkinson, who had sadly exhausted his treasury of excuses regarding the inhabitants of the scalp of that famous Duke, yet with a different beak, who was no less immovable in his wigged revulsion towards the defendant, Keith coughed a plea of 'guilty' to three similar misdemeanours whilst in charge of a motor vehicle; being the failure to produce a valid licence, his similar embarrassment when requested to furnish the arresting officer with an insurance certificate, and his indecency of amateurism in as much as he had been advancing along the carriageways of London's West End entirely disrobed of 'L' plates.

On this last point, the mercurial Parkinson executed a remarkable balestra of mercy, informing m'Lud of his client's domestic nuisance, the lusty sleuths and their habit of scavenging their idols' property for souvenirs, of which those plates would most certainly have been ripe for worship, and source of much misery to Master Richards, still grieving as he was for the loss of his treasured collection of caps in similar circumstances. In response to which, His Honour banged his gavel to the figure of ten pounds as an appropriate fine for reckless motoring, lusty sleuths or no lusty sleuths.

Thus the noose of righteous anger first fell, in separate slumps, around the shoulders of Mick and Keith: so loose, and so light, that neither could feel the weight of its loop as it continued to shrink, in the tiniest of creeps, one day at a time.

CHAPTER

XXXI

⤎⟋⤏

Is an appreciation of music and divine composition.

SO MANY HAVE been the sensations of vice and disruption encrusting these pages, like the bedsheets of a schoolboy hopelessly addicted to the pleasures of self-administration, that it may all too easily be forgotten that – when not laundering virgins, befouling garage forecourts and spontaneously combusting packets of digestives for sport of vandalism – the true vocation of The Rolling Stones was music. Music of a kind that hissed and scratched, moaned and purred, pumping the heart and engorging all botany of human union with the sticky nectar of desire. For theirs was a pure art free of care or shame, owing nothing to the petty needs of those dry minds and drier loins who demand education and moral instruction. Just as some books (and by 'some' I humbly volunteer this one as the very quintessence) are not intended to *teach* their reader as if sat in the classroom but to *ravish* them as if supine in a woodland thicket, so the songs of the Stones were like a good, rough shag – as opposed to the more refined and less potent blends for sale in most tobacconists. And so, packing our pipe with a pinch of that shag, we settle in for a long, hard smoke; to savour its rich fumes while considering that which their shenanigans of bed, bladders and biscuits have hitherto successfully distracted our thoughts away from.

It is not every mind which awakes like a once empty stave suddenly fresh with wet crotchets of cerebral ink. To the majority of mortals, whose powers of composition are confined to sporadic bars of discord after gluttonising on a prune-based dessert – all such burbles of flatus in any case being entirely spontaneous and thus orphans to authenticity of authorship – all muse is mystery: their call like a foreign signal their skulls' transistors can never receive, no matter how energetically they twiddle their knobs. Rare are that maestro breed of Beethovens, who live in permanent hurricane of tones and sounds roaring and storming about them until they have set them down in notes. And rarer still are those who – even whilst slumbering, their consciousness astray in the aphoristic foothills of Bedfordshire – are blessed with such genius as can leisurely hitch up a trio of Bs, skip through a quick C# to wriggle on D, then back again in nine notes of such sublimity that Apollo himself might be enraged to smash his lyre in a pique of jealousy. Yet such a phenomenon of chromatic subconscious indeed existed in the cerebellum of our own picaro, Master Richards.

Between the last chapter and this, the lusty sleuths of Hampstead had tormented the domesticity of their quarries with such zeal, stealing so many caps, records, sealskin anoraks, boots, belts and other personal effects for purposes of private ceremony, that the victims of their amorous larceny had no choice but to flee their separate ways. Mick, to a mews address in Marylebone. Keith, scarpering southwest to a small apartment in St John's Wood where, alone one night, during comatose chimeras of fretboards and cigarettes, he hitched, skipped and wriggled that afore-described nonet from the slumberous ether, its volume increasing inside the echo chamber of his prefrontal cortex to such decibels as finally shook his cognisance awake.

The echo vivid, he stirred for immediate company of guitar and Philips' cassette recorder: the first not so very difficult in that such a serpentine-curved beauty had been lying in the sheets beside him; the second just as readily available, specifically primed for emergency of melodic posterity upon his bedside cabinet. The strings vibrated and the apparatus employed, Keith repeated the tune his brain had kindly bequeathed him, crooning as complementary an accompaniment as his vocal chords could muster at that cockshut hour, on the theme of discontentment. In the latter focus, taxed as he was by the numbing vice of drowsiness, he was aided by the muses of that other Mount Olympus, on Chicago's South Michigan Avenue: the Stones' baptiser, Muddy Waters, who had provided them with a song on their last album entitled 'I Can't Be Satisfied'; and Chucky Berry, who in another tune of considerable punch called 'Thirty Days' had been heard to cry, *I don't get no satisfaction from the judge* – a predicament which all who understand this Author's position on members of the bench in the previous chapter will not find the least portion surprising, and here join me in extending posthumous sympathies to Mr Berry for such inevitable maltreatment by those powdered trollops of justice.

Having plucked and recited long enough to be assured comfort of dictation, Keith fell back into the arms of Morpheus, blissful oblivion flooding his senses and the rasps of somnolency rippling through his nostrils in erratic snuffles: as he was privileged to appreciate the following day when he rose to find the cassette had inscribed but five minutes of acoustic sketching and another forty of his wind passage's tuneless nocturne in Z minor.

The sketch was but a few sleepy lines, yet strokes of such conviction as coalesced in contours of a *coup de maître*: or so Mick, being learned of the French tongue, may possibly have thought when Keith passed it on to be signed off for the board of Jagger & Richards in the first week of May; at which precise time the Stones were again in the land of liberty, and Mick in a lounger of luxury, recumbent beside their hotel swimming pool under the cloudless skies above Clearwater, Florida. Those contours, as stood, consisting of a solid melody and the signature motto: 'I can't get no satisfaction'.

Distant now is that era when such a turn of phrase may have been considered the complaint of a true gentleman of the world who, having taken offence and thrown down his glove, had not yet been given his due pleasure of redress on the field of honour; as was proper in those halcyon days when the cream of male society forwent the barbarism of the courtroom to settle their affairs by more civil means of flintlock pistols. It was, therefore, understandable that Mick's sentiment of lyrical embellishments strayed far from such a once rational exegesis: instead voicing the contemporary frustrations of his youthful peers, whose want of satisfaction was largely provoked by commerce and a hatred for broadcast advertising; save some added admissions of male coital privation, especially regarding their advances towards those females who deny themselves all prospects of coalition during those weeks when the moon's phase of gibbous prompts bloody imbroglio of the menses.

It seemed proper to both Mick and Keith that, given its cultivating influence upon this child of chagrin, the Olympus of Chess studios should be the theatre of operation in which it be delivered, and so went into labour there when visiting Chicago a few days later: from whence they were discharged with a far uglier new-born than anticipated, one they would have happily surrendered for adoption were it not for the persistence of Andrew, who saw in its podgy flesh enough to yet fashion an attractive weanling with the proper tools of encouragement. A tool such as the miracle of capacitors, resistors and circuit board manufactured by the firm of Gibson in the exotic province of Kalamazoo, and purchased when the Stones next sallied on to Los Angeles.

The Maestro Fuzz Tone was confidently christened in so far as it was, amongst the myriad electronic guitar accessories available, the master of its kind and productive of tones that those with the most limited vocabularies would still likely describe as possessing a 'fuzzy' quality, and those of only slightly greater intellects might fumble in the amateur dramatics of metaphor by likening its sound to any variety of insect genus trapped inside any variety of electric domestic appliance, deluding themselves that in doing so they have successfully evaded the flypaper of cliché upon which they, and a thousand other novices of wit, were already fatally affixed. Keith thus furnished with such a device, when the Stones next attempted the song in the Hollywood studios of RCA Victor, the buzz of the Maestro vibrated the magic necessary to mutate the previous grubby duckling into the sparkling swan, so ringed '(I Can't Get No) Satisfaction'.

Satisfaction! A word the observant Reader will recognise as not insignificant amidst the prose of this History, buzzing its own magic of secret meaning. For if books were bugles, the toot of this horn would be the very same 'Satisfaction' by The Rolling Stones; anthem of these adventures and, in the wet smooch of Bill's bass, the tremble of Charlie's pelvic pacemaker, the hiss of Keith and the purr of Mick, singularly the roughest shag of a song as was ever cut and smoked during the Nineteen-Sixties.

At which interval, any persons with access to that piece of music, Decca diskette F.12220, should henceforth place it on their turntables, stand stiffly to attention and salute its majesty as it spins at forty-five ravishments-per-minute, savouring every delicious pant and tremor, before proceeding to the next constituent.

CHAPTER
XXXII

Treats of divers little matters which occurred in the Americas.

ASSUMING THE READER took fullest advantage of the liberty afforded them at the close of the preceding chapter and thus are now enjoying this volume in a spent repose void of any fleshly anxieties which might easily twist their concentration out of focus, we now fandango forwards with our story whilst simultaneously gavotting a backwards step in time; to recount the antics of our Rolling Stones during the same visit to the land of gallon-hats and fried cuisine in which that glorious ode to 'Satisfaction' was fashioned for purchase.

That voyage commenced with a brief excursion to the colossal waste of living space which balances atop America like the airy brain of a village idiot; almost entirely empty save a few clusters of bison and a disproportionately small human populace; most lost in crises of identity as to whether their tongues were English, French or aboriginal, yet all aggressively intolerant of those who assume them to be citizens of the United States, based upon an accent that is, to the majority of foreigners, indistinguishable, rather than of that vacuum, as named: 'Canada'.

Having never previously entered that portion of the continent, the Stones presupposed as favourable a welcome as that in the territories south of the border. In this optimism of humour they were to be sorely challenged; making immediate adversaries of the guild of Canadian hoteliers, all of whom expressed public shame that they had been duped into accommodating their custom through the most devious of conspiracies: telephoning advanced bookings under their own individual surnames rather than that collective professional soubriquet, infamous throughout the international lodging community as a byword for trouble, disruption and the likelihood of all upholstery being maculated with baked goods in methods unimaginably indecent.

That black reputation preceding them overseas, so did their infamy as a menace to all hymens and the scourge of all upstanding fathers whose every prayer to heaven concerned the preservation of that gossamer gateway to the sweetest of sweet deaths; a mania no different in London, the finest metropolis on earth, than in its audacious namesake in Ottawa, where the Stones commenced their Canadian cavalcade. The success of the locksmiths of this lesser London in supplying due security to keep those precious articles bolted in their bedchambers could be measured in the overprovision of eager damsels flooding through the turnstiles of Treasure Island Gardens, which, numbering a couple of thousand, would therefore constitute those best efforts of latch and key a sin to chastity and a crisis to the patience of the Ottawa Provincial Police. Theirs being the task of maintaining order at the concert, all hopes resting on the blockade of a ribbed fence, of a style designed to direct drifting snow rather than restrain free-hearted ladies.

Even those policemen with the weakest grasp of physics – being the majority, the prerequisites of enforcing 'laws' as such persons are employed excluding any understanding of those established by Sir Isaac Newton – invested the grimmest hopes in this defence strategy, which jangled their nerves to the precipice of terror before Keith had plucked a single note, or Charlie so much as tickled a cymbal. Only when, after fifteen minutes, three *virgo intactas* squeezed between the fenceposts like a blast of frizzle and flung themselves at Mick's convulsing hips did the badged stewards respond, as dictated by their presages of death and hysteria: severing the supply of power to the stage until it was as short of direct current as their heads with reason and their country with land hospitable to any sentient being other than moose. The Stones' racket so reduced to the unamplified shake of Mick's maracas, Keith's clapping and Charlie's muted snare rolls, the self-fulfilling prophecy of riot came to pass in a detonation of which kind this History has already provided umpteen examples.

Quitting that scene, and that country, our heroes next sauntered south over the border to the increasingly familiar comforts of New York City; where an uncommon oversight in the vigilance of their hotel connived many curious instances in their private chambers when all, except the immune and impenetrable Charlie, succumbed in divers degrees of fear to dwell on matters of the supernatural.

Returning to his room alone, Keith had not long kicked off his boots and reclined on his bed, cradling his guitar in yet another pitch of divine inspiration, when his attentions were unsettled by an eerie ague of having company. The same unease befell Mick, sat at his bureau penning a sweet epistle to his Chrissie back home, and to Bill, similarly occupied with ballpoint pen in the margins of his diary and all its meticulous calculations of expenditure, his instincts bristling at the sensation of an invisible presence all too close to his person.

So too Brian, who had grown especially susceptible to delusions of spectral company ever since his New Year nocturne in Lincoln sixteen months past, and who was thus reduced to such wild ripples of gooseflesh as to feverishly fling open wardrobes and cupboards stammering high-pitched demands for any intruder to reveal themselves. In course of which investigations he discovered a fragrant delight – fully-clothed, make-up smudged by perspiration – who had admitted herself through most daring escalades of drainpipe, defiance of altitude and subjugation of window lock, sat staring back at him from behind a rail of wire coat-hangers as if he were now suddenly the victor in a game of hide and seek which, for the frightened life of him, he hadn't the dimmest recollection of ever having started.

Similarly dynamic intruders in contortions of concealment, under beds, skulking in baths and secreted in the curtains like a pain in the arras eavesdropping on a Danish prince, were to be unearthed in those of his cohorts; all of whom had exploited the absence of the usual protective security to pursue their own salacious whims, to be ejected or indulged depending on the moods and mercy of their startled prey.

That the city's fair sex were thus attracted to the Stones like nancy-flies to dilberries was a point of fact not all indigenous New York males respected, especially that increasingly obsolete minority who still measured masculinity in terms of bare necks and exposed ears untroubled by ringlets, and so misjudged our five Englishmen to be the epitome of fringe-swishing sodomites, even as they were in transit to that legendary sauna of testosterone, the Playboy Club.

The cry of 'faggots' sounding, and not for want of minced pig's liver or kindling, Mick, Keith and Brian's attentions were called to a nearby convertible from which several shorn oafs had hurled that taunt with undue pride. Reputation, honour and country at stake, with Brian sounding the rally to 'get the colonists!', all three dived upon those critics of manhood, and so proceeded to administer such retribution of fist and boot as left parts of their victims looking, themselves, like rissoles of breaded offal aching for accompaniment of gravy and marrowfat peas.

Trouble and violence now clung to the tour like the smell of week-old fat from an undrained fryer, that greasy odour intensifying as they reached Florida, where between conceiving 'Satisfaction' and correcting the behaviour of Brian – deserved of its own chapter, and indeed detailed in the next – they were obliged to broil the tempers of four-thousand fresh-faced amorists at a baseball stadium in Clearwater; to degrees of impatience as licked the heads of the local police in flames of tossed toiletries and paper cups, finally igniting in a savage stampede towards the stage that would have furnished the average Canadian steward with such fodder for recurring nightmares as to assure them a gibbering end to life's journey in a buckled jerkin, hopping on the spot in a cushioned cell. The customary fare of adolescents and emergency services stirring as one in a bloody stew of ripped fabric and rampaging truncheons, our five soldiers made hasty retreat by station wagon, only narrowly avoiding multiple amputations of lower limb amongst the hormonal hordes falling into its path with all the heroism of suffragettes at an Epsom Derby. After which, the city fathers of Clearwater stretched a firm hand of solidarity across the pond to those of Blackpool, in whom they joined in banning The Rolling Stones from ever clouding their corner of the so-named 'Sunshine State' ever again.

Assuming that the civic bodies of Clearwater, of the lesser London, and of all battlefields between had been united in prayer to erase those spoilers of stall seating and schoolgirl sanity, their appeals were almost answered a few days hence in Long Beach, California. Having completed their performance at the Civic Auditorium, its audience especially rambunctious in their shews of gratitude, the Stones made routine shift to contain their persons in their chosen escape, being a limousine of appropriate dimensions to carry all five. Their passage, however, was effectually obstructed by a flank of feverish women, numbering many hundred, who quickly encircled their vehicle; the closest squashing themselves against the windows in an unsettling collage of hot breath, saliva, flattened cheeks and scraping fingers.

The driver thus unable to proceed without risk of mass murder, their circumstances became all the more dire once the more dextrous females started clambering upon the limousine's roof for want of air. As one became five, and very soon twenty, in due course the ceiling began to creak, altering its shape until that of a humungous pair of sheet metal buttocks, irreversibly descending to suffocate the persons within.

This sinking anus of doom was inspiriting to an uncommon pitch of courage, as Mick, Keith, Brian, Bill and Charlie each automatically adopted artful poses improvisational of winch and capstan, their backs to the floor while pivoting their feet hard against the ceiling, in which position they successfully strained for a full forty minutes: thus owing their lives to the past two years of constant practice in such exertions of joints, albeit to infinitely more gratifying ends; with the ever exception of Charlie, the beacon of monogamy, whose strength of *rectus femoris* was but a blessed dividend of his vigours of bass-drum pedal.

The buttocks repelled, their limousine was finally allowed to speed away, its passengers' lower limbs throbbing in want of analgesic balms, if still in lesser agonies than some of the young wounded scattered on the ground where they'd been parked, between them missing enough body parts for a Genovese scientist to stitch together and animate by diabolism into a credibly proportioned sixteen-year-old. Whereupon, we, like the Stones, drive away from these toeless casualties of rock 'n' roll warfare. They, forwards towards to San Diego; but we, backwards, to frame these same events through a different perspective, so as to twist the softer edges of narrative tension into urgent focus.

CHAPTER

XXXIII

The focus on Brian; and the detail unpleasant.

SINCE THE CLOSE of our second volume, little has been mentioned of the plight of Brian, his fragile psyche and its strange shivers of paranoia; our attentions on him instead confined to trifling incidents of horseplay, bareback, scrimmage and, twice, urine. The printed season for those neglected enquiries now falling, we thus flip open his box of Pandora, unleashing all evils of Jones into the Reader's eyes in as brief a torrent as might be reasonably stood without compromise of eupepsia.

The first demon that springs towards us is Fear. The fear of a child seated at a birthday party who, looking around the table, assesses every other jammy-lipped brat to have been supplied with a fatter slice of sponge than theirs, and so sees indisputable evidence of wicked conspiracy against them. The jammiest-lipped brat being Mick, and that cake being the rich gateau of public attention, therein this metaphor of juvenile gluttony translates to Brian's position in The Rolling Stones, as he perceived it: exacerbated by a conviction, borne out by his frequent bareback conquests, that he was yet the bonniest-looking child at that table, and that all malice of cake-knife was on account of the cruellest jealousy towards his angelic beauty, sparkling charisma and superior talent. For why else would he be mocked, teased and rebuked with such frequency? Why else would they sit silent in interviews, allowing him to caress the ears of their interrogator with his fascinating soliloquies on learning the clarinet and his 'new interpretation of love', then later mimic his every syllable in the most vicious pantomimes of lisping affectation? And why else would they be so spiteful as to steal and hide his beloved driving cushion, so needed to elevate his compromised height to a respectable eye-level above the steering wheel of his Humber, only returning it after exhausting every Hop-o'-my-thumb insult at their beastly disposal?

Behind the demon of Fear, next leaps Delusion. The delusion of a child, capering at the same birthday party who, struggling to compete in a harmless ball game, decides that sphere of communal fun belongs to him and so picks it up, abruptly halting the contest. The game being songwriting, and the ball being 'Satisfaction', therein this metaphor of sporting inadequacy also translates to Brian's position, as he perceived it: spreading rumours of the thinnest substance that Keith's dream tune was, in reality, his waking one, and that, by rights, the composer brackets beneath its title ought to contain the phrase 'B. Jones'. And just like the child who seizes the ball that doesn't belong to them is gently reminded to return it to its rightful owner, but instead responds in puncturing tantrums – spoiling the merriment for all – so Brian would try to sabotage 'Satisfaction' in concert; playing not Keith's divine air but, in its place, the theme tune of a popular cartoon series following the scrapes of a Jack Tar with swollen forearms and his addictions to pipe smoking and tinned vegetables: *viz.* 'Popeye The Sailor Man'.

Chasing the heels of Delusion now gambols that reddest of devils, Anger. The anger of a child who, given a cuddly toy to amuse themselves, instead kicks, bites and rips its head off before hurling it to the floor in a shower of stuffing. The toy being a young air stewardess and that stuffing being the bruises on her face the morning after spending the night in his bed at Clearwater's Fort Harrison Hotel, therein this metaphor of choler once more translates to Brian's position, as everyone else perceived it, when the unfortunate object of his untender mercies surfaced from his chambers bearing those contusions. And just like the child who mutilates a prize teddy ought to be yanked across the nearest lap and leathered till grizzling, so Brian was taken to task by the Stones' tour manager, a Yorkshire tussler named Mike, who concluded, to the approval of all, that the unacceptable treatment of this daughter of Eve was best highlighted by breaking two of her assaulting Adam's ribs; necessitating that fiend don recuperative apparel of a medical girdle while excusing his injury to the press on a freak accident of 'amateur karate'.

Fear, Delusion, and Anger flying free, they are hence chased by the phantom of Gluttony. The gluttony of a child who, allowed freedom behind the counter of a confectioner's, cannot but help stuff his face with every drop, cube, chew and gobstopper he can lay his sticky fingers on; until the rush of sugar to his brain sends him altogether giddy with fierce hallucinations. Those drops being of the chemical variety, and those hallucinations reptilian, therein this metaphor of excess again translates to Brian's position, as considered by those who witnessed his turn of humour at their hotel in Los Angeles; pirouetting down corridors as if in odd caricature of the risible Freddie, explaining those gambades on his need to avoid the abundance of deadly snakes littering the carpets. A fantasy conjured by a sweet tooth for his new discovery, appropriately referred to as 'acid' in that it disintegrated all reason in the frontal lobes, leaving in its wake hot vapours of insentience, dementia and nincompoopery. And though not the only Stone to savour the delirious compounds of this growing fad, while his backstage brethren palliated such rations with the less hazardous giggles of herbal stimuli, Brian alone subjugated all will to acid's cankerworms of logic, as was his gourmand's craving.

The box of Jonesian horrors almost empty, one last demon slithers towards the rim in shape of feelings Unfeeling. The unfeeling of a child who, walking along a country lane suddenly spies a lamb, its hind quarters trapped in a barbed-wire fence, and merely stands and stares, his hands in his pockets, apathetic eyes blinking as he listens to its sorrowful bleats. That lamb being any of his sons, those bleats any of their mothers, and that barbed-wire fence the trap of poverty, therein this metaphor of cold hearts and crying tots sadly translates to Brian's position, as perceived by poor Pat and poor Linda, both denied their due maintenance for their poor Julians, and both now raising their complaints through the dilberry channels of Law.

All demons released, they swirl around his golden nest like ribbons: a maypole of intertwining terror, fantasy, hatred, greed and callousness, as vivid as any of his wildest pharmaceutical trances. For Brian, at the age of twenty-three, was, in every way, still but a child. Or, as Mick, Keith, Bill, Charlie, Andrew and everyone else in his immediate circle was often heard to repeat, regardless of whether his ear was pressed against their door or not, and in sentiments that few persons of any moral fibre having digested this chapter could possibly argue with – even if their privilege of education, attendance of church and straightness of laces may yet prevent themselves from uttering aloud with the same succinct passion – Brian was, in every way, moreover 'a cunt'.

And yet, the annals of procreation serve to tell us that Brian was but one of an inevitable slew of such persons worthy of that runt-rhyming denomination that are a necessary waste product of life's human banquet, of all shapes and sizes; whether frizzle-haired or buck-toothed, pot-bellied or bandy-legged, wart-faced or whispery-voiced; whether, like he, named Jones of Welsh extraction, or christened Lewis, Brian or, indeed, Allen. Thus, keeping our thoughts pressed firmly in shape of nether-eyes, we grimly proceed to meet another.

*The theme rests between cunning and cup, where a new
character exemplary of that quarter is introduced.*

THAT MOST DIVISIVE of words beginning with the letter
C – which prudence often demands we mask in asterisks,
and which this narrator has journeyed huge distances in
the backwaters of strange slang and ancient argot to amuse and
educate his audience with as wide a variety of synonyms for that
which is, in fact, the girdle of Venus, and in phrase, the worst
scoundrel in Hades – would not exist were it not so essential a valve
of human expression. Without it, the public bars packed with
docker, riveter and hod-carrier would mourn the loss of its sharp
bounce between nicotine-stained ceiling and sawdusted floor, as so
many wet tongues toast damnation to the foreman; and the
innocent citizen would not be armed with that expletive salve
which, when screamed to the highest heaven, instantly lessens the
pain of accidental bodily abrasions to head, limbs and especially
testes; nor possess that equally fitting noun of impolite conversation
to properly describe those persons in employ of the Inns of Court.

And, just as the girdles of Venus alter dramatically in height
and width, from skinny to plump, from pale to rouge – each framed
in its own distinctive topiary – so the worst scoundrels of Hades
are no less diverse a breed in their physical appearance: no two
unutterable C's looking quite the same. Some, squat, blond, short

of neck and baggy of eyes like our subject, Brian. Others, plump, oily of hair and with a chin that would break any fist fool enough to hit it, much like that proud specimen which now creeps quietly upon our stage.

We thus introduce him by name as Mr Allen Klein, and by initials 'A.K.'; the coincidence of that abbreviation being shared with a Russian assault rifle having some due poignancy with regard to his character. Except for being Russian: when he was in fact an American lattermost, the son of Hungarian Jews secondmost, and a New Yorker foremost, born just across the Hudson River. Yet Mr Klein was otherwise such a firearm made ample flesh: his bullets contracts and clauses, his bullseyes big businesses with even bigger bank vaults. This ballistic humour might have been avoided were it not for the tragedy that befell him not long after he'd been shot from the womb, that matronly shooter passing away before his first birthday. Forced by this cruel circumstance into an orphanage exclusively populated by fellow Israelites similarly victimised by their wrathful Creator for reasons none could fathom, young Allen was furthermore condemned by rabbinical wisdom to a childhood of regulation woollen underpants; so abrasive to his infant delicacies that, come adulthood, his intolerance of that prickly fabric had assumed maximum abhorrence of phobia.

The gaping abyss of motherly love he filled with scholarship of accountancy, finding hugs in sums, kisses in division, tenderness in percentages and comfort in counting: each addition and subtraction hardening his heart until it was more abacus than organ, and he destined to join that fraternity of inhumane wretches so labelled by that sobriquet which forms this segment's chosen theme. This fresh and evil genius he decided to apply to the mechanics of America's popular music industry, after recognising a discrepancy in the ratio between noise and purse: that those making the former were incapable of rectifying to the benefit of their latter. That is, the ones executing all hullaballoo of quivering lips and hips were being rewarded with cents while all dollars were filling the pockets of their double-breasted company bosses; who spent their days in comparative silence, puffing on pungent Cuban tobacco behind mahogany desks, listening to the gentle creak of their expanding waistlines and the slothful throb of their clogging arteries.

Through combination of wile, belligerence and a mastery of calculus so bewitching to those same administrative walruses that all honked surrender to his stipulations, the young Mr Klein accrued himself a respectable roster of singing talent, all of whom had been wooed by his remarkable ability to improve their finances through the discovery of large funds that had slipped between the columns of their paymaster's books; awaiting the retrieving shine of his devilish brilliance and, when necessary, even more devilish imagination. These windfalls sent his yodelling paupers into such ecstasies that all were prepared to trust Mr Klein with their financial lives; never questioning what motives fuelled his righteous warfare through those mysterious ledgers of swindle and deceit on their behalf, and so oblivious to the secret of his success: that, where once they were paid little by those who earned much, they now earned only slightly more from one who hoarded their fortune.

By the year Nineteen Sixty-Five, Mr Klein's fiscal sorcery had enticed such renowned British pop minstrels as Herman's Hermits and The Animals into his clutches; though his prize catch, The Beatles Pop Group, still eluded him on account of being loyally lassoed to their Mr Epstein with such robust rope as even his sabre-teeth of negotiation couldn't lacerate. But there was yet another prize, almost as lucrative, and in such ease of reach that he didn't have to grab it; for it, in shape of their twitchy young manager, reached out and grabbed him.

Mr Klein's reputation preceding him, Andrew was impressed by the mythical sums he was rumoured to have sequestered as advance artists' payments, and even more pleased upon meeting him in the flesh – of which he had plenty – to find a gentleman who, in curl of hair, knuckle-breaking of face, weight of paunch and cut of New York gib, fitted his fantasy business partner of a fearsome racketeer of Italian extraction; specifically the kind who appealed to his less reasonable creditors with concrete footwear and friendly discussion on how they might cope should inconvenience of amputation befall any number of fingers, thumbs, toes or other bodily projections. So vivid was this novel interpretation of Mr Klein in Andrew's mind that his mirage made no allowance for the reality that he was of Hebrew rather than Sicilian blood, habited himself not in suits of pin-stripe but in silken sweaters that drew the eye towards his heavy bosom, and all the while puffed on a briar packed with tobacco of such rancidity as to throw doubt as to whether it might be rotting compost.

Such was the blob of silk, Brylcreem and smoke that greeted not only Andrew but also Mick and Keith when arriving for a first informal conference at The Scotch of St James: a new London nightclub where both the Stones and The Beatles Pop Group had recently taken to mingling in darkened booths of elite luxury, and where Mr Klein carefully commenced piping them into his clutches with the softest notes of charm and flattery. The trio smitten, Andrew signed the necessary papers; handing Mr Klein their purse strings which, in the same stroke of ink, he also fashioned into a suitable cord with which to strangle the oblivious Mr Easton, and so remove his body from their strained partnership once and for all.

Mr Easton, though promptly asphyxiated from their business as intended, didn't suffocate without adequate struggle, and being a proper fellow of proper means consulted the proper advice of those gowned villains of legislature. Instructed to issue a writ for breach of contract, that stratagem proved unusually difficult for, it being procedure to serve the summons to the accused in person, none expected Andrew to be so slippery of palm and so light of foot. Thus, even the most aggressive clerk – who having staked their territory and bidden their time to leap in his path hoping to thrust their damning document into his hands – found themselves outrun by Andrew's heels and outwitted by his eeliest manoeuvres of torso, rendering delivery of Mr Easton's grievance nigh impossible.

The swift and bloodless dispatch of Mr Easton was conducted without unnecessary consultation with Bill, Charlie or Brian who, having hitherto enjoyed the benefits of that gentleman's favouritism, would have surely voiced unwanted protest: all three unenlightened until they too were requested to join Andrew, Mick and Keith for another conference with Mr Klein in the splendour of London's Hilton Hotel. A conference by name, yet a *fait accompli* by nature. For in truth Mr Klein had already hived his queen bees, and so enticed the remaining drones with minimum ceremony, if maximum charade, his words wafting melodious promises of improved deals, lump sums and global domination.

These entreaties caressed all ears with immediate favour bar those cautious shells affixed either side of the head belonging to Bill: that most financially shrewd member, rarely in a position of ignorance as to the health of his savings, thanks to his custom of noting every penny that passed to and from his pocket in the margin of his diary; thus offering a contrastingly sober narrative to its predominant serialisations of laundry detail. Yet even Bill was at liberty to set aside his misgivings after witnessing Mr Klein in full majesty of performance when he next beckoned them to join him for a decisive joust in the highest turret of Decca towers with that mummified phonographic oligarch, his grace, Sir Edward.

Prior to arrival at that tired knight's quarters, Mr Klein passed firm instruction to Andrew and his five new clients to attire themselves in dark sunglasses so as to affect appropriate menace, to tread behind him at all times – he the piper, they the bubonic rats in tow – and to remain silent throughout the ensuing arbitration, which he alone would conduct with the unswerving objective of renegotiating their contract to handsome advantage.

In such a stern and intimidating aspect the Stones, Andrew and Mr Klein duly presented themselves before their titled foe: much as a pack of hounds presents itself before a weary old fox hunted to its dying breath and hemmed in a copse with no opportunity of escape, moments before they tear it sinew from sinew. As the appointed bearer of fangs, Mr Klein so administered the first bite: savaging Sir Edward's sentiments with the revelation that The Rolling Stones would not be recording another semi-quaver for Decca without renewal of terms, conditions and a suggested monetary advance so large that, had the ancient gentleman been so compromised of vision as to rely on a monocle, it would have surely bolted across the room like a shaken champagne cork. Taking a moment to gather his wits – first plunging his little fingers into both ears to loosen any wax which might have compromised his understanding of these unthinkably saucy demands – the noble Sir politely requested Mr Klein to please consider everything he had already achieved in signing and promoting those minstrels in the first place; his generosity of spirit, even after the recent chagrin of the country's blind community; and his upstanding labour force, there being 'a great many good people' in his employ who had worked on the group's behalf for two years running.

'Well,' replied Mr Klein, not a facial muscle flinching, 'I hope they can sing. Because you've just lost The Rolling Stones.'

There followed the oddest outbreak of shaking, stammering, screwing of eyeballs and slobbering of lips before, by degrees of attrition, Sir Edward was moved to croak surrender: his fingers soon trembling for relief of goose-quill and inkwell to scratch his title as many times as was required on the papers the confidently presumptuous Mr Klein had scrupulously drafted; along with a banker's cheque, to be cashed immediately and converted into whatever Rolls-Royce Phantoms, Chelsea townhouses and country manors as the visored mutes present saw fit.

Our awed subjects, like every warbling pauper before them, hence believed Mr Klein to be not merely a God amongst businessmen, but the jolliest of fellows, so say all of them, and as far removed from a mother-of-all-masons as their combined estimations of character could segregate. That opinion, quite possibly, destined to change at some future interval between this page and our very last.

CHAPTER

XXXV

Annus Urinus.

WHILST OUR FIVE Beau Brummells had been engaged in all pleasure and perils as recently described: that, is, while Mick was having his Holly Hill wardrobe ransacked by thieving jezebels, while Keith was composing the genius of 'Satisfaction' in his slumber, while Brian was escaping into acid hallucinations of locusts gobbling his feet, while Bill was exhausting all adjectives for laundry exploits in his diary, while Charlie was reducing yet another reporter to an apology of trembles with his inscrutable silence, and while Andrew was scarpering into the distance as Mr Easton's writ failed to leave the clutches of its outfoxed messenger, the noose, unnoticed, had been carefully tightening. Tight enough that a fresh fever of excitement now stirred deep in the burrows of English Law, its shivers those of virtuousness, its temperature hot with vengeance, breaking out in rashes of wild whispers that a national wrong may soon be righted, and with it faith in the statute books restored in the injured breasts of the champion Sparrow, and all his imperial ilk. For the noose swinging, and the sabre of justice rattling free from its sheath, a date had been fixed to hold to account those exasperating villains, The Rolling Stones, for all that had occurred in forecourt and foreskin between themselves, Mr Keeley and the famous Mr Lavender of front-page posterity.

That the charges, though obscene, were not historically punishable by execution, redoubled the endeavours of the prosecution counsel, for whom no second was worth sparing in the search for some bylaw in the most arcane scroll of public legislature: one which might, peradventure, warrant the chairman of the bench to recommend medieval tradition be upheld and the guilty felons suffer bone-pulverising pain of breaking wheel; while deeds dusty and ancient pertaining to the precise location of the abused edifice in Forest Gate were consulted with equal vigilance, in hope the perimeter of the Francis Service Station may yet be found within some royal charter as still belonging to the Crown, so necessitating a mandatory sentence of high treason and appropriate hanging, castrating, disembowelling and fractioning in fours.

The regrettable failure to uncover such clauses was still not enough to puncture the optimism of their appointed persecutors, whose tempers sustained the giddiest of pitches as judgement day dawned on Thursday, the twenty-second of July; by which hour all wigs had been brushed, all gowns washed, all silks pressed, all breeches dry-cleaned, all collars starched, all benches dusted, all gavels polished, all floors mopped, shiny new nibs affixed to all pens and all inkwells replenished with the slickest Indian variety. So infectious were these gleeful presages that they extended far beyond the parish of the crime itself, animating all legal professionals the length of these isles; with one magistrate in Glasgow quite overcome with passion when circumstance cast a young man into his court arrested for smashing a window in the aftermath of a recent concert by the very same urinary rascals. To whom that Clydeside wig exhibited ruddy impulse to froth: 'What's the attraction for you with morons like that? They wear hair down to their shoulders, wear filthy clothes, act like clowns, and you buy a ticket to see animals like that?'

Our heroes – thus already found guilty of being morons, clowns
and animals before they'd taken their seats in West Ham
Magistrates Court – dutifully assembled at that appointed place,
jousting their way through some three-hundred palpitating female
pulses encircling the building in faithful vigil. Another fifty of
their creed crammed the public gallery within, shaking shoulder
to shoulder with reporters, notepads and pencils poised: all eyes,
like those of the bench, affixed on the three suited defendants,
languishing in variations on a theme of nonchalance beside their
playful aide, Mr Parkinson. Keith and Charlie, both of whose
superior bladder control had spared them the ignominy of joining
them in the dock, were present nonetheless as moral support –
though what morals either possessed that could possibly aid the
fate of their comrades was difficult to distinguish from their
countenance, giving such yawns, smirks and muffled raspberries as
won them the opinion of those sat on the opposite table as
embodying the most impudent rascals on earth. That latter
estimation, naturally, formed by the chief prosecutor Mr Richardson,
in whom all hopes of tugging the noose had been officially invested,
and his star witnesses: Mr Keeley, barely recognisable having
swapped mechanics' overalls for Sunday best, and Mr Lavender,
gracing the court with his radiant celebrity.

Hush demanded by Mr Morey, the chairman of the bench,
already ogling the accused with an emphasis denoting regret that
his authority on this occasion fell short of draping a black cloth
atop his wig, Mr Richardson was requested to proceed and so
sprang upon the floor to remind the assembled of the sins for
which this session had been called. That at half-past eleven p.m.
on the eighteenth day of March, a vehicle carrying the accused
trio stopped at the Francis Service Station, Romford Road; that
they demanded privilege of the toilet facilities using the most
obscene and intimidating language; that they were accordingly

refused by the attendant, Mr Keeley; that they then informed him of their belief they were at liberty to toilet where they chose, this conviction soon finding chorus in 'a gentle chant' and an accompanying exhibition of what might broadly be termed 'dancing'; that the accused duly toileted in full view of Mr Keeley and a fellow witness, Mr Lavender, who received verbal threats of violent retribution as he attempted to make note of their vehicle registration; and that, having besmirched the brickwork of the Francis Service Station with a cocktail of urine, the accused vacated the scene in the same vehicle, flicking 'a well-known two-fingered gesture'.

'These three,' bellowed Mr Richardson, pointing a finger at the seated Mick, Brian and Bill with so dramatic a flourish his gown flapped beneath his armpits like a torn sail, 'assume they have the right to treat other people and property with sheer contempt!'

The pencils in the gallery scribbling furiously, the witness Keeley was first called to the stand, where Mr Richardson fed him gentle enquiries to encourage as gory a tableau of all he had suffered as his constitution could muster. In this obligation Keeley excelled, discovering himself to be a natural embellisher of mundane detail, the scene he described akin to that of a defenceless sentry box in the planes of the Sudan besieged by fuzzy-wuzzies, he the heroic sentry protecting Her Majesty's water closet, they the marauding tribesmen of heinous pompadour. The wilder Keeley's descriptions, the more Mr Richardson's eyes glistened with approval, his oratory climaxing in a crescendo of excitement; the bestiary of his imagination running amok, and so conveying his horror to the court at being violated by 'shaggy-haired monsters'.

This pearl of dramatic licence, though intended to provoke shock, awe and admiration for the courageous Keeley, instead acted only as a pin with which to burst the balloon of amusement brewing in the gallery, so popping in a rush of teenage howls and giggles. Lightning flashing across the brow of the chairman, Mr Morey smacked his gavel upon the block.

'Order!'

SMACK!

'This is a very serious matter!'

SMACK! SMACK!

'This is no place for mirth!'

SMACK! SMACK! SMACK!

The backside of levity thus soundly smacked and sent to bed, Mr Morey prayed Mr Richardson to continue with his next witness, so ushering to his stage that contemporary sensation of the nation's newsstands, Mr Lavender.

It is among nature's crueller mysteries that, too often, when a man has spent so long possessed with thoughts of an upcoming performance, come the moment to manifest those glorious fantasies in physical actions they discover their spirits inexplicably sagging, their armoury limp and their train of hope derailed by the most ghastly attitudes of panic and anxiety. Pity, then, the famous Lavender; who months earlier had relished the propinquity of his name printed several times parallel to those royal kneecaps from betwixt which Her Majesty, Elizabeth Regina, had first plopped into this world screaming in umbilical gore, swearing upon the holy book of the *Daily Express* to bring vengeance. Only, now, to quiver in uncertainty before the bench, his valour disintegrating under the glare of the gallery, the howlers and gigglers; of whom he found himself so afraid he begged permission for the court not to disclose his home address lest their painted fingernails tear it down, brick by brick, and bury him beneath it.

So miserable a presence was Mr Lavender and his sorry trembles of speech that the attentions of the five Stones, the three accused and their two moral buttresses, had long since wandered to the gallery and idle thoughts of laundry: these frisky figments suddenly cooling when the name 'Wyman!' was called and Bill dutifully took his appropriate station. His testimony, as prepared, was so touching a plea for sympathy that it almost begged complement of a violin bowing dolefully in a minor key. For it was Bill's oath that he had been born – nay, cursed! – with 'a weak bladder', the circumstances of the night in question conspiring to bundle him into the group's car following their concert with such haste as to deny him due opportunity of emptying that pathetic sack, already brimming at high tide.

'Jones!' next echoing around the court, Brian mobilised into position, being sure to hold the gallery's gaze on his short passage so as to accelerate their pulses with the subtlest of pouts. Mr Richardson soon flapping in his face, he was formally reminded of the loathsome allegations hanging over him, pertaining to the rude and lappy manner in which the court had heard he supposedly addressed poor Mr Keeley. Already blessed with a voice no more robust than an anaemic old maid with scarce enough strength to pluck a daisy, Brian exaggerated his genteelness in the most feathery tones at his command; meekly protesting that he was a fellow of acute delicacy, easily embarrassed, and thus incapable of insulting so much as a fly for buzzing near his sugar bowl. Furthermore, he took exception to the charge of inebriation on the night in question since, as his good memory served, he had consumed nothing stronger than tea and Coca Cola; substances he still imbibed on a daily basis, never once transporting him to such violent flows of animal spirits as the two witnesses had suggested.

Brian dismissed, the bench now cried 'Jagger!': his arrival in the dock serenaded by audible swoons amongst the gallery, still acclimatising to the frustrating sensation of being allowed to see their idol at such close quarters in an environment decreeing they resist nature's impulse to sluice their thighs. Modelling his features into a sensible cast, Mick absorbed Mr Richardson's pokes and prods with the calmest faculties of speech. As he recalled the night in question, he and his chuckaboos were in elevated humour, it being the final night of their tour, and with their thoughts occupied with their ensuing visit to the Americas. On this point, Mick reminded the court that they were quite the well-travelled gentlemen of the world, and that having played places as far and wide as Texas and Singapore, they had always conducted themselves with the utmost civility, not once falling foul of foreign law agents.

Mr Richardson, once he'd returned his eyebrows to their normal position – having arched them to extraordinary angles of withering disbelief – then cleared his throat, licked his lips, falsified his face into a menacing smile and asked Mick how he might excuse the two witnesses' corroboration that he had shouted the damnable words, 'We piss anywhere, man.' The response was as simple as it was unexpected.

'I never swear,' said Mick.

The muscles of Mr Richardson's forehead sent into the most extraordinary ballet, Mick maintained their wild tempo by elaborating upon his aversion to cursing: that never as a schoolboy, nor a student, nor since, had he ever found cause for his humungous puckerings to enunciate any phrase so vulgar as to require his mouth be fumigated with soap flakes.

This convincing charade of propriety – helped by the secure intelligence that their accusers would have been unfamiliar with the obscure 'Andrew's Blues' and its damning evidence of a contrastingly fruitier vocabulary – was amplified by the closing address of their Mr Parkinson. The charges being 'ridiculous' and the case against them 'a storm in a tea cup', he listed the various reasons why his defendants be pardoned; championing them as ambassadors of moral virtue, so beloved by their public that, on the night in question, they had been supplied in their dressing room with an apple pie, freshly baked by one of their young admirers. Therefore, Mr Parkinson appealed, the bench ought not think of the accused as 'shaggy-haired monsters' but as role models whose celebrity encouraged nothing more corruptive in the nation's youth than the preparation of buttery pastry. Nor, he argued, should the court allow their judgements be dictated by the campaign against his clients' physical appearance still being waged in the opinion columns of the popular press. 'The Rolling Stones give good clean enjoyment to millions and should be allowed a little eccentricity,' concluded the valiant Parkinson. 'Their one is long hair.'

The chairman, Mr Morey, thus furnished with all the evidence necessary to form a sound opinion of the accused, not that it had altered from the moment he first clapped eyes on them, ordered they stand. The courtroom hushed, the verdict was delivered.

'You three have been found guilty . . .'

Guilty!

'. . . of behaviour not becoming young gentlemen! Because you have reached exalted heights in your profession it does not mean you have to act like this. On the contrary, you should set a standard of behaviour which should be a moral pattern for your large numbers of supporters.'

The gallery in commotion!

'Whether it is The Rolling Stones, The Beatles Pop Group or anyone else, we will not tolerate conduct of this character! You are each hereby ordered . . .'

The noose straining taut, the dreams of Lavender, Keeley and every Sparrow in the land now rested on that sentence's conclusion. 'Each hereby ordered?' To be taken from this place, and stripped and flogged? To be dragged through the streets and placed in stocks? To be pelted with rotten eggs while crowds of coarse children taunted them with sharpened sticks chanting 'blockheads', 'numbskulls', 'doddypoles', 'dunderheads', 'nincompoops' and 'shit-a-beds'?

'... to pay five pounds. Plus the usual costs.'

SMACK!

'Court dismissed!'

The halter suddenly slack, suddenly unknotting, suddenly unravelling, the necks of the Rolling Stones slipped free; fifteen pounds poorer, but their rakish reputation infinitely richer. For, thanks to the coffers requisitioned them by Mr Klein, they already had the fortune to spend a penny wherever and whenever they pleased and, were it their whim, could blissfully baptise the fore-court of every service station from Land's End to John O' Groats to the same maximum penalty and sweat not a bead in fear of bankruptcy.

It was with such gloomy and disappointed tumults of mind that Mr Keeley and Mr Lavender – all fame having sunk out of him like the sands from a broken hourglass – watched them leave the court, straight into the clawing arms of the adoring mob; none of whom paid the slightest bit of attention as these two star witnesses slunk past the melee of policemen, photographers, waving pens and flapping flesh, turning onto the pavement and parting. Each heading their separate way, if in the same general direction of obscurity ever after.

CHAPTER

XXXVI

Too full of adventure to be briefly described.

BY THE SECOND week of September, while the names of Keeley and Lavender had been erased from public memory, that of The Rolling Stones was still in height of printed fashion, and in prominence of pop charts: having the satisfaction of witnessing 'Satisfaction' reward them with their fourth number one single; a position it had already achieved in the Americas some weeks earlier, and was fast repeating across other curvatures of the globe with a speed of infestation that would have trembled envy in the legs of those fleas nesting in the locks of the Duke of Marlborough, fast seeking alternative accommodation as the cloud of insecticide wafted towards them.

Had Andrew seen fit to place upon the wall of his new Marylebone headquarters a comprehensive chart flattening out those curvatures onto a single sheet of the world's terrain – decorated with pins to mark those provinces where the Stones had played, most likely laundered, and, in seldom cases committed grievous flapjack harm – then such golden tacks would sparkle upon the following latitudes and longitudes: the crown nations of England, Scotland and Wales; the top and toes of Ireland; the strange little dot populated by tailless felines in the Irish sea; the isles in the channel betwixt Albion and Normandy; the northern Americas; Australasia; the mentholated sovereign state of

Singapore; and the Viking peninsula of Swedes, Norse, Danes and Finns. Yet, other than a cluster of pins in Paris, and another in The Hague, mainland Europe had so far been spared their ravishing strides so frequently inciting of public dementia; an exclusion which they now chose to fix with a trip to that nation of frothing beer and fatty sausage, which only two decades earlier had nearly snuffed their candles before the wicks were lit.

Though their own residual memories, apropos infanticide by Luftwaffe, had mellowed in intervening peacetime, as the Stones boarded their plane bound for Münster their general disposition was not unlike that of the crew of a Lancaster bomber and its cargo of bouncy explosives taking off for the same airspace twenty-two years earlier. The singular difference being they had neither bombs nor bullets with which to trouble the Germans: only the heavy artillery of loud music, long hair and licentious exhibitionism – proven sufficient means to conquer on their previous excursions abroad – and so endowed all their faith in recompensing the whinny of doodlebug with the wail of 'Satisfaction' and all catastrophes of the Blitz with Mick's hips and their every shocking function.

Fortunately, the young Huns that awaited their occupation shewed themselves to be anything but resistant to their electric pluckings, having already declared themselves apostles of that genre with the tribal classification 'Beat Fanz'. The unfortunate consequence of which was a sorry misunderstanding amongst the platoons of German police officers habitually employed to dictate order at each concert, their literal reading mistaking noun for verb and so assuming the same youth to be a cult of masochists and their appellation a request to be thwacked and thumped as their mothers might scrag-end meat before shaping into an appropriate coil of bratwurst. Such gore was the substance of familiar eyesores of hostility and violence to be seen in the stalls night after night, the carnage frequently brewing beyond the theatre and into the surrounding streets; where water-cannons turned roads into rivers flecked by islands of capsized cars and uprooted benches, and where those Beat Fanz that weren't flushed away in its torrent pelted their oppressors with what arsenal could be scrounged from surrounding dustbins: including novel ballistic use of one *rattus norvegicus* which, though plausibly alive at the time of dispatch, was most definitely *rattus mortuus* once subject to the laws of aerodynamics and impacting upon the dentures of a policeman in Essen as his lips were bent in midst of screaming '*Achtung!*'

After three concerts characterised by these disturbances, the third in Hamburg once more ending in an aggregate of limps and moans burdening the local krankenhaus, the Stones were suddenly presented with an opportunity to redress the disproportionate brutality endured by their long-suffering German admirers. Its invention was the sole cunning of Keith who, upon encountering a party of offending uniforms patrolling the backstage premises, invited them to partake in a restorative nip of strong-waters which, according to their local custom, demanded spoken ceremony of '*Prost!*' and the draining of all bumpers in a single gulp. The uniforms gratefully accepted and were thus furnished with a flask of whisky from Keith's dressing room, three-quarters full, which, in absence of glasses, made an immediate circuit of their lips; each belching that peculiar greeting before pouring a generous slug of liquid down their gizzards, eliciting much squinting of eyeball and rare spasms of neck and shoulders. That their grinning monkey-faced host himself never partook in this ritual failed to arouse their suspicions, nor were their palates so advanced that they could determine its salty vintage as being a mixture of the golden waters of Johnnie Walker, matured ten years, and Keith Richards, matured all of ten minutes since evacuating his person through intimate means which would not have surprised a certain garage attendant, nor youth worker, now obsolete to the remainder of our History.

While Keith amused himself infecting the bloodstream of the local *polizei* with his Dartford dew, Bill was struggling to fulfil his expectations of Deutsche laundry; having allowed them elevation to the greatest heights after assuming the country's fairer sex to match the calibre of their naked national ambassadors as photographed for the sorts of gentlemen's periodicals connoisseurs of the natural world, such as he, enjoyed perusing in their most private moments. His disappointment in these projections was less on account of quality, there being ample young frauleins whose security of pigtails he saw fit to test with the most vigorous endeavours of unbraiding, than quantity; the sum membership of Beat Fanz, when compared with their equivalent in other regions of the world, being by majority male, with so many more Adolfs, Fritzs and Wolfgangs than Aldonas, Fridas and Wilhelminas as to compromise Bill's usual quota of industry.

This drought of German honey was of less pressing concern to Mick, now betrothed to Chrissie, Charlie, homesick for his beloved Shirley, and Keith, whose nocturnes were commonly devoted to caressing wood and strings rather than rump and garter, but bore all too heavily on Brian's appetites, which ached accordingly. Feeding the phantoms of his mind with pharmaceuticals, his celibate slumbers in Hamburg's Hotel Lillienhof had already been shaken by the spectacle of a candlestick performing inexplicable charades, of a type he only dared attribute to the influence of a poltergeist. With wits askew, upon next arriving in the city of Munich, Brian further aggravated his train with a visit to the remnants of a labour camp; one where those sharing Mr Klein's Semitic heritage were subject to unspeakable human cruelties.

It was in this same grim and discombobulated vein that Brian reconvened in the group's dressing room at Munich's Circus

Krone, where Bill was presently the focus of attention, having taken liberties with a presentation gâteau: its surface originally bearing the name of the group, but now, thanks to his amendments, declaring the distinctly Phelgian instruction to 'ROLL IN SNOT'. With unfortunate timing, his pride in this sugary anagram coincided with the admittance of fresh laundry into their backstage quarters: one who might otherwise have made Bill's acquaintance had her first impressions of him not been that of a culinary vulgarian, and so ignoring him slunk seductively past Mick and Charlie, fluttered an eyelid at Keith, and finally placed her arresting statistics in a seated position beside Brian.

It may have been mere erotic delirium – after being denied relief of bareback for as many days as would warrant tallying on two hands, thus demolishing his sanity to its recent hysterics of ghosts and genocide – but scarce could Brian imagine what sorcery created such blonde perfection, what strange and rare ingredients were flung into the cauldron of mortal conception, and what sensual incantations were chanted to bubble and boil the first breath of life into the splendour of Italian flesh introducing itself as 'Anita'.

A strange and incalculable creature, at the age of twenty-two Anita had successfully converted her prettiness into pennies in employ as a human clothes horse, being the reason she happened to be in Munich that day participating in such a photographic assignment. Brian could not have been more bewitched had she chosen to make his acquaintance in livery of broomstick and pointy hat, happily surrendering his body and soul to whatever spells she wished to cast upon him, the first occurring later that evening in his hotel bedchambers – there being no need to scandalise these pages with any further description thereof.

The mystery of Anita's preference for Brian found plenty occasion to fascinate his fellow Stones the following day during the long passage to their final destination of Berlin, arriving there to discover a city divided, in edifice as in opinion. The edifice: a wall encircling the whole west of the metropolis so as to separate it from the east, of sufficient height that if the notorious Mr Dumpty of children's folklore should have chosen it for his perch his fall would have been not merely great but one of irreversibly paraplegic consequence; notwithstanding the strong likelihood of being first perforated by bullets from the nearest guard tower, rendering him such a mess that the first representative of the King's men to arrive on the scene would almost certainly surrender their store of all semi-digested matter with due projectile violence. And the opinion: whether The Rolling Stones, those internationally renowned vandals of boudoir and biscuit, were fit guests to accommodate; the answer being '*Nein!*' according to the manager of the Berlin Hilton, who refused their custom for fear of his finest bedding falling prey to inevitable perversions of apple strudel; that attitude countered by the merciful '*Ja!*' of a surrogate hostel acquired for their repose at the shortest notice.

Due explanation for what disfavour they encountered at certain Berlin reception desks was to be found in plentiful supply amidst the surrounding architecture: much of it still exhibiting the effects of Allied conflict two decades previous in missing roofs and mounds of rubble, and it being the assumption of some locals that, as five English varlets, the Stones had merely come to play their city as an excuse to gloatingly survey these monuments to the infuriating precision of RAF Bomber Command. Taking stock of these ruins as they were ferried through the city to the forest amphitheatre where they were scheduled to provide paid entertainment, Mick could not help but dwell upon the historic fracas between their two nations; these thoughts governing his fancy to such degrees that, upon discovering their dressing room to be a concrete bunker where Herr Hitler himself had once parked his fundaments, he was seized by the impulse to parade its length in a stiff-legged gait while making mock moustache of index finger. Witnessing the cheer this produced in his squires, Mick considered it prudent to transport himself on the stage in identical fashion for the amusement of the assembled Beat Fanz and, so encouraged, proceeded to execute this plan with the boldest strains of gusto.

To describe every attendant atrocity roused by Mick's ligaments is sadly not within my power, unless I had forty pens, and could, at once, write with them all together; thereby documenting the annihilation of the Berlin Waldbuhne plank by plank and railing by railing, annotating all boom and rattle, all geysers of blood, all screams of ambulance, all smash of parked car and train carriage window as the mob rampaged through the city for four fierce hours. That it had taken just five Englishmen to wreak so much havoc upon the former headquarters of the Reich might even have moved the late Sir Winston's rotting skeleton to suddenly bolt upright in its Oxfordshire tomb, hands rattling bony victory salutes; were not those same five Englishmen's deteriorating status at home otherwise being forged in a kiln of hatred not felt in the national breast since Herr Göring last filled the skies of Kent with Fokkers. To which disreputable end they would do better to remain abroad for the next chapter where, for the time being, we shall mercifully keep them.

CHAPTER

XXXVII

    ❧

More American experiences; involving a crisis of illumination
and an altogether more serious catastrophe.

'THE UNITED STATES has been faced with war, depression, racial discrimination, murders, disease, rapists, natural disasters, and if we fall apart just because five men from England perform in an unusual manner then this country is in great need of help!' So the nervous soothsayers of the *Washington Post* trumpeted the reappearance of The Rolling Stones upon American shores that autumn; predicting the very worst for its countrymen who'd already been ravaged by their presence thrice before, that passion reciprocated in a kind which upon their last visit, in convex shape of the anus of doom, had almost cost them their lives.

Were they of especially superstitious character, that incident may, perchance, have discouraged them from so soon a return visit. Yet, since none were so feeble of mind to indulge in the throwing of old shoes, the saluting of magpies and other such tics of that sad neurotic persuasion, the Stones' attitude towards all risk of encroaching death was one of blithe fearlessness: even if their collective intellects recognised that their untimely passing would be cause for extraordinary scenes of celebration in a great many quarters of the world, from Berlin to Scotch Corner; and that were there genuine power in prayer then the combined Our Fathers of their global foes must already have passed sentence of execution, to be delivered by the Almighty in as painful a fashion as his cruellest humour could conceive.

It being every young man's luxury to scoff in the face of mortal pother, our devil's brats, too absorbed in matters strictly terrestrial, could not have known that such a heavenly petition was currently under review of the Fates who, assessing all grievances, duly decided to send them whatever American angels of death could be mustered. The first being far from angelic, her face not simply wrinkled but ploughed into innumerable furrows, and far from deadly, armed with nothing more lethal than a parasol. This domestic implement she nonetheless wielded as if a mace, setting about Charlie's person after allowing his silent majesty audience of her irritations in a hotel foyer. The angel criticising the length of his hair, and the enigma failing to provide apology other than an innocent smirk, the hoary assassin was thus agitated into full jamboree of assault; ending only when two portly doormen hauled her from the building in ugly scenes stripping all involved of their dignity, and Charlie of several buttons.

Happily, this foolish old crone was but a rare anomaly amongst the climate of American affection which elsewhere greeted them, arriving in New York City to find themselves immortalised in Times Square as five frowning gods looking down upon the Manhattan rush hour traffic. This dwarfing billboard had been erected at considerable cost, reassuring them of the sincerity in Mr Klein's oath to spare no expense in improving their commercial fortunes: to which end he also commandeered a private plane to ferry them across the States in appropriate splendour; even if its maiden flight exposed the aircraft to be less than factory fresh and so sensitive to the quakes of turbulence that few disembarked with a pallor not by some vivid tinge mortuary green.

The fact that the munificent Mr Klein chose not to accompany them on the road, nor in the air, might have impregnated them with irrational fears that he, too, was in league with Death and had selected that monstrosity of engineering so as to see their limbs picked out like needles in a mile-wide haystack of broken fuselage, were they not so convinced of his solid character. Selflessly volunteering to remain in his New York office toting up the receipts on their behalf, Mr Klein assured them he wouldn't let so much as a cent escape his attentions if their coffers were owed, and that thanks to his careful grooming their bank accounts were already in handsome fettle. Gladdened by this news, Bill was excited to ask if he might view his statement of account to compare with the thrilling narrative of petty cash as currently stood in the footers of his diary. This request squeezed a strange yet sympathetic puff from Mr Klein who – in such soft tones as a nurse might use when applying a bandage to a child's scuffed knee – regrettably informed him the costs of administration to produce such a docket would be detrimental to the rate of interest earned, and that for the same reasons, though he could furnish each member with a shiny new cheque book for their respective shares, they would be ill advised to use it for similar complex reasons which, not wishing to bore them rigid with the abstruse jargon of banking legislature, he chose not to elaborate. Instead, and until further notice, he pledged them freedom of his endless charity. So, should any urgently require ready money for any purchases, large or small, mansion or Mini, they need only demand and he, their purses' servant, would humbly oblige. This vow inviting no reasonable cause for quibble, the Stones drowned any suspicions in a toast to his sublime benevolence, and so left Mr Klein to add and subtract in the godliest of peace.

The abacus of Bill's brain nonetheless rattled for want of arithmetic, in which numerological humour he removed himself to his hotel chamber to ponder those fascinating anecdotes of expenditure inscribed in his journal. His fiscal train had not long gathered speed when its progress found just cause for derailment in that volume's more engaging inventory of ingoings and outgoings, to which he could also boast vigilance to amass those of his bandfellows. Setting aside the issue of his personal finances, he thus changed his destination to the sum of all flapdoodles since their operations began, applying himself to that task with an enthusiasm which betrayed much confidence of victory. As he predicted, Charlie fell at the first hurdle of monogamy, with Keith similarly shy of double figures and Mick, though ruined for choice, too discriminating a judge to reach a century. This left bareback Brian his only worthy rival, though still not so worthy that he could gallop anywhere close to Bill's own finishing post of two-hundred-and-seventy-eight.

It is not to be supposed Bill arrived at this total without serenity, the wealth of his joyful exhaustions transporting him to raptures of self-congratulation so overwhelming that, after screwing his eyes tight with joy, when he opened them again all was black; the shock of his tally having evidently robbed him of sight. Until this bowel-chilling trice he had never believed that common gossip of old wives warning their menfolk of the perils of disbursing their essence in too great a quantity for fear of becoming blind. Yet how could it not be otherwise, that the very instant he took stock of his liquidations – O! Fool of vanity, marvelling at his own excess! – heaven extinguished his light like Samson, cursed never to ogle the mossy beauty of a Delilah ever again. Fraught with grief, the universe swallowed in darkness, he began desperately patting his hands across his shaking body, his palm suddenly touching upon the oblong of a cigarette lighter in his trouser fob. Extracting it with the utmost care, he struck a tremulous thumb against its wheel, the scene suddenly illuminating with a yellowish-blue flame spurting from a strip of metal, clutched in a hand which he and two-hundred-and-seventy-eight brassieres knew all too well.

Similar scenes of temporary hysteria were occurring the length of New York City, the electrical supply to that great metropolis and its surrounding boroughs having been rudely snipped, plunging all inhabitants into the same groping terrors. His fellow Stones, too, were moved to varying shades of panic for as long as it took each to grasp their murky predicament as one of power shortage, with the solitary exclusion of Brian. The blackout striking whilst his mental engine was clogged with the chemical oils of cloud-cuckoo-land, he was fain to imagine the day of judgement was nigh, his wits surrendering under the power of the most insupportable dread. A whinny of fright travelling the length of the corridor beyond, Bill recognised its distinct Jonesian timbre and nobly rushed to his aid, guided by the flicker of a candle, having had the fortune to find such an article in his bedroom. With the taper at chest height so as to cast ominous shadows upon Bill's bone structure which, even in broad daylight, was of an arrangement capable of petrifying minors, he burst into Brian's room. The gloom abruptly broken by flame and boggling face in chiaroscuro, and the juices of Brian's understanding still at their thinnest, he instead identified Bill as Satan's own emissary come to escort him to an eternity of fire and toasting fork and so, emitting another scream draining his pep to its last reserve, promptly fainted away.

How easily Death might have leaped upon this scene as ripe for misadventure, closing Brian's slim volume of a life at twenty-three years, were his pulse not so robust as to repel the chilly inertia of rigor mortis, laying where he fell in a sorry diabolical stupor until revived at his own leisure. But The Reaper, and all human hopes of justice invested in its scythe, would not have to wait long for providence to place another Stone in easy swipe, biding patiently three more weeks until means and opportunity aligned with guarantee of extinction in Sacramento.

With appropriate poignancy of location, on the night in question the band were performing on stage in the city's Memorial Auditorium – serenading some five-thousand young Californians to a supreme pitch of ecstasy – when with equally appropriate poignancy of repertoire they sprang into their popular hit, 'The Last Time'. The opening verse executed without flaw, as the chorus approached Keith bumped his way towards a microphone stand so as to lend Mick's yodels required undercoat of harmony when, before his vocal cords had pleasure of phonation, the neck of his guitar struck the microphone stand, the air about him raged with sparks, a bang sounded loud enough to be mistaken for a shotgun and the smell of burnt crumpets engulfed the stalls.

All of this occurred in the space of less than one second: the same period witnessing Keith's body arc backwards high into the air, his legs forked, his arms stiff as a scarecrow, landing in the same fixed position having sailed a full breadth of the stage at a speed and elevation so taxing to this Author's quiver of description that, to properly translate, I surrender all pretence of originality and defer to those audacious doodles of the genius of *Tristram Shandy*. Thus, to follow in the stroke of Mr Sterne, Keith's electrocuted bones travelled thus:

There, at point B, beneath steaming grey vapours of scorched flesh and copper, Keith remained entirely motionless. The music stopping, dismay distorted the visages of band and audience, their chorus of confused shrieks and sobs worsening until the safety curtain plummeted to shield them from the horror – as I must now shield thee, Reader. For that curtain doubling as ours, let us not dwell a sentence further on this tragedy, but forget our grief in lighter scenes of saucy jades; such as that your merciful Author has prepared, impending.

CHAPTER

XXXVIII

⤜⤛

Reports progress in certain homely matters.

SHE HAD NOT yet been married a year, had borne a child, but
being only a girl of nineteen she still craved excitement
beyond all conjugal vows. So Mrs Dunbar sought and Mrs
Dunbar found in sinful supply – less than a mile from her marital
bed in a den of vice tucked around the corner of Gloucester Road
tube station. If she was rarely ever Mrs Dunbar in her head, she
was even less so once her petite carriage skipped across the
threshold of Number One, Courtfield Road; where her hosts were
kind enough to never once refer to her as 'Mrs Dunbar', and where
she could relinquish all wifely cares sprawled on exotic silks,
inhaling exotic smoke, lost in exotic conversations on life, art,
Camelot, magick and extraterrestrial activity. In Courtfield Road,
she could simply *be*, and being her was not to be Mrs Dunbar but
to be, exquisitely, Marianne.

Of course, she had never been less than Marianne, even in her
few domesticated duties as Mrs Dunbar. Nor could she ever forget
she *was* Marianne, her name already stamped on a brace of albums,
upper case on one, lower on the other, along with her face; whether
holding sharp focus in a haze of colour, or in knee socks in
coquettish monochrome, curled up in The Salisbury on St Martin's
Lane as if waiting for a handsome stranger to force upon her the
Dubonnet she'd been too bashful to order herself. Marianne at

thirty-three revolutions, and Faithfull at forty-five: trilling top-ten tears of past lovers, fragile birds and little cafés in a voice trembling like a partridge slowly dying of a broken heart. A singing sensation beloved by thousands, but still the same maddening confusion of matchgirl and dollymop who had strangled Andrew's senses in a lattice of butcher's knots over a year and seventeen chapters ago: the same Virgin Mary with a cracking pair of tits.

Her celebrity, like her wedding band, was irrelevant in Courtfield Road, where she was still a star on account of being indubitably Marianne; twinkling in an orbit of garrulous oddities together forming a human constellation of a shape and character that might be appropriately distinguished in the astronomy of anthropology as 'The Joint'. The sweet young boy dressed in all the colours of an impressionist's palette named Tara, whose genes lay in Ireland, whose inheritance lay in black stout, and whose head, even when on the cushions of Courtfield Road, lay somewhere on the far side of Uranus. The former Captain Fraser, now demobbed as 'Groovy Bob', collector of art and eater of opium. The incorrigible Gibby, who had first discovered Courtfield Road, demanding it be bought by those under his spell so that he might take his place as one of its more decadent ornaments, which being by trade a designer of interiors he achieved with all the genius of his profession. And the brightest star of all, whose gravity held the others in place, the soul that animated the whole society and whose name, thanks to dear Gibby, was that on the leasehold: the bewitching Anita, now living in London, now conjoined with Brian, two profligate knaves together in their tiny duchy of SW7.

Brian had never been able to shift her from his thoughts after that first night in Munich; Anita haunted him, so that when oceans apart she yet walked beside him like the phantom of all he desired, until he could bear the agony no more and begged her to fly over and attend his throbbing inclinations on tour in America. From the hour she arrived, Brian was only ever seen by the other Stones when duty called him to the stage, the rest of his time and energies spent in the most clamorous consummation of animal passions as had ever shaken ceiling plaster. Their abnormal ululations defied all attempts at interpretation in the mind's eye of those unfortunate enough to find themselves hostelled in the adjoining rooms, unable to sleep for the erratic syncopation of slap and snivel. That neither emerged from their chamber the morning after these savage pleasures assisted by splints and crutches seemed the substance of miracle to his bandfellows, all of whom had pressed enough ears against their door on enough occasions, all coming away with the distinct suspicion Anita's was the whiphand and Brian her scolded nag.

In Courtfield Road, Anita and Brian could indulge their bareback barbarism at blissful leisure, or at least when not indulging their relentless company of adopted pets, all impeccably housetrained so as not to upset the wickedly dégagé status quo. Dear Gibby, Tara, Groovy Bob and, not least, darling Marianne. They the constellation, squinting through curls of mulberry-grey smoke up at the deep space of its high-vaulted ceiling; their floppy limbs supported by rolls of cloth, tasselled rugs and Moroccan cushions, leafing through an antiquarian volume of erotic vulgarities; considering the stuffed goat atop Brian's amplifier (none so familiar with the history of that caprine legend Billy G to wonder aloud whether this was the very same William, forever immortalised in taxidermy); lost in circular conversations about Tarot cards and Stonehenge, every pair of eyes in the room expressing the same perplexed vacuity that puzzled souls generally stare with.

Some days, rare days, other foreign bodies would flit between its musky fabrics, among them Mick: his visits brief; his purpose to divine the complex weather system in Brian's head; his stomach challenged by the kitchen which in bacterial spectrum prompted many an unhappy flashback to the septic crockery of Edith Grove;

and his gaze sometimes lingering on Marianne long enough to pipe the blood to the stage of her cheeks and so cry out in a chorus of blush she wished she wouldn't sing.

And there were other days, rarer days still, when Marianne would scurry to the sanctuary of Courtfield Road and find her heart's playground all but empty. Anita gone, no Gibby, no Tara, no Groovy Bob, not even Mick with his sly peeps and unsettling puckers. Just the cushions, and the rugs, and the record player, and the goat, and the little staircase leading up to the wooden minstrel's gallery with its unmade bed. And Brian. Alone.

He welcomed her inside without ceremony and together they sat and they smoked, they pondered and they puffed, they bellowed and they billowed until the room became as foggy as their wits, and Marianne completely enveloped in its woozy miasma. Then a hand clasped her own and with a polite tug uprooted her from the carpet where she'd felt stuck for the past hour as together they contemplated the whereabouts of the lost city of Atlantis while referring to a Barnett's street map of Greater London. She began floating, through the clouds, higher and higher, until reaching a soft, pillowy stratosphere. She could feel wet lips and the stroke of warm skin, and when the mists parted and she saw Brian's urgent visage pressing towards her own, she sighed and smiled, and lay back, revelling in her nakedness against stretched cotton, her back already arching with want, itching for the happy sacrifice of Mrs Dunbar.

Another minute passed and all was deathly silent. Mrs Dunbar, still very much alive, propped herself up on her elbows and looked about her surroundings. She saw she was lying on the mattress up in the minstrel's gallery. Beside her lay Brian: very much unconscious, his mouth agog, breathing noisily like an overfed hog, immune to her every effort to rouse him; having evidently consumed opiates of a magnitude so gluttonous as to impound those tools necessary to fulfil any enterprise of adultery.

'The Devil And Mrs Dunbar'

The defeated Mrs Dunbar duly got dressed and climbed the winding stairs down to the living room, her every unsullied step heavy with vexation. She slumped on a chair beside the record player to allow her fuzziness a moment to settle, idly picking up the nearest album leaning against it, which so happened to be one of Brian's own labours. There he was on the cover, crouching down between two crates in handsome poise, looking so frustratingly capable. And there were the rest of his band standing above him. Inscrutable Charlie. Granite-faced Bill. Gorgeous Keith. And exasperating Mick, with that same strange look on his face that trembled the stitching in her knickerbockers every time she fell in its beam.

From up in the gallery, she could still hear the hog snuffling. 'Poor Brian,' thought Marianne, who took a last longing look at the album cover before standing up, tip-toeing over scatter cushions and ashtrays and letting herself out; trying to ignore the pleasingly persistent tremble in her knickerbockers as she walked home to Mr Dunbar, as slowly as her feet could carry her.

CHAPTER
XXXIX

A resurrection.

THE DULL MIST had driven the rain away over the azure of the fields, ushering the golden sunlight to illuminate this Sussex Eden. The grass by the laneside was dry once more to the touch, white dust lifting gently in tiny clouds before the breeze. The grasshopper began his cheery music among the bracken as every rose-bell peeking from the hedgerows yielded its honey-dole to amber bees. Here and there on the steep roadside bank a glistening raindrop still trembled in the crimson cup of a foxglove, or lit up the fronds of silverweed with its sparkling white. And in the deep oak wood behind, the pattering of the water yet lingered intermittently, as each leaf-reservoir discharged its burden upon the thirsty ground below.

Against the distant percussion of waves softly lapping the coastal beaches came the song of the wind, sweeping through the elm tops; warm and joyous and free. Straight from the ocean it had come, its voice rich in salt and the scent of brown seaweed torn from the garden under the deep. It carried along the dunes, whistling between the thickets of coarse coppery grasses, blowing the horns of strange shells shining like opals through their pale enamel with delicate veining of soft grey blue. It sang down narrow country lanes, inviting choral symphony from larks, robins and blackbirds, stirring floral applause from dandelion, stitchwort and buttercup, and the arias of a hundred gate hinges creaking in gay soprano.

It was such a hinge upon such a gate that the skinny young cove swung open, leaving his Oxford-blue Bentley and its chauffeur parked on the verge behind, proceeding along the driveway on foot; his gait slowing in awe as every step brought him closer to a large house crowned by a thatched roof of a splendour which only the brush of Constable might have honoured in oil and pigment. The idyllic vista was enriched by the dappling diamonds of light glistening in the surrounding moat, a modest trench yet wide enough to deter all but the most gymnastic imbeciles from vaulting across; and the necklace of flowering bushes caressing the ledges of the lower windows, from which sills he could easily imagine the dainty fingers of Anne Boleyn reaching down to pluck herself a nosegay before inserting it in her tresses and retiring upstairs, where her sovereign suitor awaited between four posters to tremble its petals loose. For though not a palace it was a home fit for a king: a detail which made plain sight of its resident emerging from the front entrance all the more remarkable, lacking as they did any regal air and dressed as any toiling layperson.

The ordinary king greeted his guest with a polite wave, assuming him to have taken a wrong turning off the main trunk road and in need of establishing his bearings. The swarthy young wanderer admitted that, indeed, he wasn't where he ought to be, though neither was he in a hurry, having spent the morning cruising the vicinity at leisure with nothing more concrete to guide him than a list of properties for sale which he intended to review for possible purchase. This confession drummed a curious smile upon the face of his highness, stroking a hand across his lips as if to mask a kindly chuckle, before inviting the stranger's opinion on whether they thought his own property to be at all desirable. The visitor responded in an eye-popping affirmative so enthusiastic it was a miracle of biology his wagging head didn't free itself from his neck and roll across the lawn and into the moat with a heavy plop.

The king asked again how much he desired it. His company reiterated again, very much. The king nodded, scratched his chin, placed both hands in his pockets and announced, that being the case, then he was willing to part with his paradise of muchness for a sum no smaller than twenty-thousand pounds.

The clock had not long struck an hour past midday. Four more times did the iron register of time beat on its sonorous bell-metal before both king and usurper were in embrace of hands and toasting of bumpers; during which period the dark blue Bentley had dashed to London, its passenger placing a telephone call to New York City to request funds, which he duly withdrew from a bank in the city, before hurtling back to his south coast Shangri La. The money counted, the deeds signed, the king wished his successor all happiness upon the throne, and so concluded that day's swift business to the utmost satisfaction of both.

Even with the key fob squeezed tightly in his palm, the new king still could not quite believe his fortune as he undertook a celebratory walk around the moat perimeter; his nostrils hungrily sucking in the country air making his head giddy and his heart race. With each stride, his carriage became more stately, his spine straighter, his shoulders braced, his chin jutting through a bristling Romany grin. The song of the wind still stirred through the low grass where he trod in his suede boots: the same boots to whom he owed his life when he ought otherwise to have been fried to a cinder on stage in Sacramento, had Death not been foiled by the blessing of their rubber soles.

At last he came to a rest by the entrance gate, leaning both elbows across its top, the hand that wasn't holding a cigarette bending over to pat the wooden sign affixed below as a master might pat his new dog. Laughing along with the rustling trees, he twirled his fingers in royal salute to the patches of nettle and cowslip, the breeze bending their stems back at him as if in silent curtsey. 'Hail King Keith!'

'Yes,' he thought to himself, sighing in dreamy contentment. 'Hail King Keith! King of Redlands!'

MADHOUSE

CHAPTER

XL

A necessary shift in time and temperament.

BEFORE WE PROCEED with our final act, let us behave as a footsore traveller who, knowing they have only so far left in their journey, pause to turn around and glance back over the distance covered with a keen sense of achievement. What lengths have we trekked since the backwoods of poverty and mucus from which our incorrigible rakes first scrambled free in shape of the musical quintet The Rolling Stones! We have witnessed them flourish, in fame, in riches, in love and in notoriety; unhindered by all sentinels of authority with regard to etiquette, neckerchiefs, biscuits and latrines. We have seen the noose of Law loop and tighten around their throats only to slip free, their foes humiliated. And we have seen the broth of dissension stir within; the artful politics of leadership tearing the tiniest of fissures, widening slowly into yet unpaperable mental cracks.

In short, we have gathered momentum of dishonour, sin and subterfuge demanding of a moral conclusion, such as that which now lies ahead like an ominous black mountain upon the horizon calling us to our unavoidably sombre terminus. But first, to reach there it is imperative that we spring across a chasm in time, both to hasten the narrative bolt of these last thirteen stages and to spare the Reader an extended account of all minor jinks to the detriment of this plot and their triceps; straining as they would be with the carriage of a work bearing such superfluous leafs as could be defined morbidly obese. In taking this liberty I trust those offended will be but a grumbling minority; of a kind preferring to be sedated with the insipid tonic of uninteresting facts and irrelevant dates brewed by painful historians who feel obliged to fill up as much paper as can be bound in a single volume. Such slaves of such manuals are so unexcitable a breed that if presented with the legend of Rapunzel, they would surely remain unmoved by the cruelty of her incarceration: expressing only exasperation at the penmanship of the siblings Grimm for failing to impart the specifics of height and elevation of her prison tower, the number of bricks employed in its construction, the breaking-strength of her celebrated tresses and the comparative weight, in imperial measure, of her princely saviour. So let us hope at this late stage in our voyage such apostles of tedium will have already abandoned our fearless ship of romance, returning to the icy grey straits of academia where we bid them good riddance; allowing us to happily continue our course, full sail, into wild seas of fancy.

The chasm in time is that of an entire rotation around the sun, numerically recorded in the Gregorian calendar as the year Nineteen Sixty-Six; the need for this chasm not because the activities of our subjects during this period were much too uninteresting, but because the Reader will already be familiarised with their ilk to the very cusp of indigestion. Therefore let us not allow our drama to sink in the quicksand of déjà vu; advancing in the knowledge that throughout that year the Rolling Stones continued to consolidate their wealth and success, topping charts at home and abroad, partaking in what pleasures of doodlesack and permanent damage of upholstery appealed to their fancies in all quarters travelled. For such scenes, though plentiful enough to fill several chapters and an entire page-a-day diary of Bill's, would be best bridged by a single one summarising only those incidents posing the greatest influence upon the remainder of our chronicle: this being that very episode of efficiency.

Their eminent diarist naturally began the year with the purchase of such a fresh journal, which over the course of the next twelve months Bill had cause to cake in as much ink as his nightly swashbuckling required, maintaining a healthy lead in the group's accumulating laundry total to the distension of his pride, the amazement of his eyesight and the acquisition of one especially unwelcome pestilence of the undiscussables; the latter placing him in an especially sore humour when its microscopic hauliers extended their distribution to the corresponding province of his soon-to-be ex-wife.

No such marital crises disrupted the breakfast table of the Watts household, Charlie shewing no alteration in his monogamous enigma other than a new growth upon his glorious philtrum: the advisability of which was called into question one day in September when coerced to don skirt, stockings, fur coat and felt hat, adopt the name of 'Millicent', and pose in broad daylight in Midtown, New York City with the purpose of being mistaken for an aged member of the female populace – a perverse folly in which he failed miserably by virtue of those very follicles. Nor was Charlie alone in this degeneracy, taking his position on the paving stones of East Twenty-Fourth Street beside his fellow Stones, all of whom were in livery of the same queer masquerade: Mick, a bespectacled spinsterly 'Sarah'; Keith a sour old-maidenly 'Molly'; Bill, an unsightly air corps cripple answering to 'Penelope'; and Brian, a painted army strumpet named 'Flossie', in platinum-blonde wig and corporal-teasing pencil skirt.

This ghastly ensemble was yet another twitch of Andrew's rare genius, deciding it a capital means of promoting the group's forthcoming disc which, containing the word 'Mother', was ample justification for them to be photographed in as convincing a condition of matronage as hosiery, cosmetics and wadding might achieve. That it served only to double the irritations of their many disparagers in civilised society should not be considered remarkable; Andrew having lost none of his relish for scandal, only narrowly backing down with his plans to christen their new album *Could You Walk On Water?*, hoping the wilful fantasists of the Christian religion might interpret it as sceptical of one of their wizard's more preposterous miracles and complain in such numbers as to brighten its beacon of publicity. This, his public appetite of old for sensation, was rivalled only by Andrew's private appetite of new for hallucinatory physic; similar to that long advocated by Brian, to which some of the other Stones had also become gradually more accustomed, in spite of the aforementioned's frequent exhibitions as to the hazards of pharmaceutical intemperance.

Brian himself began the year being denounced in court as 'deplorable' and, over the course of the calendar, became only more so. This reproof was provoked by his unfortunate habit of forgetting the former fruits of his horizontal labours and his obligation to the purses of their mothers who, in absence of such charity, had since shrivelled to the very depths of poverty and despair; necessitating the firm hand of Law to remind him of his criminal neglect.

Though his cache of rational excuses lay empty, his wits were forgivably exempt of reason, whether through violent brain fever of his illegal medicine or their possession by Anita: *light of his life, fire of his loins, his sin, his soul, A-nee-ta!* He loved her cruel scent, her vampire kiss, her lupine scratch and her molten Venus. He adored every welt and weal she gouged upon his body, each a devout prayer to the black magic of her sex. He worshipped her from the tips of her boots to the feathers of her boa, a slave to her fashions and whichever she in turn decided for him.

Anita was the centre of Brian's universe – by location Number One, Courtfield Road – where he was at liberty to share his Aphrodite with the select few who admired and assisted their characters and habitat: whether in glamorous fittings of a Moorish alcazar, the supply of hashish and stronger brain-fever dosages, or endless conversation of the fantastic. The most common indentations upon their cushions were those already introduced in this History by nickname: Mr Christopher Gibbs, alias 'Gibby'; Mr Robert Fraser, alias 'Groovy Bob'; Mr Tara Browne, alias nothing that stuck; and Andrew's pop protégée of chaste sensuality, Marianne, the only planetary object to briefly eclipse Anita when – as the Reader surely cannot have already forgotten – in a moment of rare intimacy the gases of intoxication inflated Brian's amorous spirits to suggest ravishment, both realising much too late that a consequence of the same chemicals was dismal deflation of the flesh.

By the summer of Sixty-Six, the cast of Courtfield Road jesters had extended to include Keith, who having recently suffered the agonies of romantic heartache found what mirth and solace he required upon Brian and Anita's rugs: a welcome refuge for as long as it took his decorators to prepare his newly acquired home in the Sussex countryside with the skins of enough animal species as might have once formed a modest zoo. He, like Brian, took a hazy shine to the company of Gibby and Groovy Bob, and something of a secret sparkle to Anita, frequently inviting all to transfer the domestic cheer to the recording studio, which duly became increasingly foggy of air and, on occasion, altogether aimless of industry.

Though it might be supposed that their commercial produce suffered, as the smoke thickened so did their prominence, just as the beneficent Mr Klein had promised. Their old competitors, The Beatles Pop Group, had been deafened by one teenage shrieker too many and latterly decided never to wobble their heads upon a concert stage ever again: a blessed vacuum for the Stones who, after touring the United States again that year, were to be crowned that country's biggest-selling popular music group. The selfless Mr Klein continued to nurture their swelling fortune: granting them what ready capital they needed, including that for the purchase of Keith's Sussex paradise, while kindly stalling any rash requests to withdraw directly from their accounts which might compromise the abiding security of their hard-won riches.

The brilliant Mr Klein had also announced tentative steps to double their stream of income with a foray into the film world, which had already proven fortuitous for The Beatles Pop Group: acquiring the rights to a shocking novel about unmanageable youth and their suicidal elders titled *Only Lovers Left Alive*, with Mick cast as its principal actor and already preparing himself for that endeavour with private lessons in thespianism.

But now that we have finally broached the subject of Mick, our stitch in time at last pulls shut. For we can evaluate his transition during that phase by contrasting two scenes, either end of our chasm. The first, of Mick and his betrothed Chrissie, young lovers returning from abroad, stood waiting at the recently renamed Heathrow airport while customs officers comb their luggage in assiduous suspicion. The second, twelve months later, of Chrissie lying upon the floor of Mick's apartment near Regent's Park, her face pale, her features contorted in misery, a phial of sleeping capsules lying empty an inch from her limp fingers. But what occurred to generate this horrible tableau, and the fate of that distressed damsel, we shall now record in a separate tale occupying, in whole, the following portion.

CHAPTER

XLI

❧

Shewing the romantic consequence of earlier incubation.

SHE FELT LIKE a freshly squeezed grape and it was by no means a displeasing sensation. Her breathing was fast and hungry, as if she had just fallen from the very highest mountain crag and landed delirious with the joy of not being dead. Her body felt as if it were furrowed down the centre, the flesh either side turned over like soil from which a field of tulips now bloomed upon her damp and fertile skin. She could feel neither legs nor arms, only wings of the softest down fluttering around her as if gliding upon a midsummer breeze. Her blood within felt like golden syrup, pulsing through her veins in steady glugs, its happy rhythm echoing between her ears. It was as if all the atoms throughout her person were singing to her as one in soothing chorus, and as she lay back and listened to their melody Mrs Dunbar knew, finally, she had been right royally satisfied.

The bed of contentment upon which her pores now hissed in silent glee was not her own, nor that of her satisfier, whose warm chest, though bony, provided a comforting pillow for her head while she waited for her cognisance to float back down to earth. Pressed against his ribs she could hear the solid tempo of his heartbeat as, with one hand free, he retrieved the half-smoked herbal cylinder from the bedside ashtray, placed it between his lips and ignited its tip with one slick snap of a metal lighter. As he blew its vapours above her hair it formed a thin smoky halo, which sent her nostrils twitching at the promise of its lulling sweetness. It was then that she wished she could bottle up this whole scene – the warmth of the bed, the musky incense, the beating ribcage, dawn's light tapping through the hotel curtains – and keep it with her always in an ampoule about her neck, like a magic elixir she could sip whenever happiness deserted her. She gazed up into the eyes of her proud suitor who, gazing back, smiled tenderly, removed the smouldering paper from his lips and placed it between her own. The words he then spoke, however, were not what she expected.

'Mick's crazy about you, y'know.'

Marianne let out a violent cough that was half shock and half laugh, lifting her head off Keith's torso with a start. 'Crazy,' Keith repeated as with one hand he took his turn on their pungent gasper, the other still stroking her nape. He puffed and stretched his arms, then politely drew aside, stood and unhurriedly began gathering his clothes from where they'd been tossed many hours earlier in ruttish urgency. Marianne tugged the cotton sheets up around her shoulders, watching him button, zip and buckle up in wistful wonder. Finally dressed, he bent over and caressed her farewell, sending her atoms into encore of song, before he rose and opened the door with a gentlemanly bow, blowing a kiss through the last embers of weed. She giggled, and his eyes giggled back at her. The door closed behind him, and Keith was gone.

Marianne remained under the sheets, staring at the ceiling and collecting her thoughts as best she could. She had spent a night enamoured with Keith, who had left her with the intelligence that Mick was enamoured with her. She long suspected that Keith, in all his visitations to Courtfield Road, was secretly enamoured with Anita. Then there was Brian, who was enamoured with Anita, yet who had previously tried, but failed, to enamour himself with

Marianne. And there was Chrissie, who was enamoured with Mick, that sentiment evidently no longer reciprocated; only adding to the enamouring confusion now crisscrossing inside her head in a pentagram of unrequited passions. Three women and three Rolling Stones. But out of those three women only one could brag intimacy with all three Rolling Stones, and Marianne felt a furry tickling in her guts as she remembered that providential wench was she.

Somewhere between Courtfield Road and The May Fair hotel, sometime between the rolling of endless tobacco papers, someone between Brian and Keith there had been Mick. That where was Bristol, that time one Friday in early October when Marianne had been summoned to see the group play the city's Colston Hall and gladly gallivanted thither, shaking the dust of Mrs Dunbar from her shoes long before she arrived at the stage door.

What specks of marital confetti might have remained were soon obliterated by the Stones in vicious sound and lubricious sight, the excitations of youth which they typically roused encouraging her own comparable raptures in the wings. Thereafter she received further invitation to join them in their hotel lodgings for recreational fumes and the projection of a new theatrical film concerning a young woman driven to extreme acts of psychopathy on account of her being devastatingly attractive. The film was called *Repulsion* and, by the early hours of Saturday, had nearly succeeded in the aims of its titular objective in clearing the bedroom auditorium of all except its booked occupant, being Mick, and the last remaining visitor, being herself.

Though much time had passed since Mick put an end to his economic studies, his powers of numeracy were not so dulled as to misread the situation as anything other than a simple case of human arithmetic obligating immediate addition into whatever sum total might be agreed upon under cover of bedclothes. This assessment did not, however, account for the fluxions of seduction imposed by Marianne, whose engines of pleasure first required stimulus of lengthy discussion on the court of Camelot, it being her particular prerogative that no knight, however plump and persuasive their lips, might drink from her holy grail who did not know their Gawain from their Galahad. Fortunately Mick was sufficiently versed in such ancient lore and, after impressing with a detailed itinerary of the various Sirs synonymous with that circular table of legend, Marianne cheerfully granted his lance its lot.

But how strange, now thought Marianne, to be reliving that Arthurian tryst with Mick while lying in the aroma of Keith. She could have lain there for ever in paradisiacal aftershock, and possibly would have done if the bedroom was her own, but daylight's muffled cry between the slits of the woollen curtains reminded her of the painful and pressing duty to vacate.

It was late morning when she returned to the otherwise empty home of Mr and Mrs Dunbar, filling the ghostly silence with the phonographic hum of the Stones' latest release, a proud corpus of their many hit recordings to date christened *High Tide And Green Grass*. No sooner had the stylus arm dropped when its business was threatened by the ringing of the telephone, whereupon Marianne picked up the receiver, heard a voice say her name and in the skipped beat of a heart recognised it to be the very same currently singing through her speakers.

In circumstances that exhausted all probability of coincidence, conspiring instead to produce in her the wildest epiphany on the laws of fate, Mick, of that morning's 'crazy' repute, had rung to express his wish to hereon resume their courtship on a permanent footing; according to the negation of her marriage, his noble pledge of infatuation and his assurance that, after three years and an infinity of tiffs, he and Chrissie hadn't so much as a tether left between them. The matter already decided on her behalf, Marianne consented to join him that afternoon for a festive shopping soirée, some Italian supper and quite possibly the rest of her life. And so, by the time she placed the phone back in its cradle, ashes to ashes and dust to dust, 'Mrs Dunbar' was most definitely dead.

Death was similarly uppermost in the train of the future Mrs Jagger, as Chrissie had always hoped she'd become; responding to the news that her station in her betrothed's affections was now otherwise occupied by consuming enough sedatives to render her in that sorry condition as described in the close of our previous chapter. A motion she might even have achieved with success had the mercy of the medical services not intervened and restored her to the conscious infelicity of a life without further pleasure of Mick's colossal puckerings.

And yet little could poor Chrissie, in her rawest sobs, have known what dreadful shame on the horizon of Nineteen Sixty-Seven she had been mercifully spared: that to which Marianne now galloped with all the speed of King Arthur's stallion, were even she, in her nineteen-year-old lovestruck folly, so much as able to remember its name.

CHAPTER
XLII

‚‍ᘓᘒᘒᘘ

In which they accept a revision and refuse a revolution.

OR EVERY SPHERE of celebrity there is an iron gate and for every such gate there is a gatekeeper: theirs the grave responsibility to deny the great many and admit the very few. With that responsibility comes power, and with that power many a delusion of superiority, no different to that which angled the nostrils of our old friend, Sparrow of Manchester, in permanent elevation at the threshold of his sacred Grill Room, or which clogged the veins of our long forgotten foes, the Soho Jazz Mafia, with the venomous elitism of their eventual undoing.

In progressing to the very heights of their musical sphere The Rolling Stones had already passed through many such gates, often by begrudging invitation from keepers whose sensibilities were at odds with the demands of public petition necessitating their unruly admittance. Of these gates, none were bigger, and no keeper more begrudging, than that in the care of Mr Sullivan: a gentleman of such stern lips and sombre pallor as might be expected to flinch at garlic, crucifixes and daylight; who jingled his *passe-partout* as if it were a wand of stardom with which only he could cast its mighty spell, waving it in the faces of the American nation every Sunday evening through their television sets. Mr Sullivan had famously swung his gate open for Elvis Presley – subject to proportionate castration dictating the cameras never dip south of his navel – and was of particular service to The Beatles Pop Group, who allowed that country its first exposure to their stupefied chirrups and undulations of fringe on his very programme.

Where The Beatles Pop Group led, The Rolling Stones usually followed in bolder treads, and indeed circled such around Mr Sullivan during their second visit to the United States in the autumn of Sixty-Four: Mick having the audacity to clothe himself in nothing more formal than a sweatshirt, while his ruckuses of lower body were as improper as anything young Master Presley and his bamboozling trouser puppetry had previously threatened. Mr Sullivan's discretion in having allowed them to pass his precious turnpike was thus immediately taken to task by sacks of postage from correspondents expressive of the same moral violation in respect of the Stones' hair and vestments; soliciting a public apology and a severe letter to Andrew, informing him that his charges were thereby banned from reappearing on his stage, pending only the most dramatic reformations 'in the matter of dress and shampoo'.

In his haste to censor, Mr Sullivan had never taken into account even the smallest possibility that the Stones might yet become a marvel of youth entertainment more agitating than The Beatles Pop Group: one which he would be forced to beckon back through his postern within the year, and introduce twice more before the close of Nineteen Sixty-Six; always with the same waxy grimace of resentment, and with eyes betraying incredulity that any God who made man in his own image would ever breathe life into five such unappealingly rough drafts of that divine form.

Loathsome, then, was the twinge in Mr Sullivan's stomach when, barely two weeks into Nineteen Sixty-Seven, he found himself having to announce them at the top of his bill for a fifth time. And more loathsome still was the scowl which crushed his visage like a picket fence in the wake of a January storm when his ears took inspection of the new disc they intended to perform during that broadcast. As accustomed as he was to their vulgar art after suffering four previous recitals, he nevertheless failed in preparing himself for the depths of indecency to which they had now sunk; engineering a song which, in title alone, made his jaws grind in moral fury. Five words, any one chaste in isolation, but when conjoined in so brazen an arrangement, exclamatory of the most despicable sin as e'er could consign an unmarried soul to eternity of hellfire: 'Let's Spend The Night Together'!

This indignity was thrown into yet sharper relief by Mr Sullivan's accompanying bill of wholesome vaudeville including a puppet frog, a troupe of clog dancers and the combined voices of forty nuns from Pennsylvania singing 'Kumbaya'; the juxtaposition of which with the Stones' nocturnal solicitation was deemed the quintessence of blasphemy, and so necessitated urgent conference with their administrative delegates, Andrew and Mr Klein. The offending semantics debated and dismissed, both parties eventually found fair compromise, one which would allow the group their allotted airtime – having flown from London to New York that weekend for that sole purpose – whilst still performing their song in such a way that wouldn't worry the wimples of the attendant Catholic sisters.

As the guilty foghorn of insouciance, it fell upon Mick to execute the agreed bargain, formally instructed to pronounce '... The Night ...' in modus of ' ... Some Time ...', and so removing all inference of convivial society: a task to which he did not take kindly, as became apparent once Mr Sullivan's cameras started rolling. For though he adhered to the syllable, Mick ensured all substitutions were delivered in midst of the lewdest facial pantomimes his muscles could rally; spinning his eyeballs and spouting his lips into a fleshy tuba until even St Benedict's Mother Superior was left in little doubt as to how '... Some Time ...' would be best spent, and for shame prepared her tools of self-flagellation accordingly.

Leaving Mr Sullivan in a violence of remonstrances and a renewal of purpose in blockading those rapscallions from ever tainting another of his transmissions, the group flew home, where they were scheduled to promote the same disc on an equivalent televisual platform the following weekend.

It was not without poignancy that Andrew engineered their position on *Sunday Night At The London Palladium* which, not three years earlier, had almost cost them, and he, their destiny: contingent as it was upon Mr Easton forgoing the domestic comfort of his favourite programme to spend the last hours of his Sabbath scrutinising the Stones at unpleasantly close quarters in their resident Richmond infancy. And it was not without a sense of occasion that the Stones themselves approached that hour: informing the gentlemen of Fleet Street that time had marched far enough for them to place their weight upon those celebrated boards of convention, in the hope of broadening the scope of its many million viewers to sensory pleasures greater than the occasional flash of a Tiller Girl's camibockers.

Forcefully persuaded by Andrew, whose panic of enthusiasm owed much to his recent indulgence of Spanish castle supplements, the Stones conceded on condition they were awarded toppermost billing to perform four songs, including 'Let's Spend The Night Together'; thankfully failing to yield the same indications of dismay in the show's producer, Mr Locke, as it had in Mr Sullivan, and thus approved without any fuss. Mr Locke, in turn, conceded on condition that the Stones observe just one small punctilio; a trifling formality posing little inconvenience to their persons and to which every guest in its eleven-year history – from Liberace to The Beatles Pop Group – had respectfully complied without exception. The tradition involving nothing more strenuous than their taking position upon a revolving carousel alongside the evening's other turns prior to the final curtain, in which casual attitude they might also wish to animate their hands in a waving motion so as to bid the audience a gracious farewell.

Poor Mr Locke: who, for all the reverence they apportioned his polite insistence they share a roundabout with an Irish comedian, two acrobats and a company of hyperactive Cossacks, would have been as well to have asked them to fasten ties before supper; or spend a lonely evening in a hotel room with a tin of Family Circle sweet treats and not drop a crumb; or resist all exigencies of bladder until locating proper lavatory facilities. Which, it will surprise neither head waiter, chambermaid nor garage attendant to learn, amounted to tenacious refusal.

Though Andrew effected desperate efforts to appease, Mick was still prickling from the previous week's capitulation, and so redoubled his obdurance; unmoved by Mr Locke's ensuing hysteria that, by not partaking in this ceremony, they were guilty of national disgrace worse even than that committed on the forecourt of the Francis Service Station and, on that issue, might as well acquit their wastage in the faces not only of Liberace and The Beatles Pop Group but all nine million viewers of *Sunday Night At The London Palladium*.

Mr Locke's seasoned heart being a reliable barometer of public opinion, the strain The Rolling Stones placed upon his ventricles by remaining stationary at the show's close – just inches from the carousel of their sanction and to the confusion of all but those of a charitably weak mind to presume them unusually susceptible to the trauma of motion sickness – was by no means unique: that agony assuaged only by the great many provincial philosophers moved to comfort him by pen in the letters pages of the land's more upright periodicals; where Messrs 'Andrews of Islington', 'Ross of Romford', 'Heatly of Coventry' and 'Smith of Midhurst' supplied sharp ricochet of disgust.

In order to dissipate the volume of these disagreeable grievances,

Mick had recourse of a sudden invitation from Marianne to join her abroad, where she was duty bound to a festival of song in the Italian town of San Remo; and so removed himself from the dismal shores of Andrews, Ross, Heatly and Smith for happier foreign climes and certainty of amorous union. By day, they entwined on a poopdeck sailing along the Riviera and, by night, they snuggled in the most secluded corner of a local discotheque; where the fatigue of their loving labours eventually took toll on Marianne's eyelids, exhorting her to seek immediate cure. It seemed therefore fortunate that the signor supplying the music in that establishment was also a supplier of physic, and so gladly furnished her with a scantling of capsules, ordinarily prescribed to repel hunger, but equally effective in withholding slumber. She thanked him courteously, returning to their corner where she swallowed one dosage before placing the remaining four in the pocket of Mick's velvet blazer for safekeeping, having no available pouches of her own.

By the next morning Marianne had forgotten all about them. So too had Mick, who wore the same livery back to England, passing through Her Majesty's customs without incident: neither he nor they any the wiser to the small phial all but hidden in the crevices of its lining and the tiny seeds rattling within; gently germinating till the season, fast upon them, to sprout fate's deadly bloom.

CHAPTER

XLIII

A strange interview of no small importance to this History.

WITHDRAWING OURSELVES FROM the pockets of Mick, we now dip into the corresponding pouches upon Brian's person, which were rarely empty of phials, packets, tins and wrappers containing any variety of pills, lozenges, tablets, herbs and resins designed to keep his acumens in that land of the brain where the natives converse in fluent gibberish. This he achieved in blithe disregard for the Law makers of that other land, where his physical being remained during all such vacations of reason, who regarded these preparations from the dimmest vantage and had therefore erected statutes of prohibition excluding their availability from public pharmacies, and carrying severe penalties of detention for those who dared to either procure for themselves or dispense to others. None of which succeeded in dissuading Brian from the course of insensibility upon which his daily train was now fixed, and to which end he had made acquaintance with many fellows in the business of supply, thus placing himself in a position of some risk with regards to his future liberty.

In simple phrase, Brian was a criminal ripe for the cuffing, and could not be more conspicuously so: conducting himself in the few interviews Andrew apportioned him of late as an ambassador for the daft, and advertising the same mental inertia upon the façade of the Stones' latest album, *Between The Buttons*; its cover a photographic portrait of the group stood one foggy November morning on London's Primrose Hill, with Brian's features in unmistakeable rictus of simpleton.

It was with such a visage locked in much the same configuration of vacuity that Brian found himself one evening alone in Courtfield Road: his beloved Anita out of the country on a filming assignment, with neither Gibby nor Groovy Bob to play with, nor the boy named Tara, who had permanently excused himself from their company in regrettable circumstances the week before Christmas; demonstrating the incompatibility of British car and Irish brain when respectively fuelled with petrol and acid, a tragedy which further encouraged Brian to seek respite from grief using that same disabling substance.

Reluctant to risk a whole night of his own society, after filling his pockets with enough apothecary's toils to ensure his carriage jangled like a baby's rattle, he sallied out into the night, walking the short distance to the Imperial Hotel and the sanctuary of its basement, which had been lavished for the purposes of loud music and beverage, and distinguished by the name of Blaise's. The patrons of that club shared a predominance of youth and bore all the qualities of impractical tailoring and limited vocabulary pertaining to the same condition, none wishing to appear less than 'groovy' and none capable of passing compliment greater than the high esteem of 'far out'. These cogitations owing more than a little to the effects of chemical impetus, the young flames of Blaise's were similarly unmoved by those acts of parliament designed to poop the party of their recreational preference; and so ideally suited to Brian's needs of boon companionship and arrested dialogue, which his celebrity attracted with the least effort.

This night being no exception, he had not long descended the steps and sequestered himself a corner of suitably 'groovy' features when two gentlemen approached with the offer to purchase him any drink of his choosing. They were attired somewhat soberly, in dun-coloured contrast to the rainbow of fabric rippling on the nearby dancefloor, while their hair and grooming suggested intimate association with comb and scissors equally unusual in that setting. And yet their dialect was reassuringly peppered with enough interjections of 'man' and 'cool' to temper Brian's first impressions and grant them privilege to wet his tongue and join his table.

The gentlemen declaring this most 'hip' while exchanging a nervous volley of 'cool one, man', when served and seated they proceeded to flatter Brian with enquiry into his public status, having recognised him as a member of one of the country's most popular music colligations. Brian confirmed this to be the case, that he was, indeed, 'the leader of The Rolling Stones'. This solicited the enthusiastic consensus of 'groovy' from his guests across the table, who then steered the conversation in whispered tones to the fresh topic of 'gear' and where they might acquire some 'stuff'.

Assuming this to be an entreaty to deprive him of the rattling store in his current possession, Brian confessed that he had but a handful of 'Bennies' upon him, declaring 'I just couldn't keep awake in places like this if I didn't have them,' at which moment he rummaged inside his pocket, retrieved a small jar of pills and plopped one in his mouth by way of demonstration. The gentlemen concurring aloud that the climate of coolness still reigned, they probed Brian further on whether he knew where they could 'smoke some acid'.

Confused by this remark, which exhibited all the ignorance of the non-'groovy', Brian decided it must be an ironic jape, and laughingly replied that he 'didn't go much on it' of late; not since it had found popularity amongst 'the cats'. The gentlemen voicing curiosity as to when he first smoked that material, Brian's recollection concluded it must have been on his group's first tour with The Lord Bo Diddley and Little Richard, a detail which warranted full applause of 'far out' and the proposal of a second complimentary bumper of alcohol. This Brian accepted, even though his designs on the rest of the evening had since become shaped by a pair of young ladies at an opposite table. He thus excused himself from the two gentlemen to attend this female quarter, allowing them a parting glimpse of the generous lump of hashish secreted in his coat; the intended bait to lure the designated doxies back to Courtfield Road, which he executed without hiccup.

The two gentlemen waited only a few minutes after Brian's departure to down their bumpers and make their own exit, emerging into the South Kensington night, hailing the next available hansom cab and directing its driver to an address just off Fleet Street. Once there, they scurried into a large office building in a state of great excitability, having long discharged all adolescent baggage of 'man' and 'cool' from their vocabulary, each taking their station at a desk with a typewriter in a vast chamber with leaded windows along one side, hazy with smoke and noisy with the clatter of some two dozen others already engaged in the same industry.

'This is a capital scoop, old man,' hooted the first gentleman as he took a fresh sheet of paper and rolled it into his machine.

'Jolly good work, old chum,' laughed the second gentleman feeding his own contraption.

'We ought to get a handsome bonus for this.'

'Most handsome, I should say,' nodded the second gentleman, removing a flask of spirits from a drawer beside him and sloshing a measure in two paper cups from a stack which he retained for that very purpose.

'Can you believe that deuce of a man?'

'An outrage!'

'We'll hang him high!'

'I'll drink to that!'

The two gentlemen raised, bumped and drained their cups with all ceremony of facial seizure and fiery belch that practice entailed. These scenes of jubilation taking place in full view of their colleagues, professional curiosity soon demanded they explain the cause of their euphoria.

'A scoop!' announced the first gentleman to their intrigued audience.

'A scoop and a half,' added his accomplice.

'A prize catch for the next part of our "POP STARS AND DRUGS" exposé,' teased the first gentleman, winking at his friend.

It was then that the gentleman with spectacles sat at the nearest desk – a cigarette dangling in his lips and an aspect of keenest interest upon his face – urged them with much vehemence to spill their beans.

'Only a Rolling Stone!' the first gentleman crowed, both hands now attacking his machine with urgent fingers.

'Ecod!' gasped the spectacled man. 'Which one?'

The first gentleman's fingers suddenly froze above his keys as he turned to the second gentleman, the faintest shadow of a frown now crinkling his forehead.

'The leader, wasn't he?'

'Yes,' the second gentleman nodded, 'that's right, the leader.'

'Jiggins!' cackled the spectacles. 'Mick Jagger, eh?'

'Why, yes,' said the first gentleman, 'that's him, alright!' Then, smiling smugly he continued with his sentence, reading aloud as he typed.

'**Another pop idol . . .**'

CLACK! CLACK! CLACK!

'. . . who admits he has sampled LSD . . .'

CLACK! CLACK!

'. . . and other drugs is . . .'

CLACKETY–CLACK–CLACK!

'. . . Mick Jagger of The Rolling Stones.'

CHAPTER

XLIV

❧

*Containing a selection of causes, honourably
accounting for their effects.*

ICK JAGGER OF The Rolling Stones awoke the
following Sunday to the distant hum of Marylebone
traffic, the passing coo of pigeons on the wing towards
Regent's Park, and the rustling of Marianne in the bed beside him
where both had spent the previous evening in agreeable congress.
Leaving her to awake peaceably, he repaired to the kitchen,
prepared a tray with coffee and pastries, retrieved the stack of
newspapers that had been delivered through his letterbox, and
returned to bed with all the equipage necessary for a prolonged
and languorous lie-in.

Stirred by the scent of freshly ground Arabica beans, Marianne
sat up against the pillows, helping herself to the *Observer* and a
buttery croissant; gently brushing its greasy flakes from the corners
of her mouth as she began reading about angry Russians, heroin
pedlars and a scuffle in South Africa with the US Navy. Mick
quietly sipped his beverage beside her, marshalling his scrutiny
upon the *News Of The World*, flicking over its headline story
concerning the sorry victim of the even sorrier Master Hanratty,
until his lips suddenly spluttered a shower of brown liquid over
page three. This action sufficient enough to alert Marianne to the
likelihood of some disquiet in her lover's cerebration, his

supplement of 'Fucking hell!' delivered with all the intensity of a screech-owl, hastened her inquest to ascertain its cause. Whereupon, Mick tapped a shaky hand at an article headed 'SECRETS OF THE POP STARS', in which various incriminating quotations were attributed to his good self; having apparently spent an evening in Blaise's nightclub, Kensington, in discussion with some gentlemen of that very newspaper, to whom he divulged his full narcotic history in insolent candour.

'Why, that's Brian!' giggled Marianne. 'They mistook you for Brian.' And she laughed for as long as it took her to recognise that levity hadn't yet extended to the other side of the bed, where Mick now modelled his features into the most severe cast; and so reading the language of his eyes, fell silent.

Silence, of a kind no less pregnant with vexation, would not four and twenty hours later fill an office in the Bouverie Street headquarters of the *News Of The World*, where the two gentlemen last described in this work intoxicated with triumph now sat in contrasting defeat, both squirming like a schoolboy up before the beak for placing a kipper in the engine of their science master's car: neither volunteering any syllable of speech to their respective superior, being their editorial chief, who had already administered a sound verbal thrashing upon each of their sore and sorry heads. For it had been brought to his attention, in the clearest terms of legalese, that their skills of reportage were dangerously remiss in respect of that week's article on 'POP STARS AND DRUGS', since Mr Mick Jagger – he of The Rolling Stones as printed on page three, column one, paragraph four – not only denied all knowledge of having spoken to any reporter in Blaise's nightclub regarding his pharmaceutical fancies, but furthermore had instructed his team of solicitors to take their periodical to the proverbial 'cleaners' of layman's idiom, using the heaviest artillery of Law at their disposal.

There was nothing to alleviate the unceasing pangs of the two gentlemen's shame, exhausting all energies of grovelling and failing to produce so much as a crumb of an excuse to lessen their sorrow: which soon produced a torrent of sobs as their chief impressed upon them the likelihood of their incompetence draining the company coffers of a sum of six figures, being the estimated emolument to Mr Jagger for those clumsy stains upon his character; not to mention the public ignominy of the *News Of The World* falling into disrepute as a byword for malpractice, connivance and falsification; however unimaginable that might seem for a paper of such integrity that the nation's husbands had long trusted it as the only outlet of truth where they might air all grievances regarding marriage and table condiments.

The chief stood watching them snivel and suffer, taking due pleasure from all his reproof had generated, until he had tired enough of their increasingly pathetic visages to throw them mercy of reprieve and the confidence of his gleaming hopes of revenge. That no sooner had Mr Jagger's writ landed upon his table when, after assessing their office's precarious position, he immediately set into motion a plan of counter-attack: its objective to fell Mr Jagger from his moral perch by orchestrating such a setting as would provide concrete evidence of his appetite for 'LSD' and all such criminal nostrum, thus embarrassing his claims against them.

This had the intended effect of elevating the two gentlemen's spirits to one of tearful excitement, the chief nevertheless unprepared to divulge any more of this scheme lest they somehow involve themselves in its execution with all the prospects of calamity that posed. The only intelligence he dared spare was that 'his man' was already 'on it', that the machinations were fast in progress, and that he had every confidence in securing Mr Jagger's public ruin: at which time they may wish to redeem themselves, and the tarnished masthead of the *News Of The World*, with what coverage of his disgrace their rehabilitated powers of journalism thought fair and appropriate.

Giddy with this promise of retribution, the two gentlemen bid their chief the humblest gratitudes before removing themselves from his office in reverse footsteps, spines crooked and necks cowering; as we, too, now remove ourselves, albeit in more dignified stature, skipping time and postcode, four days hence and four miles north-west, to a Friday evening in St John's Wood.

Oblivious to his new eminence in Fleet Street as the intended quarry of future headlines, Mick, accompanied by Marianne, and with equipoise of Keith, had accepted an invitation from their old allies The Beatles Pop Group, who had decided to mark the completion of a new recording with a small social gathering in the studios at Abbey Road where they usually conducted their befuddlingly successful labours. The gathering centred around the spectacle of a concert orchestra, hired to supply the finishing gloss of symphonic glissando on a song of irregular design: having no discernible chorus, its lyrics a series of confused jabberations serving no coherent function, punctuated by troubling intervals of unnecessary wailing. This queer mutation they had decided to call 'A Day In The Life' and formed part of their forthcoming long-player, christened, according to the same deficit of reason, *Sgt. Pepper's Lonely Hearts Club Band*: being the result of The Beatles Pop Group's experiments with the very acronym at the centre of the *News Of The World*'s current survey of the nation's minstrels. The handicapping sway of 'LSD' on their wits was evident not only in their music, but visibly in transformations of wardrobe and toilet: now habited in the gayest coloured livery and subjecting their lips to seek shade of a diversity of moustachios; the sum of which was to be mistaken, at a glance, for four impoverished Russian immigrants who had just replaced their peasant sackcloth with the booty from a swoop of the dressing rooms of the Birmingham Hippodrome between performances of *Aladdin*.

These multiple deliriums of disordered imagination demanding medical definition, they had been apportioned the title of 'psychedelia'; by which The Beatles Pop Group had become incurably stricken, encouraging other popular minstrels to follow that example as their influence prescribed. The Stones had not yet succumbed to its epidemic other than in some courageous purchases of shirt and trousers, with Brian their keenest and bravest soldier of fashion and millinery; though as Mick and Keith stood watching the strange circus unfolding before them, both slowly warmed to its contagious absurdity and began imagining how that might enrich their own melodic travails.

The secret, according to George from The Beatles Pop Group – who though never formally declared as such was in fact their favourite member of The Beatles Pop Group: possessing a character of human porridge which, when compared with John and Paul's vainglorious potage or the oafish gruel of Ringo, that renowned housebreaker of criminal folklore, Miss Goldilocks, would have concluded to be 'just right' – was to first 'turn on'. By which he meant yielding all logic of tone and harmony to the muse of acid, such as that which had already disintegrated a great portion of Brian's cerebellum, and in which waters Mick had so far skinny-dipped, while Keith had completed several lengths without hazard.

It so happened that the following evening the Stones had allotted some studio time to commence work on their own new long-player, lacking as they were in all necessary preparations of fresh composition, if ever optimistic of divine inspiration once all instruments were plugged in and the tapes revolving. Encumbered by the now customary entourage of puffing spectators; the absence of Andrew, whose duties as their bespoke producer were slipping down his professional priorities on his own grease of hallucinogens; and a cursory appearance by Brian, whose conduct was understandably sheepish in light of the previous weekend's tabloid indiscretions, their toils amounted to a single scrappy improvisation offering little scope for embellishment. Thus it struck Mick, listening to the playback as they gathered to leave, that they, like The Beatles Pop Group, might reap more exciting crops if they too relinquished all mental poise and 'turned on'. At which moment Keith played the hand he'd been harbouring up his sleeve all week.

The cards had been placed there by Groovy Bob, who days earlier had reacquainted himself with a sovereign of the psychedelic from the United States whose extraordinary merchandise had earned him the deserved epithet of 'the Acid King'. His highness of the high had approached Groovy Bob that Tuesday, knowing him to be an aficionado of his particular chemistry: thus hoping to interest him in some fresh produce, of which he volunteered enough to entertain a small party, such as might suit the humours of, say, The Rolling Stones, with whom, so hearsay informed him, he understood Groovy Bob might have some familiarity. Affected by this generosity and all that his majesty promised in terms of synthesised paradise, Groovy Bob concurred this to be a capital scheme, immediately telephoning Keith, who took little persuasion in offering his recently refurbished manor in the Sussex countryside as a worthy stage to receive that King.

The date affixed for that coming weekend, commencing the moment the Stones had downed studio tools, with that hour now upon them the eager cortege assembled. Of the five Stones only Mick was at liberty to accept Keith's invitation of a night-time drive south, with Charlie and Bill respectively committed to previous arrangements of consort and concubine, and Brian delaying his passage till the Sabbath so he could first spend a night of love and torture at home with Anita, who had that day returned from abroad. Pending Anita's late arrival the next day, Mick's inseparable inamorata Marianne was, until that time, the lone female in their company. Joining them, naturally, was Groovy Bob, whose retinue included his personal butler, a native of Morocco named Ali; the delightful Gibby; a charming photographer named Michael; and a stylish young gentleman of no specified profession called Nicky – swelling their total to eight.

Which left ample room to accommodate the crucial ninth, his magnificence, the Acid King. Their Punch of magic potions without whom there would be no show. The keeper of the ignition key to 'turn on'. And a man, perhaps, considered by some to be very much already 'on it'.

CHAPTER

XLV

⌒e⌒

Of work, rest and play.

SATURDAY WAS STILL clinging to the ledge of time by its last hour when the procession of cars rolled up the narrow, darkened country lane into the grounds of Keith's kingdom. Its master was among the first to step out into the English night, the air cold – the seeing clear with Orion and Sirius twinkling above – shaking his keys from his pocket, unlocking the door and beckoning his visitors to follow and enter. They needed little encouragement to escape the winter chill and so bundled fast behind him, with the dawdling exception of their royal guest of honour, who emerged from the Mini which he'd chauffeured himself, gazing skywards and passing approvingly 'Cosmic!' comment on the stellar fresco overhead in an accent sunburned by one too many days on the coast of California. Once cosseted inside, the fire lit and the hearth prettily aflame, Keith led his revellers on a short tour to familiarise themselves with its amenities: the miscellany of sleeping areas, the bathroom, the kitchen, the dining room and the main living quarter; all such chambers furnished with what furry pelts and stuffed cadavers of slaughtered beasts as he considered to be homely.

Retiring downstairs, all eyes turned expectantly to his eminence, the Acid King. He was a fellow of modest height, and modest hair, resisting any preconceptions of his title to grow his dark locks to any shamanic length. Nor did his clothes cry for special attention, being just the plain side of 'groovy': favouring sweaters and slacks, which he liked to display belted and fastened at navel height, and never more than a few feet away from the leather valise containing the crown jewels of his pharmaceutical infamy – the unveiling of such gems being the just cause of communal suspense.

Acknowledging his subjects and what hopes they'd invested in his sovereignty, the Acid King requested their patience in waiting until the dirty fingers of night had drawn open their sable curtains over the universe, vowing no more than two hours after the morning cock had crowed its first to break their fast with a potation of purest 'White Lightning' conducive to a Sabbath none would ever forget. Not wishing to quarrel with his majesty, Keith and his company satisfied themselves with smoke, spirits and a late supper of bacon and eggs prepared by Groovy Bob's handsome manservant, Ali, who shewed himself to be no less a liege when handed sceptre of stove and orb of griddle.

The logs crackling in the grate, the smoke puffing, the spirits flowing and the odd lozenge popping, the cosmic colloquies finally thinned as one by one, and some two by two, they peeled themselves upstairs to their designated boudoirs. The early hours of Sunday striking their fifth register, Keith was left alone in his favourite throne listening to the gentle music of the smouldering wood; a Romany smile perched on his face, which stayed there long after his eyelids had screwed tight the jar of sleep.

A gentle tap on his shoulder screwed them open again, long after the fire had died and the morning cock exhausted its repertoire: the sun having risen above the trees, their branch tips sticky with winter buds, leafless and silent in the faint February breeze. The vision which greeted Keith – once his optics resumed duty of focus – was a cup of steaming liquid perched on a saucer, held by a hand, at the end of an arm, connected to a body; from which peeped a neck, supporting a not unfamiliar visage, which softly whispered 'time to turn on', and which, once his cognisance had fully clocked in for business, he remembered to be the Acid King. Keith gratefully took hold of the cup and saucer, his nostrils twitching over the steam, which smelt and looked like regular navvy's tea, but was not, as the Acid King assured him, of a kind that any layman might wish to imbibe at the commencement of their shift: being sweetened with a generous dash of the famed lysergic 'White Lightning', which would send any hodman into such gibbers of confusion as to toss the contents of their luncheon box into the nearest cement mixer believing it to be an especially famished elephant answering to the name of 'Cecil'.

As Keith's day, as scheduled, involved nothing in that way of manual labour, he gladly sipped it down his throat and waited, as the Acid King instructed, for its liquid electricity to short-circuit his uppermost storey. Leaving Keith to softly stew, His Royal Acidity crept upstairs, where he visited each of the bedchambers in turn; wakening their inhabitants with the same tea ceremony, wishing them 'a pleasant trip' and suggesting they all convene below in harmonious imbecility within the hour.

The Lightning took longer to strike than many had expected, its initial stages causal only to nausea in Marianne, who for a while feared she may soon be reacquainted with the handsome plate of bacon and eggs she had so enjoyed the previous evening. And then, quite suddenly, one by one, room by room, the waking brains of Keith, Mick, Marianne, Groovy Bob, his obedient Ali, Gibby, Michael and Nicky flipped like pancakes, and not one returning to the pan of their craniums in which they'd been fried.

All was colour, and all colours sang: blues screamed, and the screams crept over walls like knots of ivy; oranges hollered, and the hollers bubbled between the threads of the carpet like a field of pumpkins; yellows bellowed, and the bellows rippled across the ceiling in a tangle of glossy ribbons; whites howled, and the howls shone in rays of brilliant light from teeth, eyes, toes and fingertips; greens moaned, and the moans curled in clouds of thick emerald smoke, spinning circular dances in every direction. When they rose to get dressed their clothes licked their bodies with cotton tongues and their buttons flew away from their fingers like startled butterflies. When they sailed downstairs, their feet felt no steps and the bannisters bent and waved to the touch like bulrushes. And when they finally assembled and looked into one another's faces with the same shiny faraway eyes, all was sweetness and joy and music and love.

And then salty air, and gull cries, and the splash of waves, and they found themselves on a beach, to where they must have journeyed by magic carpet. They stared at the surf which frothed and groaned with the sad song of Poseidon, the notes leaping out of the spray and floating up to the sky in silver vapours, where they melted like the wings of Icarus in the afternoon sun. They giggled at the movement of the sand glistening gold and pearl at their feet; moving constantly, they knew, from the shift of its trillion snakes squirming beneath the surface. They trod on seaweed pods of crystal and shells of polished bronze, and when Mick bent down to pick up a lump of driftwood Marianne squealed aloud that he'd found Excalibur, which must be returned to the Lady Of The Lake, and together they tossed it into the water.

And then the gulls stopped crying, and the waves fell silent, and they found they were in a chariot speeding through fens and spinneys on a quest to find the magic castle, where they hoped to meet a wizard called Edward who collected lots of pretty pictures of floppy clocks and floating apples. But the horses pulling the chariot seemed to be lost, and all the hedgerows were yelling at them that they'd gone the wrong way, until finally they found the magic castle, but the portcullis was closed, and the wizard wasn't there. The sun was now setting over the hills, and if they didn't go home soon somebody mentioned they might all be eaten by vampire bats, and so they turned the chariot around, racing against the dusk. And by the time they were pulling up into Redlands Lane, the horses had gone, and the chariot had turned into a transit van, and though all was still sweetness and joy and music and love, it wasn't quite as sweet or joyful or loud or as lovely as it felt like it had been only a few hours ago.

The Acid King and his eight court jesters had not long resumed their slothful repose in the living room when the sound of another vehicle pulling up outside heralded the entrance of two more. Wondering at first whether it might be the overdue Brian and Anita, with all the fractious baggage they might bring, Keith was somewhat relieved to open the door and see George from The Beatles Pop Group with his wife, Pattie, now recalling that which the White Lightning had temporarily burnt from his memory; that he'd invited them down two days earlier. Welcoming them with smoke, incense, and a gallery of faces exhibiting every stage of intellectual vacancy, they found two available cushions on which to slump from whence they attempted to blend into the giggling lethargy as best they could, intellectually disadvantaged as they were in having missed all ritual of 'turning on'.

As night descended, their culinary saviour, Ali, began preparing a spicy supper of his native homeland; Groovy Bob found a quiet nook to temper his head with a pinch of opium; Mick rummaged through Marianne's small purse of cosmetics and started applying them to his own features with great tranquillity; Marianne announced that all their gallivanting had left her feeling a mite grubby and so fluttered upstairs for a recuperative soak; Keith briefly vanished then reappeared in a change of apparel, taking command of the phonograph and feeding it the latest collection of electrified whinges by a Mr Dylan; Michael lay staring up at the beams across the ceiling in his camera's viewfinder as Gibby and Nicky stared with him in empathetic paralysis; George and Pattie sat in silent calculations of etiquette as to the earliest appropriate juncture when they might be allowed to leave without being considered un-'groovy'; and the Acid King rolled smoke after sense-crippling smoke from the uncommonly fragrant herbs in his valise of delights.

The hour gone seven, Marianne at last reappeared after her bath, inconvenienced by her sudden shortage of fresh vestments, but being clever enough to make a temporary tunic of the animal pelt in the master bedroom; large enough to preserve her modesty as the novel guise in which she presented herself keenly demonstrated. The dress code now shifting towards the prehistoric, George and Pattie seized this moment as ripe for exodus, politely bidding all the merriest of evenings before driving off into the night at such speed that, after five minutes, those they left behind started to doubt whether their visit was yet another of the dissipating White Lightning's mirages of the mind.

Possibly the television was a mirage, thought Marianne, and they weren't really sat watching Mr Simon Templar and his elastic eyebrows with the volume turned down, Mr Dylan groaning a substitute dialogue, but dumbly gazing at blank space instead. And that face at the window, peeping around the gap in the curtains like a bothersome old crone, thought Keith. That must be a figment too. So he was probably wasting his time catching its eyes, flicking it two fingers and snarling 'Fuck off!' And when he looked again and saw it had vanished he thanked his wits that he had, of course, been correct, and he laughed huskily, and everyone else laughed with him, none knowing or caring why. And it was only when the chorus of mirth had finally ebbed away that it registered someone, or something, was banging very loudly on the front door.

'A Menagerie Of Mirages'

XLVI

*In which the Author removes himself, deferring all
curation of narrative to a report from the files of the
West Sussex Constabulary.*

THE NIGHT OF Twelfth of February, Nineteen Sixty-Seven, is one which I have no doubt will haunt me to my rest, but pray God not plague me any further beyond the realms of this mortal plane. It is my duty as Her Majesty's subject, a keeper of peace and a guardian of Law, to make record of that hideous evening so that it may be used by the Crown to punish the perpetrators of the evils described; but even were it not, I would still feel compelled to pen this account in the vain hope that by doing so my soul may somehow be cleansed of those abominations which yet deform my visage in permanent grimace of one who has stared into the jaws of Hell.

'It was earlier that morning of the Twelfth, a Sabbath, which only multiplies the shiftless stench of wickedness in my nostrils, that I received the call which was to set me on collision with these mental agonies described. I was sat at my bureau in the station at Chichester, reading a constable's report of a public disorder the previous evening in Bognor Regis involving a gentleman of personal acquaintance, whose character I would have happily vouched for with all masonic kinship, and yet here, in black and white, a story of gross intemperance and arrest for insulting a police officer; the crime all the more atrocious for the detail that, between police vehicle and station cell, the accused evacuated in his pantaloons. Naturally, this intelligence soured my enjoyment of the steaming cocoa the desk sergeant had courteously brewed upon my pedantic instructions of umber hue, so when the telephone rang I was pleasantly relieved, hoping it would steer me to a happier train of thought other than befouled underclothing. How pitiful a man's hope seems in hindsight.

'The caller was a gentleman from a London newspaper, the name of which our agreed vow of confidentiality prevents me from citing, though I cannot see how it should matter, other than to apportion credit where due to that courageous publication which, as is their inexplicably modest wont, professional discretion forbids me. Over the course of the next ten minutes the gentleman furnished me with such scandal that I was at pains to request him repeat every shocking particular, and had I not our conversation would surely have been over in half that time. His intelligence involved a house, not far from the coast at West Wittering, which had, in the last year, been purchased by a minstrel from a popular music ensemble called The Rolling Stones: partial as I am to the diversion of melody in the hands of the great maestro Mantovani, I could not pretend to be familiar with their craft, but I understood they were of that obscene strain whose success was solely attributable to the gullibility of youth, and so felt no cause to pardon my ignorance.

'It was the troubling claim of my journalistic confidant that the house he spoke of was, that very weekend, the scene of criminal debauchery involving the consumption of prohibited toxins. I could scarce believe such things were possible on our simple peninsula, but chose to follow his warning call with provisional enquiries of my own to establish whether the persons and location he referred to were, indeed, correct with our parish. It seemed they were and, with a sense of foreboding that was not without justification, I acted without delay.

'Over the course of that afternoon I placed, and received, several more telephone calls to and from my superiors in Lewes and the Metropolitan force in London, who advised me on the wisest methods to handle the situation; with supplementary cautions which, as egressed, were a blessed adjunct to my otherwise comprehensive procedural knowledge. By sunset I had obtained the necessary warrant from a Justice of the Peace and assembled a squad consisting of myself, a detective superintendent, and sixteen constables from the surrounding district in whom I had to place all trust that theirs was a mettle that might withstand the perils unknown which stretched before us. All wore the faces of good, just men, and women, and as our three-strong caravan of vehicles set off on our mission I experienced an unexpected paternal flush, as if I had that day gained fourteen sons and three fair daughters; and perhaps they in turn looked upon me as the benevolent papa that the lottery of genetics had cruelly denied them.

'The house was situated at the curve of a country lane, which assumed a grim and diabolical aspect as we drove at crawling speed so as not to announce our approach, and parked as close to its perimeter fence as we could in the pitch blackness. The time was half past the hour of seven. My first task was to dispatch an officer for a reconnaissance of the grounds with the purpose of noting the registration of any vehicles in that vicinity. PC Parker returned with that inventory as demanded: at which point the sagacity of my superiors bore heavy upon me as I recognised the combination "LGF 965D" as that to be granted immunity from apprehension. For I was assured it belonged to a Mr Harrison of The Beatles Pop Group, a distinction which failed to awake my sympathies until that opinion was corrected in point of him being Her Majesty's subject, a Member of the British Empire. Whatever weakness of the brain possessed this Harrison to socialise with these vipers, I concurred his was a medallion not be tarnished, and so it was with immense relief when at five minutes to eight o'clock that same number plate was seen vanishing away from the premises down Redlands Lane – the Member of that Most Excellent Order at the wheel – and we could finally proceed at no ignominious cost to the Palace.

'My adopted children snaking behind me, I led the advance on foot, in what PC Witchem referred to as a "conga line"; an inappropriate moment of levity that I ascribed to the young lad's nerves, and which, in my pity, I let pass without reprimand. Guided by the distant lights through the trees from inside the house, we trod along a dirt path, then across a small bridge spanning a moat until secreting ourselves in the bushes opposite the front elevation. I could hear music echoing from within the house of a grisly variety, all marrow bones and cleavers; though I was somewhat thankful for its provision of a welcome muffler to any tell-tale sounds of boot crunching on twig and gravel as our ambush took formation.

'I instructed PC Fubbs, a woman officer who wore her experience on her face like the rough jottings of long division, to undertake a cursory inspection of the downstairs windows; the curtains all drawn except one which she sidled beneath, craning her head above the sill until the rest of us could define its silhouette against the yellow glow within like the pupil of a cat's eye. Unfortunately, what she was at pains to observe so discombobulated her sense of diligence that she was seen by one of its occupants, who acknowledged her in the coarse and discourteous fashion PC Fubbs will no doubt make plain in her own accompanying narrative, as requested by the Crown.

'The upper hand of surprise now falling limp, I raised the signal to attack and pressed ahead to the threshold, my officers forming a line in flank so our united front would assuredly overwhelm the spirit of anyone opening the door. I then braced my knuckles and knocked. Half a minute passed with no answer, and so I knocked a second time, harder still. The third time I banged. The fourth, I kicked. The fifth, the door finally opened, and the infernal music within flooded out into the night air.

'The creature confronting me was, as established in the first transports of the ensuing interview, the proprietor, a Mr Richards: apparently just twenty-three years of age, though the ducts of his vagabond visage seemed gouged by centuries of turpitude. It was immediately obvious from his unusually serene character and incongruous lack of alarm at the sight of a chief inspector and over a dozen uniformed police that he was most likely under the influence of strong liquor or some other potent minister to insentience; indeed, it is my understanding – gathered from overhearing his remarks to several officers during our occupation – that he was sufficiently enfeebled of mind to misconstrue us for "hobgoblins", and I their appointed "emperor". I produced the warrant from my trench-coat and formally declared my intentions: that I was a Police Chief Inspector of the West Sussex Constabulary, and that I possessed a warrant to search those premises and the persons in them under the Dangerous Drugs Act of Nineteen Sixty-Five. If he comprehended the sudden gravity of his predicament, his features failed to exhibit as much, and so pressing him aside, I stepped across the doorstep, my detachment following behind. And into the bottomless pit we fell.

'Lord, forgive me that blasphemy mine eyes have seen! For I had not entered the living area more than two seconds when I knew every word of the Good Book to be gospel, not that I ever doubted it. As here, blinding my innocence for all eternity, was Sodom and Gomorrah. An unutterable horror filled my bosom and appalled my every sense. The music still polluting our ears now assumed the hideous strain of a nasal warlock engaged in indecipherable pagan summons. The air was stagnant and foul. But as to the odour itself, how shall I describe it? It was not alone that it was composed of the ills of mortality, and with the pungent, acrid smell of musky flora, but it seemed as though corruption had become itself corrupt. Faugh! It sickens me to think of it. Every breath exhaled by these monsters seemed to have clung to the place and intensified its loathsomeness.

'Undead, so they looked, for more dreadful apparitions were never raised in a churchyard. Waxy-eyed slaves of torpescence, slithering across one another like the reptilian tresses of Medusa; their bodies benumbed, their faces rotten with venal intent. I counted eight such aberrations of man, though at least one I knew not what sex I was scrutinising: for though their physique betrayed the boyish, my faculties were obfuscated by their luxurious curls and the shine of lipstick, unable to distinguish if they were a pansy fit for whipping or the ugliest woman of the stews in Christendom.

'The one exclusion was as brazen a whore as might be found in the darkest crevice of Babylon, who presented herself in clear ache of immoral satiation; naked as sin, the natural tools of her depraved trade shrouded in the hide of a wild beast, which she squeezed so tightly to her person as to appear one and the same. This she-wolf was, indeed, an animal untamed by clean society, as I was to discover when PC Fubbs led her upstairs to search her person. Need I begin to describe how stiff my rod of disgust when she dropped her pelt in full view, basking in her creamy nakedness which she bent, hind-forward, towards the aghast officer and enquired: "Where would you like to start?"' Ay, hers was a sauce fit for hanging!

'I immediately turned away, lest the dimples of her soft translucent skin and the delicate bounce of her strawberry locks upon the cherry tips of her fleshly cissoids sear themselves upon my conscience; adding to that night's gathering conspiracy of perspiring nightmares to which I have since become hapless victim. But even in wilful circumvention, there was no escaping her impiety, for no sooner had I peeled my eyes away from her lustful frame than I caught sight of this fallen Eve's bedside accessories: being a book on witchcraft and two stray ostrich feathers, their purpose a mystery my throbbing unease had no righteous desire to solve.

'I instead abetted in the search of the surrounding cupboards and drawers, whereupon I located a green velvet blazer, its pockets containing a small vessel with four white capsules. My blood cooled and the most uncomfortable dryness spread throughout my mouth. I had found that which we had sought, and that which we had most feared: the chemical sacraments of Satan himself!

'I carried them downstairs, where I demanded their owner identify themselves. The villain quickly came forward, the epicene imp of miscreation who had so aggravated my internals upon arrival. He was a Mr Jagger, twenty-three years old, whose substantial orifice was the subject of unnecessary ribaldry in the police van on our return journey, when PC Witchem and his colleagues speculated on how many Mars bars Mr Jagger might be able to consume at once; a thread of conversation which soon stooped to vile conjectures of coital practice which, too sickened to rebuke, I feigned not to hear; though their twisted caprice has since become a sick, contagious gossip throughout the constabulary. This I mention only to reiterate the debasing environment my squad had been cursed to endure, and how it contaminated the minds of otherwise perfectly decent police officers. But I digress.

'Mr Jagger's defence was that the capsules I had unearthed were legal stimulants to combat the onset of tiredness. A picture formed in my mind as to his motives for resisting sleep, and how they might involve late nights of ostrich feathers, lipstick, fur rugs and that comely harlot who we shall refer to only as "Miss X". I cannot deny the impulse to lay him by his heels there and then was overpowering, but to my credit I resisted, informing Mr Jagger that they would be taken away for scientific tests which, if proven to be the contrary to that which he claimed, would carry the direst consequences. His suspect container was added to the formidable cache of highly irregular artefacts my officers had elsewhere located and bagged for examination: including the physic in possession of a Mr Fraser which he purported to be prescribed for diabetes; several dozen cigarette ends, some bearing the demonic markings "B&H"; a candlestick of especially dubious design; and a shady looking selection of sachets from the kitchen containing ill-smelling preparations marked "Mayonnaise", "Ketchup" and other such arcane jargon of the criminal under-world. I had seen enough.

'There was only one fellow left to be frisked, a gentleman with a high waistline and a grating North American accent who, despite these afflictions, was by far the most amenable, as my superiors in London had earlier primed me he would be. His effects included an attractive leather valise, the contents of which he assured me were many rolls of unexposed film – landscapes, nature subjects and the like, as I recall him describing – which, were I to open that case to verify, would be ruined through exposure to the surrounding light. I consider myself a shrewd judge of character, and so I have every confidence that by complying with his petty request I in no way compromised the objectives of our investigation.

'My last exchange was with Mr Richards once more, who I took aside while my officers boxed up the impeaching tokens of vice before returning to our vehicles. His devil-may-care countenance had not altered in the hour we had ransacked his lair, so I reminded that devil that he very much ought to care, and should the results of our laboratory tests show that dangerous drugs had been used on that premises but were not related to any individual, he would be held responsible. The fiend had impudence to scoff in my face.

'As I walked back across the lawn, my poisoned lungs gasping for clean air, the noxious music seemed to grow louder, as if it had leapt into my ear like a parasite, refusing to leave, tormenting me with Beelzebub's grizzling curse repeating *"Everybody must get stoned"*. O Lord, let he without sin cast the first! But I think I need share nothing else of that unholiest of nights, though I could yet add page upon page of forensic horrors. What black details vex my slumber are mine own burden to bear, and bear them I must. Pray let justice prevail, and God save the Queen.

'Her faithful servant,

'Chief Inspector _____

'West Sussex Constabulary.'

CHAPTER

XLVII

*The narrative returned to its rightful Author: who wastes
no time whipping it towards the last lap.*

THE TWO HANDS belonging to Mr Klein pressed
themselves together, spread fingertip to spread fingertip,
like an axe-head of meaty flesh and steely bone; as was
customary during those first pulsations of blood and knitting
muscle which roused the orchestra of his features to play their
unhappiest facial symphony. Conducting it was the knowledge – as
fresh as it was overpoweringly putrid – that the money-printing
mechanism he'd carefully assembled, regularly oiling and polishing
it for maximum efficiency, had suddenly developed gremlins in its
works which, if untreated, would assuredly conspire to permanent
malfunction and a regrettable end to the flow of crisp century notes
necessary to fan him to the temperature of cool contentment he
preferred. Or so he received the telephone call from a frantic
Andrew, informing him in gasps and panics of speech that two of
his Rolling Stones had, again, fallen foul of the police: this time on
account of their unhealthier recreational appetites, their fate as yet
unknown until the completion of scientific analyses; the conclusions
of which posed dire risk, not merely of prosecution but, at worst,
the sewing of mail sacks and enforced jaspery.

Mr Klein was not a fellow who took well to being made a fool,
as he now feared the bells of such were jingling around his ears.

For he had long regarded his five English scamps as his winning hand at the card table of life; one at which he had elevated his genius to mark the deck in such a way as to assure all immunity to loss, consummate in the art of play, whether at Pope Joan, bezique or whist. And yet he found himself entertaining the prospect of having been all this time carrying a brace of jokers who, in their ingratitude for the opulent sums he hoarded with such vigilance that even they were scarce allowed to withdraw more than the occasional sous, had been so reckless to compromise its future expansion. So his fingertips pressed and his brow tightened and, by degrees, the volume of the symphony increased until it battered the whole universe about his ears.

It kept battering, day after day, as whispers in the newspapers became polite coughs creeping ever nearer to the front page, whence they screamed in boldest type. Adding undue timpani to Mr Klein's adagio of anger was the insolence of Mick who, over the course of the following week, when he ought to have behaved the model of contrition, found new means to antagonise the spears of Fleet Street already jostling to pierce his hide. Invited to attend a gala performance by the Royal Ballet in the presence of Princess Margaret, he and Marianne had arrived in their seats eight slovenly minutes after the curtain had risen, when the famous Mr Nureyev was already hurling his tightly trussed periwinkles from one end of the Covent Garden Opera House stage to the other. It was only by mercy of this same phenomenon – so keenly observed through Her Highness' opera glasses in all sharpness of focus and with all the vigilant speed of a tennis umpire following the ball in play at all times – that the Princess did not personally witness the ensuing commotion in the dress circle as the tardy lovers were shooed to their seats; a disturbance which nevertheless came to be recorded in the next day's periodicals in such language as emphasised its affront to the Palace: also serving to rob Mr Nureyev of the headlines his airborne baubles might have ordinarily garnered had they not been so disrespectfully upstaged.

The Stones, so it seemed to Mr Klein, were making unnecessary problems of prosperity, the situation in no way improved by Andrew's own chemically dependent twitchings. Thus, when the sorry delegation of Mick, Keith and Brian requested his charity of emergency funds so they might temporarily escape their domestic witch-hunt and remove themselves abroad, though Mr Klein seldom enjoyed siphoning their riches, he concurred: believing their taking a foreign refuge to be a strangely sensible motion in the current climate, and so forwarded them the necessary assets in vain hope the ancient tonics of sun, sea and sand may yet cure the pox of social idiocy infesting their functions.

Their destination was Morocco – a land which had already impressed upon their fancies in home furnishings and the fumes that clung within – where they planned to convene with their traumatised compatriots Groovy Bob and Gibby in the city of Marrakesh, albeit by separate modes of transportation: Mick by air and Keith by road, caravanning through France and Spain in his 'Blue Lena', as he had latterly christened his Bentley, and in company of Brian and Anita who, in compensatory solidarity for absenting themselves from his recent weekend retreat (soured as it was by the eighteen interlopers from the West Sussex Constabulary), happily accepted his generosity of wheels and chauffeur to join him in that leisurely expedition.

The journey had not long begun when Keith allowed his troubles to dissolve in the upland Gallic vistas and the comforting exchanges of Anita: whose teeth and eyes had long purred at him in a language of their own making, to which he now believed himself close to fluency. So too was Brian – sat between them in the rear of the Blue Lena while their chauffeur steered her over river and valley – whose sight, though compromised by its customary fog of linctus, caught enough flutters and blushes to decipher his own translation. These furtive linguistics continued to squeeze the trigger of Brian's melancholy until, when climbing in altitude towards the city of Toulouse, his visage drooped to such a picture of ill health that even Keith and Anita were moved to halt their coquetry, concurring they should seek him medical assistance forthwith, and instructing their driver to find the nearest infirmary.

Such a haven was located in Albi, a town of charming medieval design upon the River Tarn, where Brian was delivered into the care of its local sanatorium and the arms of one Nurse Marie. First diagnosing her new patient as a woman of grim physiognomy, only after persuading 'Mademoiselle Jones' to change into a hospital gown did the folly of Nurse Marie's assumption swing into clearer perspective: correcting her professional opinion to that of a young gentleman suffering from *'les diables bleus'*, whose only hope of exorcism was to spend several days recuperating at blessed grace of her cold compresses and any fusses of pillow propping and chamber pot his poorly condition required.

As Brian lay horizontal, in his first weary transports of convalescence he detected the warm touch of Anita, stroking her fingers atop his own as she whispered her pledge that she, and Keith, would remain in the vicinity for as long as it took him to recover his faculties and resume their passage to the North African coast. So satin was her voice, so soothing his pillows, and so woozy the analgesic Nurse Marie had prescribed (oblivious to the infusion it affected with that already sloshing around his skull), that Brian was moved to regard Anita as an angel of mercy, one so beautiful and compassionate that he could not allow himself to clip its wings; and so granted her full permission to fly on to Morocco, where he would join them as surely as his strength would soon return, comforted as he would be by the knowledge she would be feathering their bed ready for his arrival.

It was only when, following a brief but delirious repose, the analgesia weakened and Brian awoke, realising Anita had vanished and Keith with her, and that he was alone in a strange bed in a strange town in a strange country that his heart began to palpitate, his hair to bristle up and his thoughts teem with presages of betrayal and cuckoldry. Remembering all he had seen unfold in the Blue Lena, he could not help but speculate what might progress in his absence and thus underwent a severe paroxysm of dismay which tested Nurse Marie's powers of sedation to their very limits.

Sleep offered no respite to the pictorial torments that capsized his dreams, and when he finally opened his eyes, bagged by panic and grooved with misery, he found waiting by his bed table a telegram, informing him that Keith and Anita were presently enjoying all the Spanish hospitality of a hotel in Marbella, and his despair intensified.

Brian asked Nurse Marie to dispatch an immediate response, requesting Anita drop all castanets and return to comfort him without loss of time. When another day's bedridden anguish passed without answer, he sent another: its language desperate, its sentiment begging, its tone demanding and its intelligence assuring her that, as he would soon be fit enough for discharge, she had best prepare herself for their amorous reunion: the speedier the better.

This second missive was infinitely more successful than the first, soliciting a short but courteous reply acknowledging its receipt, and assuring Brian that Anita was already on her way, a detail which greatly decreased his disturbances of thought as he counted the hours until her advent – at which time they returned with a vengeance to confirm his terrors. For there was something inexplicably odd about Anita. A look upon her face that he had never seen before. The look of a by no means displeasing sensation, much like that of a freshly squeezed grape. And Brian did not like it one bit.

CHAPTER

XLVIII

The whipping continues and a spirit is broken.

IT HAS BEEN noted, even by minds lesser than those which have devoted their life to the field of biology, that a wound received on Monday may yet scab over by Wednesday and be gone entirely come the hour for bathing on Sunday. Or, as that note usually finds favour in popular idiom, 'Time is a healer'. Which, while true for some casualties, only applies if the urge to pick that prickling scab is resisted: for if not, the wound is reopened and the risk of pus, infection and permanent scarring greatly increases, making mockery of that same fishwife wisdom and all who invest their faith in its clockwork.

So it was for Brian who, from the moment Anita collected him from the hospital in Albi, though cured by Nurse Marie of his dismal *diables bleus*, had allowed the passage of their days apart to scab his soul with jealousy; an itch he could not help but scratch until it seeped thoughts green and rotten into every fissure of his cerebral tissue. The Anita he once knew had vanished and in her place stood a once cherished instrument he was convinced had been strummed by another's hand; its tuning unfamiliar and its frets foreign to his touch. When she stared into his eyes it was with a twinkling otherness, as if she saw not Brian but somebody stood one pace behind him. Her laugh, too, seemed to ring with a cold queerness, like she was sharing a joke with some unseen spirit at his expense. And then he realised that, where once she had been the phantom of all he desired, walking beside him always even when oceans apart, she now must have taken a new phantom of her own.

Thus Brian's scab grew itchier and the seepage fouler with every mile that brought him closer to Morocco and the enemy of his suspicions, who he duly found waiting in the desert city of Marrakesh, sat by the pool of their palatial hotel in company of Mick and an elderly gentleman who introduced himself as 'Mr Beaton': a fellow Englishman abroad whose reputation preceded him in most civilised quarters as a photographer of fashionable society. That Brian made no effort to ingratiate himself to Mr Beaton's famous lenses was omen enough that he was out of his usual humour, having already focused all force of his envy elsewhere so as to have none spare for Mick: the centre of the old gentleman's attentions at the exclusion of all others, for reasons Brian would never have fathomed, and which Mr Beaton himself confided only to the pages of his diary; the crux a conundrum of some delicacy as to whether Mick was 'beautiful' or, conversely, 'hideous'.

Alas, before Mr Beaton could form a more solid opinion of this mysterious pulchritude, Mick returned to London; apportioning blame for his exodus on the sudden change in convivial climate since Brian arrived, and since Anita's eyes simultaneously resumed their gay tarantellas with those of Keith. Though trifling gestures, light as air, they were strong as proofs of holy writ to Brian's scabrous apprehensions. And yet he could do nothing, only sit and let their gazes tickle at tame distance: looking to all others who observed him like the meekest wittol in Marrakesh, yet inwardly boiling with blackest Venetian fury.

How like the Moor, indeed, was Brian, and what juicy meat to the green-eyed monster's mockery did his bitter senses carve. Ever it is the cuckold's curse that the very image he fears most is that which illuminates the stage of his waking fancy in grotesque exaggeration; positioning their loves in strange akimbos, obsessing over the fine details of how her parcels of hair may bounce in riggish rhythm, how her clammy fingers may grip support of bedpost or hoist of oak branch in hornbeaming tango, and how every gasp of encouragement may change in pitch until forming a melody of moans smashing between the sides of his skull like the clapper of a bell. These, the screaming peals of Anita's pleasure, now deafened Brian's processes; drumming fraught shockwaves across his visage which, already much too pale and worn, could ill afford to add more scribbles to that unappealing sketch.

Pity, then, the two employees of Marrakesh's oldest profession obliged to entertain that terrible portrait when on his second evening in the city Brian – who by that stage had become dishevelled of all sane thought – took advantage of one of Anita's frequent absences of flirtation to request that duo's custom in his hotel suite. Desperate men are oft driven to desperate measures, and desperate indeed was Brian's prayer that, through art of his rival promiscuity, Anita would soon feel the taste of jealousy's poisoned brew upon her own scarlet tongue, recognise the error of her wandering ways, pine for forgiveness and restore herself to the path of fidelity.

Let it not be assumed Anita made this discovery without emotion: for upon returning to her chamber and catching Brian in flagrante delicto with a pair of frisky Arabian trulls, earning their dirhams in scenes which prompted both to reconsider their future services with a much firmer eye on the rate of inflation, she allowed the organs of her repulsion all energy of voice. Mistaking her cry as a gasp of defeat, Brian poured oil upon the pyre of his fatuity by suggesting that Anita show due submission by joining him and his accomplices, the names of whom beggared the life of him at that present interval, in that same private festival of easy virtue. Only when she refused, sparing no hostility towards those anonymous tradespersons who were quick to robe and withdraw, did the hopelessness of his cause bear heavy on Brian's delusions and shrivel his dignity. The battle lost – oh, unsmiling villain! – he raised his hands, and in that drastic action stooped to the very lowest gutter of his sex: as all such brutes who strike or shove a damsel, be she innocent seraph or deceiving harpy, castrate the scrappy remains of their manhood.

It was the following morning, when poolside levity was in noticeably short supply, that Mick grimly read on Anita's swollen face the forecast for the next few days and made expedient his escape, passing mumbled apology to Mr Beaton who was led to understand that 'things' were becoming 'fucking heavy'. Having no desire, now their prince had flown, to remain in consort with those he considered vulgar gypsies, Mr Beaton beat a similar retreat, as did the equally wary retinue of Groovy Bob and Gibby; no more charmed by Brian's company and its unhelpful influence upon all efforts of relaxation. Which left only Keith, Anita, her bruises, their creator, and the handful of loose acquaintances they'd befriended in the hotel bar: bonding whether over mint tea or other more flammable local horticultures.

Through invitation of one such new confrère, Brian was provided with opportune excuse to spend a few hours' grace away from Anita – now shirking from his touch and affecting infuriating hypnosis by the duck and splash of Keith's diverting display of 'peekaboo' in the shallow end – when coaxed on an afternoon's shopping expedition of the city's ancient medina. Wandering through the perfumed smoke and haggling chorus of its tightly packed bazaars, he happily forgot his troubles, and during the rare flashbacks of grief when he lacked the will to do so, there was always a pipe on hand to help puff his train of oblivion back to speed. He even bought one of his own as a souvenir, a bone-encrusted hubbly bubbly that gurgled joyfully whenever he inhaled and, for the first time in more weeks than he could remember, a fixed grin, warm and true, took hostage of Brian's lips.

It was dusk when he returned to the hotel with a gay spring in his stumble to show Anita his purchase, hoping that it may yet find function as a pipe of peace to put an end to any further unpleasantness. Heading straight to the pool, he saw she was no longer there. Nor, when he checked, was she in their bedroom. Nor her clothes, her case, her hairbrush nor her other effects.

His every pore starting to sweat, he flew down to the bar and restaurant but she was nowhere to be seen. Then, running with shaky steps, dread bellowing his lungs in gasps, he knocked on Keith's room. His heart thumped as its door opened, thumping harder still when he found himself staring at a maid with a duster in her hand, a shrug upon her shoulders and a crater in her vocabulary where the answers to his questions should be.

Fortunately, the concierge at the front desk with the fez and pencil moustache fared much better in translation, and it was from him that Brian learned 'Miss Anita' had checked out that afternoon. As had 'your friend, Mr Richards'. But however impressive that foreign gentleman's command of English, even he struggled to find the right words of comfort when Brian sunk to his knees there in the foyer and screamed and screamed till his tonsils bled raw.

CHAPTER
XLIX

ᖇᘺᕊ

Portrait of a picaro.

TWO MONTHS PASSED and Brian, who had finally stopped screaming, was back in the numbing womb of Courtfield Road; singeing his mind with smoke, powders and all such bon-bons of stupefaction as were required to maintain a serene countenance. Little had changed in his domestic kingdom by way of cushions, rugs and the empathetic gleam of doom in the glass eyes of his mummified goat: only the addition of a hubbly bubbly pipe and the removal of all articles belonging to She whose name alone, if spoken aloud, was enough to pop the cork of a fresh magnum of agony and send him into evil fits of face scratching and teeth gnashing until that flask was dry. But he yet whispered it within his thoughts, a haunting three syllable pulse of the light now dead and the fire turned to ashes.

The pulse ever throbbed, and with it memories of all that had happened between a foyer floor in Marrakesh and his present state of paralysis. He had, he recalled, stepped off the plane in London, his eyes puffy as a couple of wasps' nests, and returned to an already emptied home. From that moment forth he had no choice but to make a permanent enemy of sobriety, and equipped himself with all the liquid artillery for that purpose: stoking the cannons of his courage and setting them upon the door of the unfurnished domicile in St John's Wood that Keith had retained as an easy alcove of repose when in the capital, and where Brian reasonably assumed its one mattress was now sweet with Her scent. And so he fired his cannons thither and the door gave way, but only because its keeper had sense to open it. Whereupon seeing Keith, and hearing Her cry of concern somewhere behind him, Brian's hostilities crumbled; as did all strength of knees and all restraint of emotion, which thus began to wet his cheeks and cascade from his nostrils.

Some kindly Samaritan must have mopped him up, for his next hazy recollections were of being back on a plane, with Keith, Mick and the other Stones, who may at one time have been his fellow Stones, but were now less fellow than foreign; as foreign to Brian as the ogres of chevron and brassard who barked them into airport corners in jagged vowels none of them understood. There they were subject to as thorough an investigation of their persons as was possible without the proper tools of internal surgery: under suspicion of being international smugglers of the demon physic, made to stand all but naked in their underclothes, while the contents of every suitcase were ripped, torn, shaken and snapped, as if the crumbs of sinful contraband may be hidden between the tightest stitch of silk or cotton.

He remembered being on a stage, but not in which city, not that it ever seemed to matter. For whichever stage in whichever city it was always the same wild wassail of screams, sirens, blood and destruction; the same sick tremor in his guts that he had somehow already died and this was his fate, for all eternity: to play stage right in the house band of Hell. A fate that could be no worse for the unshakeable vision, stage left, of the damned Scaramouche on guitar responsible for the mocking flames of cuckoldry lapping at his heels, scalding the scruples of his honour and pressing on his will to seek everlasting relief in the vapours of fantasy.

Only then, in fragrant clouds, through eyes of purple mist,

could he obliterate all life's toil and trouble in the hubble and bubble of his fertile fancy. Just a quick huff and puff and, behold: the Sultan's long procession, the clashing cymbals, the ten thousand scimitars flashing in the sunlight, the thrice ten thousand dancing-girls strewing flowers, the white elephants caparisoned in countless gorgeous colours, infinite in number and attendants. And all in miniature, snaking up the walls and weaving across the ceiling of Courtfield Road as he lay on his back, waving at the occasional dervish and blowing kisses at the bejewelled nymphs showering rose petals upon his crown, and that of his goat, and that of the strange gentleman of similarly scattered consciousness flopped on the other side of the living room.

He was a prince, at least in name, though the kind who, were they to stumble upon a glass slipper, would in all probability happily pawn it for sums equivocal to the purchase of a bag of magic beans. It was not merely for this eventuality that his full title was that of 'Prince Stash', a welcome truncation of his consonantly gluttonous Franco-Polish lineage Stanislaus Klossowski de Rola: though his given abbreviation fitted his character more snugly than any crystal shoe could a foolish scullery maid with bourgeois delusions, in as much as his pockets were seldom devoid of the tickets to oblivion, bean-shaped or otherwise, necessary for Brian's regular commutes of mind to that very vicinity, and from which both were presently returning to the terminus of sad reality after another blissful sojourn.

Greeting them at that station was a rasping tannoy announce-ment, its voice fuzzy and urgent, echoing what sounded an imminent departure to 'Oppenhup!' As neither Brian nor Prince Stash had designs on that location they chose to ignore it, until its metallic cry repeated, louder and ever more frantic. At which season this geographical mystery perished: in the sudden separation of syllables, 'Open up!'; in the late dawning of intelligence that the tannoy was the inter-communication system of Brian's flat; and in the sequel supplied by his royal guest, who took pains to stand and stagger to the front window, from which he peered through the curtains down into the street below, all blue blood sapping from his cheeks as he exclaimed in a queer yet distinct whinny:

'Milordy! The police!'

Brian's hope that Prince Stash was mistaken – that his brain were merely belching phantom figures as a satisfied diner hiccoughs a gaseous reminder of the hearty meal he has consumed many hours earlier – slimmed into thin air when he looked for himself and saw that regal observation to be an honest account of the activity of trench-coats swarming outside his door. The ebbing tides of delirium nullifying what might, in his more earthly humours, seize with all the frenzy that takes possession of any cornered prey, he admitted them without further delay: sacrificing all measures for his own preservation by leaving their traces of abandon undisturbed; all ash and apparatus, all residue and wraps, all pillboxes and pipes ready to be scavenged by the dozen or more shadows of Law who thus burst in upon him with gleeful assiduity of purpose.

There was something familiar about this scene, so Brian thought with what thrift his weary faculties could spare, as if he had already witnessed it, or it had recently happened to somebody else, somebody he might have once known, but the finer details escaped him. As did his own name when the policeman asked him, and for a second he thought he heard himself say 'Elmo Lewis', being uncertain as to whether that may or may not be true; having but a vague reflexion of mind as to the correct answer to that simple enquiry. And so, as the police led him outside Courtfield Road, past the winking bulbs from waiting photographers, into the back of a car beside his poor perspiring prince, he decided he would do his best to try and remember.

They drove him the short distance to the local station in Kensington, his thoughts already flinching with past sounds and smells of nights on cold linoleum, aerated bread, damp ceilings, Italian suits and Höfner guitars. He was still entranced as he was led into the custody of a back room where a man with thick-rimmed spectacles and stains on his tie started reading from a sheet of paper, though his words became buried in another voice from another room in another time altogether.

'And now, we've got a guest on guitar. He's come all the way from Cheltenham, just to play for you. Give it up for – Elmo Lewis!'

The man with the thick-rims and the stains was still moving his mouth and he thought he heard him cough the word 'charged', for Prince Stash turned yet paler, then something very silly about a 'Dangerous Drugs Act'. But he really couldn't be certain for the new noises rushing between his ears, of chaffing steel and trembling valves, and *'I believe I'll dust my broom!'* And in another amplified twang the stained tie vanished, and the man who wore it, and the desk in front of him, and Prince Stash beside him, and the ceiling of Kensington police station. And in their place the heat and cramp of the Moist Hoist, his nostrils twitching to sweat, beer, cologne and the spike of reefer; for he was five years younger and five lifetimes happier. He was Elmo Lewis, after all.

The reverie evaporated, but its glow lingered as he was marched along a corridor, out into fresh evening air and a squealing chorus of young girls, and in his head he could not conceive a more tremendous figure than Elmo Lewis must now have exhibited. And so he smiled and they squealed even louder, till one of them shrieked *'We love you Brian!'* and he suddenly froze as if he had been struck across the back of his skull with a pickaxe.

'Brian!'

So the blows began to rain, *'Brian!'* after cruel murderous *'BRIAN!'*, and in less than a minute the maimed body of Elmo

Lewis slumped dead at the feet of Brian Jones. But the girls outside Kensington Police Station just kept screaming and, from behind his dark glasses, Brian just kept smiling. And it was only by their opaque grace that not a sinner amongst them could see his tears.

CHAPTER

L

❦

And another.

MICK HAD SPENT an entire day acquainting his eyes with the external masonry and internal woodwork of the courthouse in Chichester: lingering in its corridors until such times as designated; listening to its wigs mutter formal charges and conditions of bail; and touched by the knot of admirers who'd camped as close to its threshold as police would allow, there to trumpet forth their support for himself and Keith, who had been obliged to appear in company of Groovy Bob – all three submitting their preliminary pleas of 'not guilty' prior to a trial date to be hence decided.

He had done tolerably well throughout, his manners polite whenever addressed by the bench, sparing affectionate smiles for the gathered fans and enjoying a pleasant luncheon at a local hotel. Though he and Keith left on the understanding they would be returning in seven weeks to face a jury, Mick had the comfort of his counsel, and the protective glare of Mr Klein, who had flown over from New York especially to hear the proceedings in person, reassuring him that he was innocent of all allegations, and the Law without means to prove otherwise, and so was of peaceful humour upon the drive back to Redlands: the blemished paradise where the seeds of this miscarriage had been sewn three months earlier.

It was only then, after he and Keith had loosened ties and decanter tops that a telephone call brought news that Brian had been arrested and charged that very afternoon under identical offences. Whereupon Mick's deepest fears of conspiracy redoubled, his high feather plummeted and dungeon-dark storm clouds rent the blue skies of his mind.

Work provided only minor distraction to that gnawing terror as summer bloomed: the hydrangea in flower, the horse chestnut in full candelabra and the Stones in their studio, if comparatively sapless. For they had little in the way of tunes, but too much in the way of stimulants, and thus spent a surfeit of vigour labouring over trifles and inflating fripperies in the vain hope that something might suddenly leap out of the vacuum and arm them with recognisable song. Brian was barely ever there, and of far more use in his absence than in the hindering plucks of lethargy he tossed into the ether on his few surprise visits. Nor was Andrew, who had been gradually retreating for six months past: away from all responsibility as the producer of their psychedelic shambles; away from all skulduggery in the calculus of Mr Klein; away from all association with phials, trials, and tabloid headlines; and backwards into his own chemical sanctuary. He would thus appear only occasionally: a pale apparition in the control booth, hand twitching a limp salutation through the glass, his head lolling to the heavens as he listened to the Stones make something less of the desperate nothing they started with. Nobody noticed him arrive any more, just as nobody noticed him depart. He was but a spectre, a twitch in time, till one evening when Andrew telephoned the studio to tell Mick he wasn't ever coming back. Mick didn't try to change his mind. And so the catapult was gone.

The seven weeks swam much too quickly down the gutter of time, and Tuesday the Twenty-Seventh of June dawned with frightening eagerness through the curtains of Redlands, where

Mick and Keith had both chosen to rest the night before the trial. Mick had thought it only chivalrous to request Marianne not accompany him; thus avoiding the gantelope of the popular press and with it all encouragement of gossip already circulating in that company regarding the identity of a certain 'Miss X', notwithstanding certain unprintables of courverture chocolate. Bill and Charlie had also volunteered what moral stanchion they could but were similarly discouraged in the interests of unnecessary public sensation. As was Brian, who with his own impending tribunal would have been as cursed a choice of courtroom mascot as the Acid King himself, had that elusive gentleman with the leather valise not eluded all efforts to subpoena him to that place, baffling the combined intellects of every European border agency to whom he had become an untraceable figment of no fixed abode.

As accustomed as he now was to courtroom interiors and all appurtenance of horsehair, cape, gavel, bench, scribe and police sentry, the sight of that which greeted Mick in Chichester – though familiar in outlay – still increased what disturbances of thought had kept him awake through most of the previous night, also accounting for his pallor, which was not without its tincture of the jaundice of dismay. The curator of his fate was a Judge Block, a surname its face had seen fit to honour with expressive implication of medieval beheadings, and who first caught his eye with a terrifying ogle as if already engaged in private calculations of blade width. This disquiet of mind then multiplied twelvefold when Mick turned to survey the members of the jury and read the story of his ruin, complete and unabridged, in a dozen glaring chapters of man. He knew not their names, but their like he had seen before, time and again, in umpteen guises: behind hotel desks and guarding grill rooms, in late night garage kiosks, in a blur of batons thumping down on innocent youth, in mortar board and sash, in short back and shorter sides, in polished shoe and bowler hat, and in all whose laps suddenly vanished in erection for 'God Save The Queen'.

Mick's fickle prayers of salvation fell squarely upon the powers of his defence counsel, Mr Havers – an esteemed gentleman of Law who, fortunately, was not at task to be addressing a judge of Scotch extraction who might otherwise interpret his appellation as denoting an orator of gibberish – and those of his local practitioner, Dr Dixon-Firth of no less respectable a London borough than Knightsbridge.

Having settled all preliminaries of standing, seating, thumping gavel and a necessary 'order!' to quell the hysterical exhalations from those devoted young maidens who'd managed to secure themselves a prime position of vantage in the public gallery, Judge Block called the prosecution to advance their arguments against the accused. This opportunity they seized with evident relish: a Mr Morris, Queen's Counsel, inviting a sombre-faced gentleman to the witness box who announced himself as a Chief Inspector of West Sussex Constabulary, and whose report of what had occurred on the evening in question was commended by the bench for its measured presentation of the facts. He was thus implored to reiterate those same details for the benefit of the jury; occasionally lapsing into digressions of a Biblical nature and cautioned only the once when, having finished his forensic monologue, he felt compulsion to point a shaking finger towards the bench where Mick was seated and rage in gravelly tones, 'Get thee behind me!'

The moral heights established, the prosecution next requested a pharmacist in employ of the Metropolitan Police to furnish the court with the intelligence from their scientific analysis of that which was discovered in the blazer pocket of the accused. The pharmacist, speaking as slowly as he believed necessary for his wisdom to register upon the jury's minds, which he collectively suspected to be of dulled parochial limitations, explained that Mr

Jagger had been in possession of four tablets of an amphetamine compound known as 'Ben-ze-drine'. These pills had found favour amongst the young for invoking unnatural levels of pep, and though readily available for purchase on the continent – where iniquity typically flourished in the lands of greasy victuals and popery – was here prohibited by Her Majesty's government and supplied only on condition of written prescription from a registered physician.

Had Mr Jagger been able to provide such a docket?

'Mr Jagger had not,' answered the pharmacist.

And was Mr Jagger, then, in that professional gentleman's opinion, guilty of possessing an illegal substance without prescription?

'Mr Jagger was.'

Judge Block stroked a bony finger across his chin, swivelling his eyes from the witness to the accused, the same glint of cold steel in his beady pupils.

Mr Morris then withdrawing, Mr Havers was next requested to entertain the court with his tokens of defence: beginning with a digest of Mick's educational achievements and sundry references of good character before ushering Dr Dixon-Firth to help fumigate the evil odour of prosecution while still fresh. The doctor thus proceeded to clear that air, and with it any misunderstanding of the circumstances surrounding the defendant's carriage of the aforementioned substance. That the 'pep pills' had been purchased in Italy, in all legality of that province, and that upon returning to England Mr Jagger had sought the advice of his physician, that is himself, who sanctioned their use at such times that the rigorous demands of Mr Jagger's working schedule required armour against fatigue. The doctor's verbal advice being, by authority of medicine, tantamount to a prescription, the defendant was therefore innocent of the charge, an opinion that Mr Havers politely directed the jury to accommodate to the best of their common sense.

This last appeal roused Judge Block into full swing of gavel and objection, his estimation of the defence counsel having latterly veered towards the penetration of the Scotch; that Mr Havers was, indeed, the embodiment of all nonsense his ancestral name suggested. For the doctor's consent, lacking all validity of written documentation, was no more equivalent to a prescription for dangerous physic than a banker's cough a promise to pay ten pounds to the bearer of a dirty napkin.

'And so,' said Judge Block, his grin curving sharply like a headsman's axe, 'as a matter of Law, it therefore follows that the defence open to Mr Jagger is not available.'

Mick's innards turned to glaciers. 'I therefore direct you,' continued Judge Block, narrowing his field to the blinking jurors, 'that there is no defence to this charge. I now ask you to consider your verdict.'

The jury exited the courtroom as instructed, returning in six agonisingly swift minutes. Judge Block licked his lips, tapping his forefingers together in impatient rhythm.

'Have you reached a unanimous verdict?'

The foreman of the jury replied that they had.

'And how do you find the accused?'

The foreman answered him, and as he did so a scream burst from the gallery, the light forsook Mick's eyes, his knees knocked together and he fell at length insensible on the floor. The noose, taut and unbreakable, had finally found its voice.

'Guilty!'

CHAPTER

LI

A trinity is crushed.

THE SHORT SUMMER night blinked much too fast and
the following dawn Keith awoke in a humour no better
than that which had stirred Mick the previous morning,
and rather the worse for reviewing all that had taken place in the
four and twenty hours between. He had accompanied Mick to
court that first day, and observed his will ground into powder by
twelve stony hearts and their judicial miller. He had seen Groovy
Bob suffer the same fate, forced to confess wilful carriage of opium
tablets and doomed to modify his plea to that of guilty. He had
watched both men shiver at the gavel's bang, and felt his own
marrow tremble as they were led away in confused tears and steel
bracelets; knowing that the next day his would be the neck assessed
for severance, and only then would all three be enlightened as to
the measure of their separate punishments. And he returned to
Redlands, without comfort of Anita – unable to extract herself
from what she'd described as 'a very pretty, pretty' filming commitment in Rome – and so slept alone in broken dreams of clanging
doors and rattling chains, wondering if that night would be his
last at liberty.

Keith's disturbed fancies were the sound of Mick's reality, a
condemned man obliged to spend the night in custody of a local
gaol until the appropriate hour when Judge Block would pass

sentence. He sat upon the hard bed in his cold cell, his visage a fracas of tics and twitches, his lips flapping like a shotten herring, his orbs boggling big as the moon that teased him with all the freedom of the night sky through the bars of his high window. He grew so terrible, at last, that one gaoler could not bear to witness the torture, and in charity of distraction supplied him with a jigsaw puzzle, though he made no effort to alleviate despair in its tedious assembly, and fell only further into the nettle patch of melancholy and all its sleepless stings.

The verdict had made the front pages of that evening's papers, and many were the Sparrows, Keeleys and Lavenders who bespoke themselves a heartier dinner than was normal for a Tuesday, their appetites encouraged by the portrait of a Rolling Stone in all humiliation of chains and cuffs: a circumstance productive of much gloating mirth, though not in all, and least not Marianne, who could no more honour her pledge to keep away from the court and so hurried to Chichester the following day. She was allowed but a brief conference with Mick, who could only weep into her silken hair and beg her to importune whomsoever she could to secure his freedom, before being escorted to her seat in the public gallery; her presence encouraging a thunder of murmurs, all pealing with the same spluttering vowels.

'Mussix!'–'Missex!' –'M' sex!' –*'MISS X!'*

The commotion of Marianne and the figure of Keith occupying the station beside Mr Havers where Mick's prospects had hitherto perished was all that distinguished the scene from that of the previous day; the jury still the same firmament of gleaming eyes, and the basilisk gaze of Judge Block still flinty with purpose. Order called, the prosecuting Mr Morris oiled his engines of eloquence and detailed the specific charge against Keith: amounting to his wilful condoning of mental paralysis by foul and forbidden means in his private domicile. The court was reminded of the wicked

'Jagger In The Condemned Cell'

physic responsible for the verdicts already passed upon the heads of Mick and Groovy Bob, of the equally incriminating apparatus supposedly belonging to that erstwhile pimpernel 'the Acid King', and of the unnatural behaviour of 'Miss X' who, though granted anonymity of court and exempted from the witness stand, was, argued Mr Morris, the very emblem of narcotic debauchery as only Keith could have choreographed.

To furnish the jury with grisly yet necessary particulars of that innominate slut, a policewoman answering to the name of Fubbs was summoned and forthwith flourished in that capacity. 'Miss X', as she recounted, had abandoned every scrap of clothing along with her character, a shame she revelled in save for a rug of unspecified animal origin with which she made but cursory efforts to shield her indecencies. It was the further opinion of PC Fubbs that 'Miss X' was in a state of merriment beyond all sober pleasure, and welcomed the serious formality of a search of her person with inordinate gaiety; subjecting the eyes of all assembled constables to a feast of naked flesh and directing that officer to commence her inspection in the crevices of – begging the court's pardon – the young lady's quim.

This gripping testimony, supplemented by the interruptions of Mr Morris, who considered it useful to repeat choice passages from that celebrated report of the Chief Inspector of West Sussex Constabulary with regard to the offending minx and her 'creamy nakedness', greatly affected the jury, who read in all the havoc that time and nature had seen fit to play upon PC Fubbs' face that she herself was a woman whose private parlour had seldom been visited, and therefore such vulgarity was not merely an affront to the badge of Law but a cruel slur upon the blessed martyrs of spinsterhood. Mr Morris thus summarised by placing before the court his conclusion that these actions could only be those of a wretched girl who had not long ingested some outlawed fillip to cretinism, as Mr Richards must have been aware; so failing in his legal responsibility as the lord of his own manor, as the jury must surely now doom him accordingly.

The reins of procedure passing to Mr Havers, he began Keith's defence with some divisive comments on the members of the press, inciting much 'pshaw!'-ing from their representatives present, scandalising the court with the suggestion that this entire hearing was a strategy of war against the Rolling Stones invented by one particular Fleet Street periodical, the *News Of The World*, as retribution for Mr Jagger submitting a libel claim against their offices not seven days before the night in question, and with full conspiracy of the Metropolitan Police and their long departed pigeon, codenamed 'the Acid King'. This defence was not merely unpopular but, as Judge Block objected, raising all cudgel of voice, unfounded, and since those associated with that publication were not on trial, he advised Mr Havers to resist the afflictions of his cognomen, spare those innocent scribes the malice of slander and restrict his business to excusing the conduct of his client – if indeed that miracle were within his already questionable powers of attorney.

Mr Havers voicing many supplications for mercy and forgiveness, he admitted Keith to take the stand where he was led gently over the coals of enquiry; cooling them as best he could with a plea, not merely of innocence, but of ignorance to the various residues of 'Indian hemp' and all other sinful detritus collected by the police, which he apportioned to the corruption of his fugitive highness, the so-named 'Acid King'.

Mr Havers thanking the court, Mr Morris then bounded to the witness box to pick up that which the defence had conveniently neglected, apropos the curious mood and doxyish habits of 'Miss X'.

'We are not old men,' said Keith, holding the prosecutor's stare without weakening blink. 'We are not worried about petty morals.

She was not under the influence of drink or anything. She had been upstairs and bathed. She had taken off her dirty clothes and had not brought a fresh set with her. She came downstairs for a cup of tea and was sitting there when the police arrived.'

'Sitting!' scoffed Mr Morris. 'Did it not come as a surprise to you that she was prepared to go back downstairs wearing only a rug?'

'No, sir,' replied Keith, making sure not to turn his head and steal a tender glance at Marianne, by now transfixing the focus of the jury. 'I thought the rug was big enough to cover three women.'

Mr Morris tightened his vision. 'You do not, Mr Richards, think it was because she had been smoking Indian hemp? And it had got rid of her inhibitions?'

'No, sir.'

Mr Morris cocked a slow, deliberate eyebrow that rippled in turn across the bench, clerk to clerk, finally crashing in a surf of incredulity on Judge Block's forehead. It remained there, a scarring froth of muscle, as he instructed the jurors to displace from their thoughts all gibbers of 'petty morals', but fix the sights of their integrity upon agreement of whether the accused was knowingly hospitable to all improperness committed under his roof, or the oblivious fool of his protestations. These cogitations lasting a little over an hour, they returned in concurrence of verdict. There were groans in the gallery, but none were surprised, and nor did Keith's knees surrender when the foreman declared.

'Guilty!'

All three pretty white necks now in the noose, Mick and Groovy Bob were brought up from their cells, united with Keith, and braced for the fife and drums of execution to play their sentence song. A trinity crushed, or so they looked to Marianne, whose choking sobs were all that spoiled the dreadful hush as Judge Block delivered. Were the black cap balancing upon his crown, his neck could not have been stiffer, nor his leer more frightful. Then, oh, how the trap did snap and the bodies did swing!

'Keith Richards. You will go to gaol . . .'

GAOL!

'. . . for one year. You will also pay £500 towards the cost of the prosecution. Go down!'

Keith did not go down. He stood, a stunned pillar of defiance, and stared with a look that pummelled the flinching foes his fists could not reach. The gallery in grizzling hubbub, Judge Block continued, thrusting into Groovy Bob.

'You will go to gaol for six months. You will also pay £200 towards the cost of prosecution. Go down!'

Marianne now shaking in the gallery, the pitch of young screams rising, Keith yet to go down, Judge Block licked his tomahawk lips and swiped at Mick.

'Michael Philip Jagger. You have been found guilty of possessing a potentially dangerous and harmful drug. You will go to prison . . .'

PRISON!

'. . . for three months. You will pay £200 towards the cost of prosecution. Go down!'

The noose jerked and all went down. And with them Marianne's heart, and the hearts of all beside her screeching 'No!', some fainting upon the deck, as Mick thought he might, as Keith daren't allow him. Down, down into the pit where all hope was dead.

Down, down fell the Rolling Stones.

CHAPTER

LII

‿❧‿

In which the Rollaresque is concluded.

I
T WAS A morning many thought the most beautiful as had
ever dawned, awaking town and country, street and field with
its midsummer newness; a golden light they could almost
savour upon their tongues like a warm, sweet milk, swishing it
around the corners of their mouths until its giddying effects had
rendered them insensibly serene. A morning so pure and pristine
as must have seemed on the seventh day of Creation, and the
grateful smiles of men, women and children rose up into the sky
in a million unspoken 'Amen's, each its own humble prayer of
thanks. To be alive, and to be British; to have tea in the pot, and
jam on the table; to have beer in the pump, and skittles in the bar;
to have Dom's pills for backache and Snug cushions for false
teeth; to have a Queen on the throne and a Tory petition gathering
ink to 'Bring back the rope!'; to be servant heirs to all won by Sir
Winston Churchill, Admiral Nelson, the Duke of Wellington and
all who died vanquishing foreign swine at their command; and to
be rid – at last! – of The Rolling Stones.

It was not such a beautiful morning for our slain picaros:
bringing only the unfamiliar smell of damp cell and stale sackcloth
pillow and the waking woe that these fetid ills were not the
torment of sleep. Nor was it such a beautiful morning for this
Author, who in placing the Reader there in all sunrise and dew

must now acknowledge, with great concern to his earthly purpose once the last period of this History is blotted, that the sands of his time are almost run out and very shortly he too must, 'go down!' For having knotted the ribbon of this sordid chronicle with appropriate moral bow, his parting duty herein is to close it tight with the fortunes of those who have occupied the bulk of these censurable leafs so the spectre of their wrongdoing, which might otherwise plague the Reader's conscience, be extinguished proper without fear of Sequel.

Of Charlie, we may comfortably assume that he remained not merely an enigma but an ideal husband who, by now, must surely boast a collection of vintage pistols as handsome in order and variety as that of his celebrated handkerchiefs.

Of Bill, it is only known that he continued to maintain a fresh diary every year; which in order to sustain their predecessors' high quality of incident obliged him to conduct his personal affairs in much the same fashion as worthy anecdote of expenses – whether in finance or fluid – necessitated.

Some delicacy surrounds Brian, whom we left weeping three chapters past, and whose further adventures do not lend themselves to any great improvement in that grim countenance. It is better, therefore, that I not impart these gruesome particulars, but instead leave the Reader, now more than adequately conversant with Brian's nature and all its blemishes, to conclude his story as they wish according to their fancy; whether for unlikely reprieve of happy ending or the tragic denouement his dance through these pages might deserve.

And so, with the chilling clink of the gaoler's fob, we come to Mick and Keith, trembling in their separate dungeons, nine miles and a river apart. Mick in Her Majesty's Prison Brixton, where the ghosts still groaned with the exhaustion of the treadwheel. Keith in Her Majesty's Prison Wormwood Scrubs, where the midnight corridors yet echoed with the stifled sobs of Wilde's traitorous lover, Bosie. Two Stones, their bodies isolated yet their souls as one. Unfit for any kind of company other than bricks, bunk, window bars and the vice of despair squeezing free what little juice of understanding had soaked their nocturnes as to 'HOW?' and 'WHY?' their deeds had brought them hither. 'HOW?' the hammer and 'WHY?' the nail, rhythmically beating into their skulls, slowly, steadily, second by second.

'HOW?' – *THUD!* – 'WHY?' – *CLANG!*

Were they not fair fellows? True, they had, in their twenty-three summers, trifled with the knickerbockers of many a consensual young lady. But they had since found their own princesses in Marianne and Anita, to whom each had pledged full industry of love and lust to the exclusion of all others, and so could not be here through any lapse in gallantry.

'HOW?' – *THUD!* – 'WHY?' – *CLANG!*

Were they not harmless knaves? True, they had, in their few years of professional minstrelship, committed mischief against hoteliers, head waiters, shopkeepers, the poor-sighted, singing milkmen, garage mechanics and the carousel of the London Palladium. But in all that giddy-goating they had not harmed another living creature, shedding not a drop of blood, only the occasional splash of pot-water and a lone shower of crumbs, and so could not be here through any malice of forethought.

'HOW?' – *THUD!* – 'WHY?' – *CLANG!*

Were they not innocent troubadours? True, they had frequently been the catalyst for terrible scenes of mayhem and public disorder as had not been witnessed in the near two centuries since Lord Gordon's rioters stormed through Newgate hollering 'No Popery!' But such anarchy was never their intention, merely the misplaced affection of those too young and excitable to know better, and so could not be here for any provocation to incite or destroy.

'HOW?' – *THUD!* – 'WHY?' – *CLANG!*
'HOW?' – *THUD!* – 'WHY?' – *CLANG!*

The hammer hammered and the nail nailed until their wits were trampled and all that remained was a shared memory so sad it fair skewered their hearts. Of platform two, Dartford railway station. Of a copy of Chuck Berry's *Rockin' At The Hops*. Of a simple dream born of Rhythm and Blues that began one morning service to Charing Cross. And yet derailed, to end here, in a Victorian gaol.

How the tears did flow down the cheeks of the wretched duo. Oh, if there be a God in Heaven, show these miserable sinners some mercy!

'HOW?' – *THUD!* – 'WHY?' – *CLANG!*
'HOW?' – *THUD!* – 'WHY?' – *CLANG!*
CLICK!

And, Lo! – the key of mercy turned.

The long, long while that Mick and Keith had been eroding in lachrymals, their agents of Law had been begging and bartering on their behalf till their quill hands were limp with scribbling, their horsehair sodden with perspiration and their gowns frayed with flapping protestations. These heroic efforts they directed at the noble trinity of Diplock, Brabin and Waller: being three of the finest wigs from the highest court in the Land, who listened and frowned and mulled and decided that – pending surrender of passports – application of bail should be granted at the price of seven thousand pounds upon each of their heads.

This sum of considerable consequence was fetched and filed to the court from the purse of none other than Mr Klein, viewing it as a relative pittance to unshackle his two most profitable labourers, whom he had no doubt would reimburse him many times over at the very next opportunity of active business; and hopefully ever after until the day, were it ever to come, that they should amend their opinion of his character and practices to somewhere in the vicinity immediately south of 'cunning': a detail that sadly lies beyond the jurisdiction of this otherwise embarrassingly rich History.

They had been gaoled on Thursday, and it was not until the afternoon of Friday that the wardens of Brixton and Wormwood Scrubs opened their cells, where Mick and Keith both received the intelligence of their conditional liberty laughing and weeping by turns. Within the hour they had been collected from those houses of correction and ferried to the Temple offices of their legal saviours where, properly reunited, they exhibited yet wilder extravagances which are known to be symptoms of hysterical affection, before repairing to the nearest hostelry, named The Feathers, and so sharing the lightness of spirits on which they floated in with much alacrity, seating themselves at the bar to take welcome pleasure of their cups.

Their first toast was to clemency, their second to the goodness of Mr Klein, and their third a bump to lessons learned – every second in their cells a lash of the cat leaving permanent scars to remind of past follies – and new beginnings.

Never again would they cause upset or create nuisance, nor sicken nor scandalise, nor dabble with forbidden concentrates and queer powders, nor promote virtue of rakishness and immorality. They would strive to avoid association with all things rascally, wicked and diabolic and behave with impeccable courtesy and manners at all costs. And no more would they be mistaken for 'gentlemen of the road', or 'shaggy-haired monsters', for they would henceforth habit themselves as men of wealth and taste.

For here, in the bar of the Feathers inn on Tudor Street, on the last day of June, Nineteen Sixty-Seven, they could begin afresh, just as they had done on platform two of Dartford railway station not six years before. And as they sipped their strong-waters, transported on these shiny reflections of importance and solidity, it was as if they were making one another's acquaintance for the very first time.

'*Pleased to meet you.*'

They bashed glasses and gulped heartily, the taste soft on their tongues and glowing warm in their bellies. But it wasn't that of Mick's vodka and lime, nor Keith's whisky and coke. It was a shared taste of something infinitely sweeter, something now twinkling in their eyes and curling their lips into a pair of not undevilish grins.

SATISFACTION!

A brief GLOSSARY for the MODERN READER of the OLD and VULGAR TONGUE

altar of Venus	shrine of love: that is, the vagina
arbor vitae	tree of life: that is, the penis
bareback	raw and sheathless sexual congress
bedcraft	sexual congress, sheathed or otherwise
bingo	brandy
bit o' jam	a comely maiden
black cap	a dark cloth ceremonially worn by a judge atop their wig when passing sentence of death
bobbery	a commotion
castrato	a male vocalist surgically separated from his testes prior to puberty and thus only capable of a very high vocal register; that is, like the shrill coos of The Beatles Pop Group
chuckaboo	a close acquaintance
convivial society	shenanigans of a sexual nature
creature, the	alcoholic beverage
cunnigate	a term best not abbreviated in polite society
Cyprian	relating to 'the Cyprian' deity Aphrodite: Goddess of love and all feats of human pro-creation; e.g. *Cyprian fountain*: the vagina; *Cyprian instrument*: the penis, etc.
dandiprat	a bothersome person

dilberry	a bauble of dried excreta as found stuck in the anus hair of horses, livestock etc.
dollymop	a woman of easy virtue
doodlesack	the vagina
Don Cypriano	the penis
'Ecod!'	an exclamation: 'my God!'
flapdoodle	the vagina
foxtrel	an especially vulpine young woman; *cf.* vulpette
fundaments	the buttocks
gantelope	a military punishment, as in running the gauntlet
giddy-goating	being foolish; as in 'acting the giddy goat'
glister-pipe	the penis
gulf of Venus	similar to the altar of Venus
hornbeaming	the use of sturdy trees as a supporting scaffold for sexual congress in a woodland setting
inexpressibles	trousers
Irish toothache	erection of the penis, especially if involuntary and inappropriate
itching Jenny	the vagina
jaspery	male homosexual congress
lappy	to exhibit the influence of having consumed more strong-waters than is sensible; to be drunk
moll	a young woman of severely abandoned character
mother of all masons	the vagina
nancy	the buttocks
nether-eye/ nether-mouth	the vagina
nonesuch	the vagina
pikestaff	the penis

pot-water	urine; as in chamber-pot water
privy-counsel	the vagina
quim	the vagina
rollaresque	a rock 'n' roll picaresque
shady spring	the vagina
shit-a-bed	a person who evacuates whilst still asleep with terrible consequences for their linen
silent flute	the penis
strong-waters	alcoholic beverage
sweet death	an odd fit of physical pleasure: that is, an orgasm
swived	past participle of 'to swive'; to have sexual dealings
toodlewag	the penis
tool of generation	the penis
trinket box	the vagina
trull	a woman who uses her natural resources to furnish her purse
tuzzy-muzzy	the vagina
vulpette	a woman of vulpine quality; that is, a 'foxy' lady, *cf.* foxtrel
whistle and bells	the penis, and its neighbouring appendages
wicket and stump	respectively, the vagina and the penis
woman of the stews	being not unlike a *cf.* trull, or dollymop
Zam-Buk	an ointment for chilblains, rashes, sores and similar afflictions, of English manufacture

A brief DISCOGRAPHY of
THE ROLLING STONES
as issued in GREAT BRITAIN
during the period of this
HISTORY

∽

NINETEEN SIXTY-THREE

June
'Come On'
b/w 'I Want To Be Loved'

November
'I Wanna Be Your Man'
b/w 'Stoned'

NINETEEN SIXTY-FOUR

January
The Rolling Stones {EP}
i: 'Bye Bye Johnny', 'Money'
ii: 'You Better Move On', 'Poison Ivy'

February
'Not Fade Away'
b/w 'Little By Little'

April

The Rolling Stones {LP}

i: 'Route 66', 'I Just Want To Make Love To You', 'Honest I Do', 'Mona (I Need You Baby)', 'Now I've Got A Witness', 'Little By Little'

ii: 'I'm A King Bee', 'Carol', 'Tell Me', 'Can I Get A Witness', 'You Can Make It If You Try', 'Walking The Dog'

June

'It's All Over Now'

b/w 'Good Times, Bad Times'

August

Five By Five {EP}

i: 'If You Need Me', 'Empty Heart', '2120 South Michigan Avenue'

ii: 'Confessing The Blues', 'Around And Around'

November

'Little Red Rooster'

b/w 'Off The Hook'

NINETEEN SIXTY-FIVE

January

The Rolling Stones No. 2 {LP}

i: 'Everybody Needs Somebody To Love', 'Down-Home Girl', 'You Can't Catch Me', 'Time Is On My Side', 'What A Shame', 'Grown Up Wrong'

ii: 'Down The Road Apiece', 'Under The Boardwalk', 'I Can't Be Satisfied', 'Pain In My Heart', 'Off The Hook', 'Susie Q'

February

'The Last Time'

b/w 'Play With Fire'

June

Got Live If You Want It {EP}

i: 'We Want The Stones', 'Everybody Needs Somebody To Love', 'Pain In My Heart', 'Route 66'

ii: 'I'm Moving On', 'I'm Alright'

August

'(I Can't Get No) Satisfaction'

b/w 'The Spider And The Fly'

September

Out Of Our Heads {LP}

i: 'She Said Yeah', 'Mercy Mercy', 'Hitch-Hike', 'That's How Strong My Love Is', 'Good Times', 'Gotta Get Away'

ii: 'Talkin' Bout You', 'Cry To Me', 'Oh Baby', 'Heart Of Stone', 'The Under Assistant West Coast Promotion Man', 'I'm Free'

October

'Get Off Of My Cloud'

b/w 'The Singer Not The Song'

NINETEEN SIXTY-SIX

February

'19th Nervous Breakdown'

b/w 'As Tears Go By'

April

Aftermath {LP}

i: 'Mother's Little Helper', 'Stupid Girl', 'Lady Jane', 'Under My Thumb', 'Doncha Bother Me', 'Goin' Home'

ii: 'Flight 505', 'High And Dry', 'Out Of Time', 'It's Not Easy', 'I Am Waiting', 'Take It Or Leave It', 'Think', 'What To Do'

May

'Paint It, Black'
b/w 'Long Long While'

September

'Have You Seen Your Mother, Baby, Standing In The Shadow?'
b/w 'Who's Driving Your Plane'

November

Big Hits (High Tide And Green Grass) {Compilation LP}
i: 'Have You Seen Your Mother, Baby, Standing In The Shadow?', 'Paint It, Black', 'It's All Over Now', 'The Last Time', 'Heart Of Stone', 'Not Fade Away', 'Come On'
ii: '(I Can't Get No) Satisfaction', 'Get Off Of My Cloud', 'As Tears Go By', '19th Nervous Breakdown', 'Lady Jane', 'Time Is On My Side', 'Little Red Rooster'

NINETEEN SIXTY-SEVEN

January

'Let's Spend The Night Together'
b/w 'Ruby Tuesday'

Between The Buttons {LP}
i: 'Yesterday's Papers', 'My Obsession', 'Back Street Girl', 'Connection', 'She Smiled Sweetly', 'Cool, Calm And Collected'
ii: 'All Sold Out', 'Please Go Home', 'Who's Been Sleeping Here?', 'Complicated', 'Miss Amanda Jones', 'Something Happened To Me Yesterday'

August

'We Love You'
b/w 'Dandelion'

All of the above phonographic recordings were originally released in Great Britain by the Decca Record Company.

The discography of The Rolling Stones followed quite a different pattern in the United States of America, especially in terms of their long-players which occasionally featured songs never released in their homeland. Of these, the most curious is that named *Flowers*, released in July of Nineteen Sixty-Seven, including an exquisite Jagger/Richards composition entitled 'Sitting On A Fence' which is fiercely recommended by this Author to any persons at such leisure as to bother to compile their own corresponding *Rollaresque* soundtrack.

YESTERDAY'S PAPERS

Stanley Booth, *The True Adventures Of The Rolling Stones*

Barbara Charone, *Keith Richards*

Pete Goodman, *Our Own Story: The Rolling Stones*

Marianne Faithfull, *Faithfull*

Mick Jagger, Keith Richards, Charlie Watts etc. *According To The Rolling Stones*

Philip Norman, *The Stones*

Philip Norman, *Mick Jagger*

Andrew Loog Oldham, *Stoned*

Andrew Loog Oldham, *2Stoned*

Mark Paytress, *The Rolling Stones: Off The Record*

James Phelge, *Nankering With The Rolling Stones*

Bent Rej, *The Rolling Stones: In The Beginning*

Keith Richards, *Life*

George Tremlett, *The Rolling Stones Story*

Paul Trynka, *Sympathy For The Devil*

Simon Wells, *Butterfly On A Wheel*

Bill Wyman (with Ray Coleman), *Stone Alone*

Bill Wyman, *Rolling With The Stones*

All of the above titles provided the bare canvas of fact which this Author may have had cause, albeit on rare occasion, to embellish as his giddy demands of drama and levity dictated. Additional research was undertaken in all due sobriety amidst the newspaper and humanities archives of the British Library, Euston Road, London.

WE LOVE YOU

᜶

Mick Jagger	William Makepeace Thackeray
Keith Richards	Hablot Knight Browne
Brian Jones	George Cruickshank
Bill Wyman	John Gay
Charlie Watts	Edward Ravenscroft
Ian Stewart	Stanley Kubrick's *Barry Lyndon*
Andrew Loog Oldham	Tony Richardson's *Tom Jones*
Jack Nitzsche	Kevin Pocklington
Marianne Faithfull	Andrew Goodfellow
Bo Diddley	Liz Marvin
William Hogarth	Josh Ireland
Tobias Smollett	Don Martin of The Ealing Club
Henry Fielding	*and to a solid rock in*
Laurence Sterne	*a world of rolling stones,*
Charles Dickens	Sylvia Patterson

The eight illustrations were conceived by the fanatical Mr Goddard
and executed by the fantastical Mr Chadwick, whose artworks are
available for admiration at www.mrchadwick.co.uk.

ABOUT THE AUTHOR

Simon Goddard was born under the same constellation as Keith Richards and similarly attended art school, though not in Sidcup.

This is his fifth book.

Chronicles certain particulars during the festive season,
concerning a variety of edibles and encounters with
the spirit world.

THEIR APPETITES FOR provincial fruits thus whetted, they'd not long scrubbed the scent of its juice from their crevices with the cleansing waters of their beloved metropolis when, capitalising on their growing success, and with motive of promoting their new disc, Andrew dispatched the Stones straight back into the surrounding countryside for second portions.

Mouths shaped for peaches, in the town of Nuneaton they were instead subject to cream, finding themselves performing an unusually hazardous afternoon matinee in a ballroom almost entirely occupied by the severely juvenile. The supply of innocence amongst these Warwickshire weanlings being as short as their exposure to the rod, they were similarly deficient in appreciation of the supplied entertainment; taking voluble exception to Mick's bodily excitations, Keith's gurns of encouragement, Brian's static repose, Bill's perpendicular habits and even the undisputed tautness of Charlie's tempos.

The organisers having taken vain precautions to mollify these imps with provisions of sweet pastries, in doing so they made the serious error of equipping them with an opportune arsenal to express their displeasure. The first volley of sticky buns acting as a starting pistol, the air above and between sprite-gathering and stage was soon a precipitation of moist dough; aimed with devilish precision to discharge all contents of preserve and processed dairy upon violence of impact. Mick having the advantage of evasive movement, while Keith, Brian and Bill each had useful shield of instrument, the military acumen of their short-trousered assailants speedily deduced Charlie to be an appropriate sitting duck; and so concentrated all efforts of marksmanship, all success of splatter and all hoots of morosis in his direction. At the end of which, their seated victim exited the stage in urgent need of ablution, his appearance so dramatically rehabilitated by custard that he resembled an exquisitely tailored pavlova.

As discouraging a brush with youth as that had been, the Stones were nevertheless coerced into devoting yet another hour of their time to the pleasure of minors, hoping to demonstrate their saintlier aspects of character by paying visit to a children's hospital in Surrey a few weeks before Christmas; it being safely assumed that this particular audience would be sufficiently challenged by polio, rickets and various other poxes to limit their abilities to pelt creamy victuals with required proficiency. These preconceptions correct, they were received with as broad a set of grins as their feeble owners could muster, the group's presence inciting the joyful rattle of callipers and such elevations amongst the bedridden as might only be thought possible of that Jewish prophet of popular folklore. Their benevolence in this gesture was, however, tempered upon sight of a poster pinned to the ward wall: a portrait of The Beatles Pop Group, which Brian took special pleasure in mimicking, treating the assembled infants to such amusing Nankers of face that, in effort of laughter, their crippled bodies emitted groans of a fashion in imminent peril of expiration.

Come Christmastide, the Stones' own seasonal carol, 'I Wanna Be Your Man', was at last in handsome position inside the top twenty, helped in no small part by its authorship: the very same Beatles Pop Group; their popularity now a national plague from which even the House of Windsor had failed to immunise themselves, inviting that unbearably illustrious quartet to play by Royal appointment, and who themselves had recorded their own version of that song on their latest long player, released to the public the day the world learned of the assassination of the American president: so rousing an international tidal wave of mourning alleviated only by the pipette of comfort that poor Mr Kennedy died never having suffered exposure to 'I Wanna Be Your Man' as expressed by the harrowing brays of Ringo, whose perverse honour it was to undertake said vocal task.

Even so, The Beatles Pop Group were clearly invincible, though the threat to their standing posed by our heroes was now a matter of printed conjecture in several parishes: whose correspondents reported with apposite drama on the Stones' provocations to the decency of the gentler sex, regularly driven to commit fierce acts of ravishment upon the group's hair and clothes, rarely satisfied until they'd undone all labours of loom and clawed plentiful souvenir of twine.

These well-intentioned violations were nevertheless on occasion of secondary menace to regional comestibles, as was instanced on Christmas Eve when, between eluding the divesting assaults of the young ladies of Leek in the county of Staffordshire, the Stones took nourishment of pies purchased from a nearby grocer's. Their contents described in the broadest terms as 'meat', it wasn't until after the concert, upon the return drive to London, that digestion took effect, and so prompted autopsy of thought as to the identity of that member of the animal kingdom who'd been thus slaughtered, boned, cubed and prepared in gravy and case of shortcrust: suspicions ranging from border collie to a distant relative of Brian's beloved Billy G, whose appointment with the abattoir had been blessed relief from lingering mange. Such cogitations voiced not so much in words but in liquid ejaculations from mouth and anus, acquitted with loud supplements of whimpering anguish, this lengthy debate necessitated frequent roadside stops, also ensuring that most appetites for the next day's obligatory turkey dinner were resolutely compromised.

Allowing a week for their movements to resume regular interval and familiar texture, the year's final engagement ushered them to the northern city of Lincoln on New Year's Eve where, for once, Bill abstained from the many stockinged temptations available after the concert, retiring to his hotel room in monastic solitude for a long, restorative slumber.

His bedside lamp had been extinguished not half an hour when his ears were suddenly alerted to the faint disturbance of moaning; not of the kind to stir envious regret of his night of celibacy, but of some altogether less pleasurable human condition in state of duress, the hideous mewls becoming louder until silenced by a slow triplet of knocks upon his door. Accelerating Bill's agitation of wits was memory of a conversation some hours earlier of super-natural attitude, the group being informed that their designated inn, the White Hart Hotel, was residence to the phantom of a murdered parlour maid, who was rumoured to make nuisance of her unrest in the corridors after nightfall.

Following a short period of deliberation, during which he considered the pleasing possibility of it being some skirted admirer intent on sabotaging his wastefully chaste designs, Bill nervously tiptoed across the carpet and, placing a hand upon the doorknob, cautiously turned it open. The passage in darkness, he poked his head into the gloom and was thus confronted with diabolical vision of shaking white bedsheet, its contours suggesting some abominable envoy of the afterlife housed within. While ordinarily these circumstances might have been just cause for shrieks of